The Narrative Bible

THE NARRATIVE BIBLE

Edited by Clifton Johnson

FOR YOUNG PEOPLE

The Tower of Babel

THE
NARRATIVE BIBLE

Edited by
CLIFTON JOHNSON

Illustrated by
GUSTAVE DORÉ

New York
THE BAKER & TAYLOR COMPANY
1910

THE
NARRATIVE BIBLE

Edited by
CLIFTON JOHNSON

Illustrated by
GUSTAVE DORÉ

New York
THE BAKER & TAYLOR COMPANY
1910

COPYRIGHT 1910 BY
THE BAKER & TAYLOR COMPANY
Published October 1910

PRINTED IN THE UNITED STATES
BY
The F. A. Bassette Company
OF SPRINGFIELD, MASSACHUSETTS

Contents

I.	The Beginning	1
II.	The Flood	7
III.	Abraham, Isaac, and Jacob	11
IV.	Joseph and His Brethren	36
V.	Job and His Friends	57
VI.	Moses and the Plagues of Egypt	67
VII.	The Ten Commandments	89
VIII.	The Israelites in the Wilderness	104
IX.	God's People Enter the Promised Land	119
X.	The Judges	132
XI.	Ruth	149
XII.	Samuel and the First of the Kings	155
XIII.	King David	184
XIV.	Solomon the Wise	203
XV.	The Later Kings	210
XVI.	The Story of Jonah	241
XVII.	Daniel in Babylon	244
XVIII.	Queen Esther	256
XIX.	The Return from the Captivity	267
XX.	The Life of Jesus	270
XXI.	The Acts of the Apostles	367

Illustrations

The war against Gibeon	*Fly-leaf*
The tower of Babel	*Frontispiece*

	FACING PAGE
Adam and Eve driven from the Garden of Eden	4
Rebekah at the well	20
Samson slays a lion	142
Jonah in Nineveh	242
The star in the east	272
The prodigal son	326
Paul's shipwreck	398

Introductory Note

THE main purpose of this edition is to condense the narrative portions of the Bible into a volume of moderate length possessing as much interest as possible for child readers.

The Bible words and the Bible's impressive phraseology are retained almost exclusively; and such changes as have been made are of a minor nature. Most of them consist in merely substituting the names of persons or things for more or less indefinite pronouns. The verbal form is as a rule that of the King James Version; but where the Revised Version or the marginal alternative readings offer words or phrases that are clearer to the youthful mind, these have been substituted for the usual text.

Great care has been taken to have the narrative as connected as that in the Bible itself, or even more so; for continuity makes the impression stronger, and attracts much keener interest than a broken series of short stories. In perserving this continuity several books of the Old Testament are printed out of their customary order, that the events they chronicle may follow each other more accurately. Likewise, in the New Testament, all the four gospels have been drawn on to yield a single full and orderly story.

Nearly every happening and circumstance is included to which young people are likely to find reference in their general reading or conversation. A knowledge of these is an essential part of education, and without such knowledge one's culture is seriously incomplete.

The text is printed in the form that children are accustomed to see in their other books, with short sentences and short paragraphs, and with quotation marks in their appropriate places. This gives the pages an increased attraction, for immature readers, at least, and makes the story more easily comprehended.

I have omitted repetitions and all that is not essential to the main narrative, and have reduced as much as I could the multiplicity of names, both of places and of persons. Yet the eliminating has very rarely been of a nature to sacrifice any incident or detail that would prove of interest and be suitable for the average reader under fifteen years of age.

CLIFTON JOHNSON.

Hadley, Mass.

The Narrative Bible

I

THE BEGINNING

IN the beginning God created the heaven and the earth. The earth was waste and void, and darkness was on the face of the deep. God said: "Let there be light;" and there was light, and God divided the light from the darkness.

God called the light day, and the darkness He called night; and there was evening and there was morning, one day.*

God said: "Let there be a firmament in the midst of the waters;" and God made the firmament.

God called the firmament heaven; and there was evening and there was morning, a second day.

God said: "Let the waters under the heaven be gathered together into one place, and let the dry land appear;" and it was so.

God called the dry land earth, and the gathering together of the waters He called seas. God said: "Let the earth put forth grass, herb yielding seed, and fruit-tree bearing fruit;" and it was so; and there was evening and there was morning, a third day.

---

*Among the Hebrews the day was reckoned from sunset to sunset

God said: "Let there be lights in the firmament of the heaven to divide the day from the night; and let them be for signs, and for seasons, and for days and years; and let them give light on the earth;" and it was so.

God made two lights, the greater light to rule the day, and the lesser light to rule the night. He made the stars also; and there was evening and there was morning, a fourth day.

God said: "Let the waters bring forth abundantly moving creatures, and let fowls fly above the earth;" and God created the great sea-monsters, and every creature that moveth in the waters, and every winged fowl; and there was evening and there was morning, a fifth day.

God said: "Let the earth bring forth cattle and creeping things and beasts;" and it was so.

God also created man in His own image. God formed man of the dust of the earth and breathed into his nostrils the breath of life; and God gave him dominion over the fish of the sea, and over the fowls of the air, and over every living thing; and there was evening and there was morning, the sixth day.

The heaven and the earth were finished and all the host of them; and on the seventh day God rested from all His work; and God blessed the seventh day and hallowed it.

The Lord God planted a garden in Eden, and out of the ground made grow every tree that is pleasant to the sight and good for food. The tree of life was in the midst of the garden, and the tree of the knowledge of good and evil; and a river watered the garden. The Lord God commanded the man, saying: "Of every tree of the garden thou mayest freely eat, but of the tree of the knowledge of good and evil, thou shalt not eat; for in the day thou eatest thereof thou shalt surely die."

The Lord God brought every beast of the field and every fowl of the air unto the man to see what he would call them; and the man gave names to all cattle, and to the fowls of the air, and to every beast of the field.

The Lord God said: "It is not good that the man should be alone. I will make a helpmeet for him;" and the Lord God caused a deep sleep to fall on the man, and he took one of his ribs and made a woman and brought her unto the man.

The serpent was more subtle than any beast of the field which the Lord God had made; and the serpent said unto the woman: "Hath God said ye shall not eat of every tree of the garden?"

The woman said unto the serpent: "We may eat of the fruit of all the trees of the garden, except of the tree of knowledge. God hath said: 'Ye shall not eat of that; neither shall ye touch it lest ye die.'"

The serpent said unto the woman: "Ye shall not die; for in the day ye eat thereof your eyes shall be opened, and ye shall be as God, knowing good and evil."

When the woman was told that the fruit of the tree was good for food, and that it was to be desired to make one wise, she took of the fruit and did eat; and she gave also unto her husband, and he did eat. Then their eyes were opened and they knew that they were naked, and they sewed fig leaves together and made themselves aprons. Afterward they heard the Lord God walking in the garden in the cool of the day; and the man and his wife hid among the trees. The Lord God called unto the man and said: "Where art thou?"

The man said: "I heard Thee in the garden, and I was afraid, and I hid myself."

The Lord God said: "Hast thou eaten of the tree whereof I commanded thee that thou shouldest not eat?"

The man said: "The woman gave me of the tree, and I did eat."

The Lord God said unto the woman: "What is this thou hast done?"

The woman said: "The serpent beguiled me, and I did eat."

The Lord God said unto the serpent: "Because thou hast done this, cursed art thou. I will put enmity between thee and the woman, and between thy seed and her seed."

Unto the woman He said: "I will greatly multiply thy sorrow."

Adam and Eve driven from the Garden of Eden

The Beginning

Unto Adam He said: "Because thou hast harkened to the voice of thy wife, and hast eaten of the tree, cursed is the ground for thy sake; in toil shalt thou eat of it all the days of thy life; thorns also and thistles shall it bring forth to thee."

The man called his wife's name Eve; and the Lord God made for Adam and for his wife coats of skins and clothed them.

The Lord God said: "Behold the man knows good and evil; and now, lest he put forth his hand, and take also of the tree of life, and eat, and live forever, I will send him forth from the garden of Eden to till the ground."

So He drove out the man, and He placed at the east of the garden of Eden the Cherubim, and a flaming sword which turned every way to keep the way of the tree of life.

The first children born to Eve were Cain and Abel. Abel became a keeper of sheep, but Cain was a tiller of the ground. In process of time it came to pass that Cain brought of the fruit of the ground an offering unto the Lord; and Abel brought an offering of the firstlings of his flock. The Lord had respect unto Abel and to his offering; but unto Cain and to his offering He had not respect; and Cain was very wroth.

The Lord said unto Cain: "Why art thou wroth? If thou doest well, shalt thou not be accepted? and if thou doest not well, sin lieth at the door."

Cain said to Abel: "Let us go into the field;" and when they were in the field Cain rose up against his brother, and slew him.

The Lord said unto Cain: "Where is Abel thy brother?"

Cain said: "I know not. Am I my brother's keeper?"

The Lord said: "What hast thou done? The voice of thy brother's blood crieth unto me from the ground. Cursed art thou. When thou tillest the ground, it shall not henceforth yield unto thee its strength. A fugitive and a wanderer shalt thou be on the earth."

Cain said unto the Lord: "My punishment is greater than I can bear. Behold, thou hast driven me out this day, and from thy face shall I be hid; and it shall come to pass that whosoever findeth me shall slay me."

The Lord said unto him: "Whosoever slayeth Cain, vengeance shall be taken on him sevenfold;" and the Lord set a mark on Cain, lest any finding him should smite him.

Cain went out from the presence of the Lord and dwelt in the land of Nod on the east of Eden.

II

THE FLOOD

ADAM had many sons and daughters, and he lived nine hundred and thirty years. His son Seth lived nine hundred and twelve years, and Seth's descendant, Methuselah, lived nine hundred and sixty and nine years.

The people multiplied, and the Lord saw that the wickedness of man was great on the earth, and that every imagination of the thoughts of his heart was evil continually; and the Lord said: "I will destroy man whom I have created, and beast, and creeping thing, and fowl of the air; for it repenteth Me that I have made them."

Only one man, Noah, found grace in the eyes of the Lord; and God said unto Noah: "The end of all flesh is come; for the earth is filled with violence. Make thee an ark of gopher wood. Rooms shalt thou make in the ark, and shalt pitch it within and without with pitch. The length of the ark shall be three hundred cubits,* and the height thirty cubits. A roof shalt thou

---

*A cubit originally meant the length of the forearm from the elbow to the extremity of the middle finger. The cubit of the Hebrews was nearly eighteen inches.

make to the ark, and a door shalt thou set in the side thereof. With lower, second and third stories shalt thou make it. Behold, I will cause it to rain forty days and forty nights; and every living thing that I have made will I destroy from off the face of the ground. But thou shalt come into the ark, thou, thy sons, and thy wife, and thy sons' wives; and of every living thing, two of every sort, male and female, shalt thou bring into the ark to keep them alive with thee. Of the fowls after their kind, and of the cattle after their kind, of every creeping thing of the ground after its kind, two of every sort shall come unto thee to keep them alive; and take thou of all food that is eaten, and it shall be food for thee and for them."

Noah did according unto all that the Lord commanded him; and in the six hundredth year of Noah's life, in the second month, on the seventeenth day of the month, were all the fountains of the great deep broken up, and the windows of heaven were opened. In the selfsame day entered Noah, and Shem, and Ham, and Japheth, the sons of Noah, and Noah's wife, and the three wives of his sons, into the ark; and every beast, and all the cattle, and every creeping thing, and every bird of every sort, went into the ark, two and two of all flesh, male and female; and the Lord shut them in.

Forty days it rained, and the waters prevailed and increased greatly, and the ark went on the face of the waters. All the high mountains were covered and all

The Flood

flesh died, both fowl, and cattle, and beast, and every creeping thing, and every man. Noah only was left, and they that were with him in the ark.

God remembered Noah, and God made a wind to pass over the earth, and the waters assuaged. The fountains also of the deep and the windows of heaven were stopped, and the rain was restrained. The waters decreased and Noah opened the window of the ark and sent forth a dove to see if the waters were abated from off the face of the ground; but the dove found no rest for the sole of its foot and it returned; and Noah put forth his hand and brought it into the ark. He stayed seven days, and again he sent the dove out of the ark; and the dove came in to him at eventide, and, lo, in its mouth an olive leaf plucked off. So Noah knew that the waters were abated from the earth. He stayed yet other seven days and sent forth the dove, which returned not again.

More than a year after the flood began, Noah removed the covering of the ark, and looked, and, behold, the ark rested on the mountains of Ararat. The face of the ground was dried, and God spake unto Noah, saying: "Go forth out of the ark."

So Noah, and his sons, and his wife, and his sons' wives, and every beast, every creeping thing, and every fowl, went forth out of the ark; and Noah builded an altar unto the Lord, and offered burnt offerings on the altar. The Lord smelled the sweet savor, and the Lord said: "I will not again smite every thing living, as I have done. While the earth remaineth, seedtime and harvest, and cold and heat, and summer and winter, and day and night shall not cease."

God blessed Noah and his sons, and said unto them: "The fear of you and the dread of you shall be on every beast of the earth, and on every fowl of the air, and on all the fishes of the sea. Into your hand are they delivered; and behold, I establish my covenant with you and with every living creature. All flesh shall not be cut off any more by the waters of a flood. This is the token of the covenant which I make: I do set my bow in the cloud. It shall come to pass when I bring a cloud over the earth, that the bow shall be seen in the cloud, and I will remember my covenant."

Many years passed and the people increased greatly, and the whole earth was of one family and of one speech. As they journeyed they found a plain in the land of Shinar; and they dwelt there. They said one to another: "Let us make brick and build a city, and a tower whose top may reach unto heaven."

The Lord came down to see the city and the tower which the children of men builded; and the Lord said: "Behold, they are one people, and they have all one language, and this is what they begin to do. Let us confound their language that they may not understand one another's speech."

So the Lord scattered them abroad thence on the face of all the earth. They left off to build the city, and the city was called Babel.

III

ABRAHAM, ISAAC, AND JACOB

ABRAHAM, a descendant of Shem, dwelt in Haran, and the Lord said unto Abraham: "Get thee out of thy country and from thy kindred unto the land that I will show thee; and I will make of thee a great nation, and I will bless them that bless thee, and him that curseth thee will I curse."

So Abraham took Sarah his wife, and Lot his brother's son, and all their substance that they had gathered, and they went forth into the land of Canaan; and the Lord appeared unto Abraham, and said: "Unto thy seed will I give this land."

Abraham was very rich in cattle, in silver and in gold. Lot also had flocks and herds and tents; and the land was not able to bear them that he and Abraham might dwell together. There was a strife between the herdmen of Abraham's cattle and the herdmen of Lot's cattle, and Abraham said unto Lot: "Let there be no strife between me and thee. Is not the whole land before thee? Separate thyself, I pray thee, from me. If thou wilt take the left hand, then I will go to the right; or if thou take the right hand, then I will go to the left."

Lot lifted up his eyes and beheld the Plain of Jordan that it was well watered everywhere like the garden of the Lord. Then Lot chose the Plain of Jordan, and Lot and Abraham separated the one from the other. Lot moved his tent as far as Sodom; but the men of Sodom were wicked and sinners against the Lord exceedingly.

Abraham moved his tent and dwelt by the oaks of Mamre which are in Hebron, and built there an altar unto the Lord. As he sat in the tent door in the heat of the day, lo, three men stood over against him. They were the Lord and two angels. When Abraham saw them, he ran to them, and bowed himself to the earth, and said: "Pass not away from thy servant. Let a little water be brought, and wash your feet, and rest yourselves; and I will fetch a morsel of bread, and comfort ye your hearts. After that ye shall pass on."

They said: "So do as thou hast said."

Abraham hastened into the tent unto Sarah, and said: "Make ready quickly three measures of fine meal, and make cakes."

Then he ran unto the herd and fetched a calf tender and good, and gave it unto a servant, who dressed it. Abraham took butter, and milk, and the calf which had been prepared, and set this food before the men, and he stood by them, and they did eat.

Later the men rose up and started toward Sodom, and Abraham went with them to bring them on the

Abraham, Isaac, and Jacob 13

way; and the Lord said: "Because the cry of Sodom and Gomorrah is great, and because their sin is very grievous, I will go and see whether they have done altogether according to the cry which is come unto me."

The two angels went on toward Sodom, but Abraham stood before the Lord and said: "Wilt thou destroy the righteous with the wicked? Peradventure there be fifty righteous within the city, wilt thou not spare the place for the fifty righteous that are therein?"

The Lord said: "If I find in Sodom fifty righteous, then I will spare all the place for their sake."

Abraham said: "Peradventure there shall lack five of the fifty righteous, wilt thou destroy all the city for lack of five?"

The Lord said: "I will not destroy it if I find there forty and five."

Abraham spake yet again and said: "Peradventure there shall be forty found?"

The Lord said: "I will not destroy it for the forty's sake."

Abraham said: "Oh let not the Lord be angry, and I will speak. Peradventure there shall thirty be found?"

The Lord said: "I will not do it if I find thirty there."

Abraham said: "Peradventure there shall be twenty found?"

The Lord said: "I will not destroy it for the twenty's sake."

Abraham said: "Oh let not the Lord be angry, and

I will speak yet this once. Peradventure ten shall be found?"

The Lord said: "I will not destroy it for the ten's sake;" and the Lord went his way, and Abraham returned.

The two angels came to Sodom at even, and Lot sat in the gate of Sodom. Lot saw them, and rose up to meet them; and he bowed himself with his face to the earth; and he said: "My lords, turn aside, I pray you, into your servant's house, and tarry all night, and ye shall rise early, and go on your way."

He urged them greatly, and they entered his house and he made them a feast and they did eat. But before they lay down, the men of the city compassed the house round, and called unto Lot, and said: "Where are the men that came in to thee this night? Bring them out unto us."

Lot went out and shut the door after him, and he said: "I pray you, my brethren, unto these men do nothing, forasmuch as they are come under the shadow of my roof."

They said: "Now will we deal worse with thee than with them."

They pressed sore on Lot, and drew near to break the door; but the two men put forth their hands, and pulled Lot into the house; and they smote the men that were at the door of the house with blindness, so they wearied themselves to find the door. Then the two men said unto Lot: "Hast thou here any others of thy family? Whomsoever thou hast in the city, bring them out; for we will destroy this place because the wickedness of its people is waxen great."

Lot went and spake unto his sons-in-law, and his two daughters, and said: "Up, get you out of this place; for the Lord will destroy this city."

But he seemed unto his sons-in-law as one that mocked.

When it was morning the angels hastened Lot, saying: "Arise, take thy wife and thy two daughters, lest thou be consumed in the iniquity of the city."

He lingered, and the men laid hold on his hand, and on the hand of his wife, and on the hands of his two daughters, and brought them forth, and set them without the city; and the men said unto Lot: "Escape for thy life. Look not behind thee, neither stay thou in all the Plain. Escape to the mountain, lest thou be consumed."

Lot said unto them: "Oh, not so, my lords. Behold now, thy servant hath found grace in thy sight. I cannot escape to the mountain, lest evil overtake me, and I die. There is a city near, and it is a little one. Oh, let me escape thither."

They said unto him: "We have accepted thee concerning this thing also. We will not overthrow the city of which thou hast spoken. Haste thee; for we cannot do anything till thou be arrived thither."

The name of the city was Zoar; and as Lot went toward it, his wife looked back from behind him, and she became a pillar of salt. The sun was risen when Lot entered Zoar. Then the Lord rained on Sodom and Gomorrah brimstone and fire out of heaven, and he overthrew those cities and all the Plain, and all the inhabitants of the cities, and all that grew on the ground.

Abraham gat up early in the morning to the place where he had stood before the Lord; and he looked toward Sodom and Gomorrah, and toward all the land of the Plain, and, lo, the smoke of the land went up as the smoke of a furnace. But God had remembered Abraham, and had sent Lot out of the midst of the overthrow.

Lot went from Zoar to the mountain; for he feared to dwell in Zoar; and he lived in a cave, he and his two daughters.

Sarah, Abraham's wife was without children; and she had a handmaid, an Egyptian, whose name was Hagar; and Sarah gave her handmaid to Abraham to be his wife. Hagar bare Abraham a son, and Abraham called the name of his son, Ishmael.

In her old age, Sarah, also bare a son, and Abraham named him Isaac. The child grew and Abraham made a great feast on the day that Isaac was weaned; and Sarah saw the son of Hagar the Egyptian, mocking. Wherefore she said unto Abraham: "Cast out this bondwoman and her son; for the son of this bondwoman shall not be heir with my son."

The thing was very grievous in Abraham's sight; but God said unto Abraham: "In all that Sarah hath said, hearken unto her voice."

So Abraham gave bread and a bottle of water unto Hagar and the child, and sent them away. They departed, and wandered in the wilderness; and the water in the bottle was spent, and Hagar cast the child under one of the shrubs. Then she went and sat down a good way off; for she said: "Let me not look on the death of the child."

She lifted up her voice and wept, and the angel of God called to Hagar out of heaven, and said: "What aileth thee, Hagar? Fear not. Arise, lift up the lad; for I will make him a great nation."

God opened her eyes, and she saw a well of water, and she went, and filled the bottle with water, and gave the lad drink. God was with the lad, and he grew, and he dwelt in the wilderness, and became an archer; and his mother took him a wife out of the land of Egypt.

It came to pass after these things that God did prove Abraham, and said unto him: "Abraham, take now thy son Isaac, and get thee into the land of Moriah, and offer him there for a burnt offering on one of the mountains."

Abraham rose early in the morning, and saddled his ass, and took two of his young men with him, and

Isaac his son. He clave the wood for the burnt offering, and journeyed toward the place of which God had told him. On the third day he saw the place afar off, and Abraham said unto his young men: "Abide ye here with the ass, and I and the lad will go yonder, and we will worship, and come again to you."

Abraham took the wood of the burnt offering, and laid it on Isaac his son; and he took in his hand the fire and the knife; and they went both of them together. Isaac spake unto Abraham his father, and said: "Behold the fire, and the wood; but where is the lamb for a burnt offering?"

Abraham said: "God will provide the lamb for a burnt offering, my son."

They came to the place, and Abraham built an altar, and laid the wood in order, and bound Isaac his son, and laid him on the altar, on the wood. Abraham stretched forth his hand, and took the knife to slay his son; and the angel of the Lord called unto him out of heaven, and said: "Abraham, Abraham."

Abraham said: "Here am I."

The angel said: "Lay not thine hand on the lad; for now I know that thou fearest God, seeing thou hast not withheld thy son from Him."

Then Abraham saw behind him a ram caught in a thicket by its horns, and Abraham went and took the ram, and offered it for a burnt offering in the stead of his son.

The angel of the Lord called unto Abraham a second time out of heaven, and said: "Because thou hast not withheld thy son, I will bless thee, and I will multiply thy seed as the stars of heaven, and as the sand which is on the seashore. In thy seed shall all the nations of the earth be blessed, because thou hast obeyed my voice."

So Abraham returned unto his young men, and they went with him to his dwelling-place.

The life of Sarah was a hundred and seven and twenty years; and Sarah died in Hebron in the land of Canaan.

Abraham was old, and well stricken in age; and the Lord had blessed Abraham in all things. Abraham said unto his servant, the elder of his house, that ruled over all he had: "I pray thee, swear by the Lord, the God of heaven and the God of the earth, that thou shalt not take a wife for my son of the daughters of the Canaanites, among whom I dwell; but thou shalt go unto my country, and to my kindred, and take a wife for my son Isaac."

The servant sware to him concerning this matter, and took ten camels, and went unto the city of Abraham's brother Nahor. He made the camels to kneel down without the city by a well of water at the time of evening that women go to draw water; and he said: "O Lord, the God of my master Abraham, send me good speed this day. Behold, I stand by the well, and the daughters of the city draw water. Let it come to pass, that the damsel of whom I shall ask drink be she that Thou hast appointed for Thy servant Isaac."

Before he had done speaking, Rebekah, daughter of Bethuel the son of Nahor, Abraham's brother, came with her pitcher on her shoulder; and the damsel was very fair to look on. She went down to the well, and filled her pitcher, and came up. The servant ran to meet her, and said: "Give me to drink, I pray thee."

She said: "Drink, my lord;" and she let down her pitcher on her hand, and gave him drink.

Then she said: "I will draw for thy camels also."

She hasted, and emptied her pitcher into the trough, and ran again unto the well, and drew for all his camels. The man looked steadfastly on her, and it came to pass, as the camels had done drinking, that he put on her a golden ring and two bracelets, and said: "Whose daughter art thou? Tell me, I pray thee, is there room in thy father's house for me to lodge?"

She said unto him: "I am the daughter of Bethuel the son of Nahor. We have both straw and provender enough, and room to lodge in."

The man bowed his head, and worshipped the Lord, and said: "Blessed be the God of my master Abraham, who hath led me to my master's brethren."

The damsel ran, and told her mother's household. Rebekah had a brother named Laban, and when he saw the ring and the bracelets she wore, and heard his

Rebekah at the well

sister's words, he went unto the man; and, behold, the man stood by the camels at the well. Laban said: "Come in, thou blessed of the Lord. Wherefore standest thou without?"

The man followed Laban to the house, and Laban ungirded the camels, and gave straw and provender for the camels, and water to wash the man's feet and the feet of the men that were with him. Then there was set meat before him to eat; but he said: "I will not eat until I have told mine errand."

Laban said: "Speak on."

The man said: "I am Abraham's servant. The Lord hath blessed my master greatly, and hath given him flocks and herds, and silver and gold, and menservants and maidservants, and camels and asses. My master hath a son, the only child of his wife Sarah, and my master made me swear, saying: 'Thou shalt not take a wife for my son of the daughters of the Canaanites; but thou shalt go to my kindred, and take a wife for my son.' I came this day unto the well, and behold, Rebekah came with her pitcher on her shoulder, and she went down and drew water, and gave me to drink. She made the camels drink also; and she said she was the daughter of Nahor's son, and I put the ring on her nose, and the bracelets on her hands. Then I bowed my head, and blessed the Lord who had led me in the right way to take a daughter of my master's kindred for his son. Now if ye will deal kindly and truly with my master, tell me."

Laban and Bethuel answered and said: "The thing proceedeth from the Lord. Rebekah is before thee; take her and let her be thy master's son's wife."

When Abraham's servant heard their words, he brought forth jewels of silver, and jewels of gold, and raiment, and gave them to Rebekah. He gave also to her brother and to her mother precious things; and he and the men that were with him did eat and drink, and tarried all night.

They rose up in the morning, and he said: "Send me away unto my master. Hinder me not."

Rebekah's brother and her mother called her, and said: "Wilt thou go with this man?"

She said: "I will go."

So they sent away Rebekah, and her nurse, and Abraham's servant, and his men. Rebekah and her damsels rode on the camels, and followed the man; and he went his way.

Isaac dwelt in the south country; and Isaac went out to meditate in the field at eventide. He lifted up his eyes, and, behold, there were camels coming, and Rebekah saw Isaac, and alighted off her camel. She said unto the servant: "What man is this that walketh in the field to meet us?"

The servant said: "It is Isaac."

The servant told Isaac all the things that he had

done; and Isaac brought Rebekah into his mother Sarah's tent, and Rebekah became his wife, and he was comforted after his mother's death.

Abraham gave all that he had unto Isaac; and these are the years of Abraham's life, a hundred three score and fifteen years; and Abraham died, and his sons Isaac and Ishmael buried him.

Isaac was forty years old when he took Rebekah to be his wife; and they had twin children, Esau and Jacob. The boys grew, and Esau became a cunning hunter, a man of the field; and Jacob became a dweller in tents. Isaac loved Esau, because he did eat of his venison, and Rebekah loved Jacob.

Esau came in from the field, and he was faint; and Esau said to Jacob: "Feed me, I pray thee."

Jacob said: "Sell me first thy birthright."

Esau said: "Behold, I am at the point to die, and what profit shall the birthright do to me?"

So he sold his birthright unto Jacob; and Jacob gave Esau bread and pottage of lentils; and Esau did eat and drink, and rose up, and went his way.

It came to pass, when Isaac was old, and his eyes were dim so that he could not see, he called Esau, and said unto him: "My son, behold now, I am old, I know not the day of my death. Therefore, I pray thee, take thy quiver and thy bow, and go and get me some venison. Make me savory meat, such as I love, and bring it to me, that I may eat, that my soul may bless thee before I die."

Rebekah heard what Isaac said, and when Esau went to hunt for venison, she spake unto Jacob saying: "I heard thy father say to Esau thy brother: 'Bring me venison, and make me savory meat, that I may eat, and bless thee before my death.' Now therefore, my son, obey my voice according to that which I command thee. Go to the flock, and fetch me two good kids of the goats, and I will make them savory meat for thy father, such as he loveth; and thou shalt take it to thy father, so that he may bless thee."

Jacob said to his mother: "Behold, Esau is a hairy man, and I am a smooth man. My father peradventure will feel me, and I shall seem to him as a deceiver, and I shall bring a curse on me, and not a blessing."

His mother said: "On me be thy curse, my son. Only obey my voice."

Then he went and fetched the kids, and his mother made savory meat; and Rebekah took the goodly raiment of Esau, which was in the house, and put it on Jacob; and she put the skins of the kids on his hands, and on the smooth of his neck; and she gave the savory meat and the bread, which she had prepared, into the hand of her son Jacob.

He went unto his father, and said: "My father."

Isaac said: "Here am I. Who art thou?"

Jacob said: "I am Esau. I have done according as

thou badest me. I pray thee, eat of my venison, that thy soul may bless me."

Isaac said: "How is it that thou hast prepared it so quickly, my son?"

Jacob said: "Because the Lord thy God sent me good speed."

Isaac said unto Jacob: "Come near, I pray thee, that I may feel thee whether thou be my very son Esau or not."

Jacob went near unto Isaac his father, and Isaac felt him, and said: "The voice is Jacob's voice, but the hands are the hands of Esau."

He discerned him not, because his hands were hairy, as his brother Esau's hands; and he said: "I will eat of my son's venison, that my soul may bless thee."

Jacob brought it near to him, and he did eat; and Jacob brought wine, and he drank. Then Isaac said: "Come now, and kiss me, my son."

So Jacob came and kissed him; and Isaac smelled the smell of his raiment, and blessed him, saying:

"See, the smell of my son
  Is as the smell of a field which the Lord hath blessed;
Therefore God give thee of the dew of heaven,
And of the fatness of the earth,
  And plenty of corn and wine.
Let peoples serve thee,
  And nations bow down to thee.

Be lord over thy brethren,
  And let thy mother's sons bow down to thee.
  Cursed be everyone that curseth thee,
  And blessed be everyone that blesseth thee."

It came to pass, as soon as Isaac had made an end of blessing Jacob, and Jacob was scarce gone out from the presence of Isaac his father, that Esau came in from his hunting. He also made savory meat, and brought it unto his father, and said: "Let my father arise, and eat of his son's venison, that thy soul may bless me."

Isaac said unto him: "Who art thou?"

Esau said: "I am thy son Esau."

Isaac trembled exceedingly, and said: "Who then is he that brought venison to me, before thou camest, and I have eaten, and have blessed him?"

When Esau heard the words of his father, he cried with a great and bitter cry, and said: "Bless me, even me also, O my father!"

Isaac said: "Thy brother came with guile, and hath taken away thy blessing."

Esau said: "He hath supplanted me two times. He took away my birthright, and, behold, now he hath taken away my blessing. Hast thou not reserved a blessing for me?"

Isaac answered and said: "I have made him thy lord, and with corn and wine have I sustained him; and what shall I do for thee, my son?"

Esau said: "Hast thou but one blessing, my father? Bless me, even me also, O my father;" and Esau lifted up his voice, and wept.

Isaac answered and said unto him:

"Behold, away from the fatness of the earth shall be
    thy dwelling,
And away from the dew of heaven from above;
    And by thy sword thou shalt live;
And thou shalt serve thy brother."

Esau hated Jacob because of the blessing wherewith Jacob had been blessed; and Esau said: "I will slay my brother Jacob."

The words of Esau were told to Rebekah; and she sent and called Jacob, and said unto him: "Thy brother Esau doth purpose to kill thee. Now, therefore, my son, flee thou to Laban my brother at Haran, and tarry with him until thy brother's fury turn away from thee, and he forget that which thou hast done to him."

Jacob went toward Haran, and he alighted at a certain place to tarry all night. The sun had set, and he took one of the stones of the place, and put it under his head, and lay down to sleep; and he dreamed, and behold a ladder set up on the earth, and the top of it reached to heaven; and behold the angels of God ascending and descending on it. The Lord stood above it, and said: "I am the Lord, the God of Abraham, and the God of Isaac. The land whereon thou liest, to thee will I give it, and to thy seed; and thy seed shall be as the dust of the earth. I am with thee, and will keep thee whithersoever thou goest."

Jacob awaked out of his sleep, and he said: "Surely the Lord is in this place, and I knew it not. This is the gate of heaven."

Jacob rose early in the morning, and took the stone that he had put under his head, and set it up for a pillar, and poured oil on the top of it; and he called the name of that place Beth-el.

Then Jacob went on his journey, and came to the land of the people of the east; and he looked, and behold a well, and three flocks of sheep lying by it; and the shepherds rolled the stone from the well's mouth, and watered the sheep, and put the stone again on the well's mouth in its place. Jacob said unto them: "Know ye Laban the grandson of Nahor?"

They said: "We know him."

He said unto them: "Is he well?"

They said: "He is well; and, behold, Rachel his daughter cometh with his sheep."

While they yet spake, Rachel came with her father's sheep. When Jacob saw Rachel, and the sheep, he went and rolled the stone from the well's mouth and watered the flock; and Jacob kissed Rachel, and told her that he was Rebekah's son; and she ran and told her father.

When Laban heard the tidings of Jacob, his sister's son, he ran to meet him, and embraced him, and brought him to his house. Jacob abode with Laban the space of a month; and Laban said unto Jacob: "Shouldest thou serve me for nought? Tell me, what shall thy wages be?"

Laban had two daughters. The name of the elder was Leah, and the name of the younger was Rachel. Jacob loved Rachel, and he said: "I will serve thee seven years for Rachel thy younger daughter."

Laban said: "It is better that I give her to thee, than that I should give her to another man. Abide with me."

Jacob served seven years for Rachel, and he said unto Laban: "Give me my wife; for my days are fulfilled."

Laban gathered together all the men of the place, and made a feast; and he took Leah his daughter, and brought her to be Jacob's wife. Jacob said to Laban: "What is this thou hast done? Did not I serve with thee for Rachel? Wherefore then hast thou beguiled me?"

Laban said: "It is not so done in our place, to give the younger before the firstborn. We will give thee the other also, for which thou shalt serve me yet seven other years."

So Laban gave him Rachel his daughter to wife, and Jacob served Laban yet seven other years.

Jacob had twelve sons: Reuben, Simeon, Levi, Judah, Dan, Naphtali, Gad, Asher, Issachar, Zebulun, Joseph, and Benjamin; and Joseph and Benjamin, who were born last, were the children of Rachel.

It came to pass that Jacob said unto Laban: "Send me away, that I may go to my own country. Give me my wives and my children, and let me go."

Laban said: "If I have found favor in thine eyes, tarry; for I have divined that the Lord hath blessed me for thy sake."

Jacob said: "Thou knowest how I have served thee, and how thy cattle have fared with me. It was little which thou hadst before I came, and thy herds have increased unto a multitude. The Lord hath blessed thee whithersoever I turned; and now when shall I provide for mine own house also?"

Laban said: "What shall I give thee?"

Jacob said: "I will again feed thy flock and keep it, if thou wilt give me every black one among the sheep, and the spotted and speckled among the goats. Of such shall be my hire."

Laban said: "Behold, I would it might be according to thy word."

So Laban removed that day the goats that were speckled and spotted, and all the black ones among the sheep, and he set three days' journey betwixt himself and Jacob; and Jacob increased exceedingly, and had large flocks, and maidservants and menservants, and camels and asses.

Jacob beheld the countenance of Laban, and it was not toward him as beforetime; and the Lord said unto

Jacob: "Return unto the land of thy fathers, and to thy kindred, and I will be with thee."

Then Jacob rose up, and set his sons and his wives on the camels, and he carried away all his cattle, and all his substance which he had gathered, for to go to Isaac his father in the land of Canaan.

Laban was gone to shear his sheep, and Jacob stole away unawares. It was told Laban on the third day that Jacob was fled; and he took his brethren with him, and pursued after Jacob seven days' journey, and overtook him on the mountain of Gilead. Laban said to Jacob: "What hast thou done, that thou hast stolen away unawares to me, and carried away my daughters as captives of the sword. Wherefore didst thou flee secretly; and didst not tell me, that I might have sent thee away with mirth and with songs? Now hast thou done foolishly."

Jacob answered: "I was afraid, lest thou shouldst take thy daughters from me by force. This twenty years have I been with thee. In the day the drought consumed me, and the frost by night, and my sleep fled from mine eyes; and thou hast changed my wages ten times. Except God had been with me, surely thou hadst sent me away empty."

Laban said unto Jacob: "Come, let us make a covenant, I and thou."

Then Jacob took a stone, and set it up for a pillar; and Laban said: "This pillar be witness, that I will not pass over it to thee, and that thou shalt not pass over it to me, for harm."

Jacob offered a sacrifice, and they did eat bread and tarried all night on the mountain. Early in the morning Laban rose up, and kissed the children and his daughters, and blessed them; and Laban departed, and returned unto his place.

Jacob went on his way, and he sent messengers before him to Esau his brother unto the land of Seir. He commanded them, saying: "Thus shall ye speak unto my lord Esau: 'Thy servant Jacob saith: "I have sojourned with Laban until now, and I have oxen, and asses, and flocks, and menservants and maidservants; and I have sent to tell my lord, that I may find grace in thy sight."

The messengers returned to Jacob saying: "We went to thy brother Esau, and he cometh to meet thee, and four hundred men with him."

Then Jacob was greatly afraid and distressed; and he divided the people that was with him, and the flocks, and the herds, and the camels, into two companies; and he said: "If Esau come to the one company, and smite it, the company which is left shall escape."

Afterward Jacob prepared a present for Esau his brother; two hundred she-goats and twenty he-goats, two hundred ewes and twenty rams, thirty milch camels with their colts, forty kine and ten bulls, twenty she-asses and ten foals. He delivered them into the hand of his servants, every drove by itself, and said: "Pass over the river Jabbok before me, and put a space betwixt drove and drove."

He commanded the foremost, saying: "When Esau my brother meeteth thee, and asketh thee: 'Whose drove is this?' thou shalt say: 'It is thy servant Jacob's, and is a present sent unto my lord Esau.'"

He commanded also the second, and the third, and all that followed, saying: "On this manner shall ye speak unto Esau, when ye find him, and ye shall say: 'Moreover, thy servant Jacob is behind us.'"

For Jacob thought: "I will appease Esau with the present that goeth before me, and afterward I will see his face. Peradventure he will accept me."

The present passed before him, and he rose up that night, and took his wives and children, and sent them, and all that he had, over the ford of Jabbok. Jacob was left alone, and there wrestled a man with him until the breaking of the day. When the man saw that he prevailed not against Jacob, he touched the hollow of Jacob's thigh, and the thigh was strained as they wrestled; and the man said: "Let me go, for the day breaketh."

Jacob said: "I will not let thee go, except thou bless me."

The man said unto him: "What is thy name?"

Jacob told him, and the man said: "Thou shalt be

called no more Jacob, but Israel.* Thou hast striven with God and hast prevailed;" and he blessed him there.

The sun rose, and Jacob joined his family, and he looked, and, behold, Esau came, and with him four hundred men. Jacob went and bowed himself to the ground seven times, until he came near to his brother; and Esau ran to meet him, and embraced him, and kissed him, and they wept. When Esau lifted up his eyes, and saw the women and the children, he said: "Who are these with thee?"

Jacob said: "The family which God hath graciously given thy servant."

Then Jacob's wives came near, and their children, and they bowed themselves.

Esau said: "What meanest thou by all the company which I met?"

Jacob said: "To find grace in the sight of my lord."

Esau said: "I have enough. My brother, let that thou hast be thine."

Jacob said: "Nay, I pray thee, receive my present;" and he urged him, and he took it.

Then Esau said: "Let us go on our journey."

Jacob said unto him: "My lord knoweth that the children are tender, and that if we overdrive the flocks and herds they all will die. Let my lord pass before his servant, and I will lead on softly, according to the

---
*The name Israel means, "He who striveth with God."

pace of the cattle and according to the pace of the children, until I come to my lord at Seir."

So Esau returned that day on his way to Seir; and Jacob came unto Isaac his father at Mamre. The days of Isaac were a hundred and fourscore years; and Isaac died, and was gathered unto his people; and Esau and Jacob his sons buried him. Esau dwelt in Mount Seir; and Jacob dwelt in the land of Canaan.

IV

JOSEPH AND HIS BRETHREN

JOSEPH, being seventeen years old, fed the flock with his brethren. Israel loved Joseph more than any of his other children, and he made him a coat of many colors. When his brethren saw that their father loved him more than them, they hated him, and could not speak peaceably unto him.

Joseph dreamed a dream, and he said to his brethren: "Hear, I pray you, this dream which I have dreamed. Behold, we were binding sheaves in the field, and, lo, my sheaf arose, and stood upright; and your sheaves came round about, and made obeisance to my sheaf."

His brethren said to him: "Shalt thou have dominion over us?" and they hated him the more for his dream.

He dreamed yet another dream, and said to his brethren: "I have dreamed a dream; and, behold, the sun and the moon and eleven stars made obeisance to me."

He told it to his father, and to his brethren; and his father rebuked him, and said: "What is this dream that thou hast dreamed? Shall I and thy mother and thy brethren come to bow down ourselves to thee?"

His brethren envied him; but his father kept the

saying in his mind. His brethren went to feed their father's flock in Shechem; and Israel said unto Joseph: "I will send thee unto them. Go now, see whether it be well with thy brethren, and well with the flock, and bring me word."

Joseph went, and his brethren saw him afar off, and they said one to another: "Behold this dreamer cometh. Let us slay him, and cast him into some pit, and we will say: 'An evil beast hath devoured him;' and we shall see what will become of his dreams."

But Reuben said: "Let us not take his life. Cast him into a pit here in the wilderness; but lay no hand on him."

This he said, that he might deliver him out of their hand, to restore him to his father. When Joseph was come unto his brethren, they stript him of his coat of many colors, and they took him, and cast him into a pit. Then they sat down to eat bread, and, behold, a traveling company of Ishmaelites came from Gilead, with their camels bearing spicery and balm and myrrh, going to Egypt.

Judah said unto his brethren: "What profit is it if we slay our brother? Let us sell him to the Ishmaelites."

His brethren harkened unto him, and they drew up Joseph out of the pit, and sold him to the Ishmaelites for twenty pieces of silver. Reuben was not with the others and knew not what they had done. When he went to the pit, behold, Joseph was not there; and he rent his clothes. He returned unto his brethren, and said: "The child is not."

Then they took Joseph's coat, and they killed a goat, and dipped the coat in the blood; and they brought the coat of many colors to their father, and said: "This have we found. Know now whether it be thy son's coat or not."

He knew it, and said: "It is my son's coat. An evil beast hath devoured him. Joseph is without doubt torn in pieces;" and Jacob mourned for his son many days.

Joseph was brought down to Egypt; and Potiphar, an officer of Pharaoh's, the captain of the guard, bought him of the Ishmaelites. The Lord was with Joseph, and his master saw that the Lord made all he did to prosper. So Joseph found grace in his master's sight, and Potiphar made him overseer over his house, and all that he had he put into his hand; and the Lord blessed the Egyptian's house for Joseph's sake.

Joseph was comely, and well favored; and his master's wife cast her eyes on Joseph and loved him. She spake affectionately to him day by day, but he hearkened not unto her. It came to pass about this time, that he went into the house to do his work, and she caught him by his garment; and he left his garment in her hand, and fled. She laid up his garment, until his master came home. Then she said: "The Hebrew servant, which thou hast brought unto us, came in unto me to mock me; and as I lifted up my voice and cried, he left his garment by me, and fled out."

When Potiphar heard the words of his wife, his wrath was kindled, and he took Joseph, and put him into prison. But the Lord was with Joseph, and gave him favor in the sight of the keeper of the prison; and the keeper of the prison committed to Joseph's hand all the prisoners that were in the prison.

It came to pass, that the chief butler of the king and the chief baker offended their lord the king of Egypt. Pharaoh was wroth against his two officers, and he put them into the prison where Joseph was; and they dreamed a dream, each man his dream, in one night. Joseph came in unto them in the morning, and saw they were sad; and he asked: "Wherefore look ye so sadly today?"

They said unto him: "We have each dreamed a dream, and there is none who can interpret them."

Joseph said: "Tell me the dreams, I pray you."

The chief butler said: "In my dream, behold, a vine was before me, and the vine had three branches. It budded, and blossomed, and the clusters thereof brought forth ripe grapes. Pharaoh's cup was in my hand and I took the grapes, and pressed them into Pharaoh's cup, and I gave the cup to Pharaoh."

Joseph said unto him: "This is the interpretation: The three branches are three days. In three days shall Pharaoh restore thee unto thine office, and thou shalt give Pharaoh's cup into his hand, after the former manner when thou wast his butler. But have me in thy remembrance when it shall be well with thee, and shew kindness, I pray thee, unto me. Make mention of me unto Pharaoh, and bring me out of this prison; for indeed I have done nothing that they should put me here."

Then the chief baker said unto Joseph: "In my dream, behold, three baskets were on my head, and in the uppermost basket there was all manner of bakemeats for Pharaoh, and the birds did eat them out of the basket."

Joseph said: "This is the interpretation: The three baskets are three days. In three days shall Pharaoh lift up thy head from off thee, and shall hang thee on a tree; and the birds shall eat thy flesh."

It came to pass the third day, which was Pharaoh's birthday, that he made a feast unto all his servants; and he restored the chief butler unto his butlership, and the butler gave the cup into Pharaoh's hand; but he hanged the chief baker, as Joseph had interpreted. Yet did not the chief butler remember Joseph, but forgot him.

At the end of two years Pharaoh dreamed he stood by the river Nile; and, behold, there came up out of the river seven kine, well favored and fatfleshed, and they fed in the reed-grass; and, behold, seven other kine came up out of the river, ill favored and leanfleshed, and the ill favored and leanfleshed kine did eat up the seven well favored and fat kine; and when they had eaten them up, it could not be known that they had eaten them; but they were still ill favored, as at the beginning. Then Pharaoh awoke.

He slept and dreamed a second time; and, behold, seven ears of corn grew on one stalk, rank and good; and, behold, seven ears, thin and blasted with the east wind sprung up after them, and the thin ears devoured the seven rank and full ears. Pharaoh awoke, and, behold, it was a dream.

It came to pass in the morning that his spirit was troubled, and he sent for all the magicians of Egypt, and all the wise men thereof. Pharaoh told them his dreams; but there was none that could interpret them unto him.

Then spake the chief butler unto Pharaoh, saying: "I do remember Pharaoh put me and the chief baker in prison, and we each dreamed a dream; and there was with us a young man, a Hebrew, servant to the captain of the guard. We told him, and he interpreted to us our dreams; and it came to pass, as he interpreted to us, so it was."

Then Pharaoh sent and called Joseph, and they brought him hastily out of the dungeon, and he shaved himself, and changed his raiment, and came in unto Pharaoh.

Pharaoh said unto Joseph: "I have dreamed a dream,

and there is none that can interpret it. I have heard say of thee, that when thou hearest a dream thou canst interpret it."

Joseph answered Pharaoh, saying: "God shall give Pharaoh an answer."

Then Pharaoh told his two dreams, and Joseph said: "God hath showed Pharaoh what He is about to do. The seven good kine are seven years, and the seven good ears are seven years. The dreams are one. The seven lean and ill favored kine are seven years, and also the seven empty ears blasted with the east wind. They shall be seven years of famine. Behold, there come seven years of great plenty throughout all the land of Egypt, and there shall arise after them seven years of famine, and the famine shall consume the land, for it shall be very grievous. Now therefore let Pharaoh look out a man discreet and wise, and set him over the land of Egypt; and let Pharaoh appoint overseers to gather the food of the good years, and lay up corn. The food shall be for a store against the seven years of famine, that we perish not."

The thing was good in the eyes of Pharaoh, and in the eyes of all his servants, and Pharaoh said unto Joseph: "Forasmuch as God hath showed thee all this, there is none so discreet and wise as thou. Thou shalt be over my house, and according unto thy word shall all my people be ruled."

Pharaoh took off his signet ring from his hand and

put it on Joseph's hand, and arrayed him in vestures of fine linen, and put a gold chain about his neck. He made him ride in the second chariot which he had, and set him over all the land of Egypt. Pharaoh gave him to wife Asenath the daughter of Poti-phera priest of On; and Joseph was thirty years old.

Joseph went throughout all the land of Egypt, and in the seven plenteous years the earth brought forth by handfuls; and he gathered up the food of the seven years, and laid up corn as the sand of the sea.

Unto Joseph were born two sons before the years of famine came, and Joseph called the name of the firstborn Manasseh, and the name of the second called he Ephraim.

The seven years of plenty came to an end, and the seven years of dearth began, according as Joseph had said. There was famine in all lands; but in the land of Egypt there was bread; and when the land of Egypt was famished, the people cried to Pharaoh for bread. Pharaoh said to the Egyptians: "Go unto Joseph. What he saith to you, do."

Joseph opened the storehouses, and sold unto the Egyptians; and all countries came into Egypt to Joseph to buy corn, because the famine was sore in all the earth.

When Jacob saw that there was corn in Egypt, he said unto his sons: "Why do ye look one on another? There is corn in Egypt. Get you thither, and buy for us, that we may live, and not die."

So Joseph's ten older brethren went to buy corn from Egypt. But Benjamin, Jacob sent not; for he said: "Lest peradventure mischief befall him."

Joseph was the governor over the land. He it was that sold to all the people; and his brethren came, and bowed down themselves before him with their faces to the earth. Joseph knew his brethren, but made himself strange unto them, and spake roughly with them. He said: "Whence come ye?"

They said: "From the land of Canaan to buy food."

Joseph remembered the dreams which he dreamed of them, and said: "Ye are spies. To see the nakedness of the land ye are come."

They said unto him: "Nay, my lord, but to buy food are thy servants come. We are true men. Thy servants are no spies. We are the sons of one man in the land of Canaan; and, behold, our youngest brother is with our father."

Joseph said unto them: "Ye are spies. By the life of Pharaoh ye shall not go forth hence, except your youngest brother come hither, and ye shall be kept in prison, that your words may be proved, whether there be truth in you."

He put them all into prison three days, and Joseph said unto them the third day: "Let one of you be bound in your prison; but go the rest of ye, and carry corn for the famine of your households, and bring your

Joseph and his Brethren

youngest brother unto me. So shall your words be verified, and ye shall not die."

They agreed to do as he commanded; and they said one to another: "We are verily guilty concerning our brother Joseph, in that, when he besought us, we would not hear. Therefore is this distress come on us."

Reuben said: "Spake I not unto you, saying: 'Do not sin against the child;' and ye would not hear?"

They knew not that Joseph understood them; for he spake unto them by an interpreter; and he turned himself about from them, and wept. Then he returned, and took Simeon from among them, and bound him before their eyes. Joseph commanded to fill their sacks with corn, and to restore every man's money into his sack, and to give them provisions for the way.

Thus was it done unto them, and they laded their asses with their corn, and departed. As one of them opened his sack to give his ass provender in the lodging place, he espied his money, and, behold, it was in the mouth of his sack. He said unto his brethren: "My money is restored, and, lo, it is in my sack."

Then their hearts failed them, and they turned trembling one to another, saying: "What is this that God hath done unto us?"

They came unto Jacob their father and told him all that had befallen them, saying: "The man, who is lord of the land, spake roughly to us, and took us for spies of the country. We said unto him: 'We are true men.

We be brethren, and one other brother, the youngest, is with our father in the land of Canaan.'

"The lord of the land said unto us: 'Leave one of your brethren with me, and go your way and bring your youngest brother unto me.'"

Jacob said: "Me have ye bereaved of my children. Joseph is not, and Simeon is not, and ye will take Benjamin away. He shall not go with you; for his brother is dead, and he only is left. If mischief befall him, then shall ye bring down my gray hairs with sorrow to the grave."

The famine was sore in the land, and it came to pass, when they had eaten the corn which they had brought out of Egypt, Jacob said unto his sons: "Go again. Buy us a little food."

Judah spake, saying: "If thou wilt send our brother with us, we will go and buy thee food; but if thou wilt not send him, we will not go; for the man said unto us: 'Ye shall not see my face, except your brother be with you.'"

Israel said: "Wherefore dealt ye so ill with me, as to tell the man ye had yet a brother?"

They said: "The man asked straitly concerning ourselves and our kindred, saying: 'Is your father yet alive? Have ye another brother?' and we told him. Could we in any wise know that he would say: 'Bring your brother'?"

Judah said unto his father: "Send the lad with me,

and we will arise and go, that we may live, and not die, both we, and thou, and also our little ones. I will be surety for him. Of my hand shalt thou require him. If I bring him not unto thee, and set him before thee, then let me bear the blame forever."

Israel said: "Do this; take of the choice fruits of the land and carry the man a present, a little balm, and a little honey, spices and myrrh, nuts and almonds. Take double money in your hands; and the money that was returned in the mouth of your sacks carry again. Peradventure it was an oversight. Take also your brother, and God Almighty give you mercy before the man, that he may release unto you your other brother and Benjamin."

The men took the present, and they took double money, and Benjamin, and went to Egypt, and stood before Joseph. When Joseph saw Benjamin with them, he said to the steward of his house: "Bring the men in, and make ready, for they shall dine with me at noon."

The steward did as Joseph bade, and brought the men into Joseph's house; and they were afraid. They said: "Because of the money that was in our sacks are we brought in, that he may seek occasion against us, and fall on us, and take us for bondmen."

They drew near to the steward of Joseph's house, and said: "Oh my lord, we came the first time to buy food, and when we went to the lodging place, we opened our sacks, and, behold, every man's money was in the mouth of his sack, and we have brought it again. Other money have we brought to buy food. We know not who put our money in our sacks."

The steward said: "Peace be to you. Fear not. Your God, and the God of your father, hath given you treasure in your sacks."

Then he brought Simeon unto them, and gave them water, and they washed their feet; and he gave their asses provender.

They made ready the present, and when Joseph came home, they brought him the present, and bowed down themselves to him to the earth. He asked them of their welfare, and said: "Is your father well, the old man of whom ye spake? Is he yet alive?"

They answered: "Thy servant our father is in good health;" and they made obeisance.

Joseph saw Benjamin his brother, his mother's son, and said: "God be gracious unto thee."

His heart did yearn toward his brother, and he entered his chamber, and wept there. Then he washed his face, and came out, and said: "Set on bread."

The servants set on for him by himself, and for his brethren by themselves, and for the Egyptians, that did eat with him, by themselves, because the Egyptians might not eat bread with the Hebrews, for that is an abomination unto the Egyptians. Joseph sent messes unto his brethren from before him; but Benjamin's mess was five times as much as any of theirs; and they drank and were merry.

Joseph commanded the steward of his house, saying: "Fill the men's sacks with grain, as much as they can carry, and put every man's money in his sack's mouth; and put my silver cup in the sack's mouth of the youngest, with his corn money."

The steward did according to the words that Joseph had spoken. As soon as the morning was light, the men were sent away, they and their asses. When they were gone out of the city, and were not yet far off, Joseph said unto his steward: "Up, follow after the men, and when thou dost overtake them, say unto them: 'Wherefore have ye rewarded evil for good? Have ye not stolen the silver cup from which my lord drinketh?'"

He overtook them and spake unto them these words, and they said: "God forbid that thy servants should do such a thing. Behold, the money, which we found in our sacks' mouths, we brought again unto thee out of the land of Canaan. How then should we steal out of thy lord's house silver or gold? With whomsoever of thy servants the cup be found, let him die, and the others of us will be my lord's bondsmen."

The steward said: "He with whom the cup is found shall be my bondman; but the rest shall be blameless."

Then they hasted, and took down every man his sack to the ground, and opened every man his sack. The steward searched, and began at the eldest, and left at the youngest, and the cup was found in Benjamin's sack. Then the brethren rent their clothes, and laded every man his ass, and returned to the city. Judah and his brethren came to Joseph's house, and they fell before him on the ground. Joseph said unto them: "What deed is this that ye have done?"

Judah said: "What shall we say unto my lord? or how shall we clear ourselves? Behold, we are my lord's bondmen."

Joseph said: "The man in whose sack the cup was found, he shall be my bondman. As for the rest of you, get you in peace unto your father."

Then Judah came near unto him, and said: "Oh my lord, let thy servant, I pray thee, speak a word in my lord's ears. My lord asked his servants, saying: 'Have ye a father, or another brother?'

"We said unto my lord: 'We have a father, an old man, and a child of his old age, a little one; and his brother is dead. He alone is left of his mother, and his father loveth him.'

"Thou saidst unto thy servants: 'Bring him unto me that I may set mine eyes on him.'

"We said unto my lord: 'The lad cannot leave his father; for if he should, his father would die.'

"Thou saidst unto thy servants: 'Except your youngest brother come with you, ye shall see my face no more.'

"When we came unto thy servant my father, we told

him the words of my lord. Our father said: 'Go again, and buy us a little food.'

"We said: 'We may not see the man's face, except our youngest brother be with us.'

"My father said unto us: 'Ye know that Rachel my wife had two sons, and the one went out from me, and I have not seen him since. If ye take this one also from me, and mischief befall him, ye shall bring down my gray hairs with sorrow to the grave.'

"Now therefore when I come to my father, and the lad be not with us, seeing that his life is bound up in the lad's life, he will die. Thy servant became surety for the lad unto my father. Let thy servant, I pray thee, abide instead of the lad a bondman to my lord; and let the lad go with his brethren. For how shall I go to my father, and the lad be not with me? lest I see the evil that shall come on my father."

Then Joseph could not refrain himself, and he cried: "Cause every man to go out from me except these Hebrews."

When there stood no others with them, Joseph wept aloud, and said: "I am Joseph. Come near to me, I pray you."

They came near, and he said: "I am Joseph your brother, whom ye sold into Egypt. Be not grieved, nor angry with yourselves, that ye sold me hither; for God did send me before you to preserve life. Two years hath the famine been in the land, and there are yet five years, in the which there shall be neither plowing nor harvest. God sent me before you to save you alive by a great deliverance. Haste ye, and go to my father, and say unto him: 'Thus saith thy son Joseph: "God hath made me lord of all Egypt. Come down unto me. Tarry not; and thou shalt be near unto me, thou, and thy children, and thy children's children, and thy flocks, and thy herds, and all that thou hast. I will nourish thee."' Ye shall tell my father of all my glory in Egypt, and of all that ye have seen."

Then Joseph fell on his brother Benjamin's neck, and wept; and he kissed all his brethren, and wept on them. After that his brethren talked with him.

The fame of all this was heard in Pharaoh's house, and it pleased Pharaoh well, and his servants; and Pharaoh said unto Joseph: "Say unto thy brethren: 'This do ye; lade your beasts, and get you unto the land of Canaan, and take your father and your households, and come unto me, and ye shall eat of the fat of the land. Take you wagons out of the land of Egypt for your little ones, and for your wives, and your father. The good of the land of Egypt is yours.'"

Joseph gave his brethren wagons, according to the commandment of Pharaoh, and gave them provisions for the way. To each of them he gave changes of raiment; but to Benjamin he gave three hundred pieces of silver, and five changes of raiment. So his brethren departed, and came into the land of Canaan unto Jacob their father. They told him, saying: "Joseph is yet alive, and he is ruler over all the land of Egypt."

Jacob's heart fainted, for he believed them not, and they told him all the words of Joseph, which he had said unto them, and when Jacob saw the wagons which Joseph had sent, his spirit revived, and he said: "It is enough. Joseph my son is yet alive. I will go and see him before I die."

Jacob rose up, and his sons carried him, and their little ones, and their wives, in the wagons which Pharaoh had sent; and they took their cattle, and their goods, and came into Egypt. Jacob sent Judah before him unto Joseph, and Joseph made ready his chariot, and went to meet his father. He presented himself unto him, and fell on his neck, and wept a good while.

Israel said unto Joseph: "Now let me die, since I have seen thy face, that thou art yet alive."

Then Joseph went and told Pharaoh, and said: "My father and my brethren, and their flocks, and their herds, and all that they have, are come out of the land of Canaan."

From among his brethren he took five men, and presented them unto Pharaoh; and Pharaoh said unto them: "What is your occupation?"

They said: "Thy servants are shepherds."

Pharaoh spake unto Joseph, saying: "The land of Egypt is before thee. In the best of the land make thy father and thy brethren to dwell. In the land of Goshen let them dwell; and if thou knowest any able men among them, make them rulers over my cattle."

Joseph brought in his father, and set him before Pharaoh; and Pharaoh said unto Jacob: "How old art thou?"

Jacob said unto Pharaoh: "The years of my pilgrimage are a hundred and thirty. Few and evil have been the years of my life, and they have not attained unto the years of the life of my fathers;" and Jacob blessed Pharaoh, and went out from his presence.

There was no bread in all the land; for the famine was very sore, so that the land of Egypt and the land of Canaan fainted by reason of the famine. Joseph gathered up all the money that was found in the land of Egypt, and in the land of Canaan, for corn which the people bought, and Joseph brought the money into Pharaoh's house. Then all the Egyptians came unto Joseph and said: "Give us bread; for why should we die?"

Joseph said: "I will give you bread in exchange for your cattle, if money fail."

So they brought their cattle unto Joseph, and Joseph gave them bread in exchange for the horses, and for the flocks, and for the herds, and for the asses.

When that year was ended, they came unto him the second year, and said unto him: "Our money is all spent, and the herds of cattle are my lord's. There is nought left but our bodies and our lands. Wherefore should we die before thine eyes? Buy us and our land for bread, and we will be servants unto Pharaoh."

So Joseph bought all the land of Egypt for Pharaoh. The Egyptians sold every man his field, because the famine was sore on them, and the land became Pharaoh's. Only the land of the priests bought he not; for the priests had a portion from Pharaoh.

Then Joseph said unto the people: "Behold, I have bought you and your land for Pharaoh. Lo, here is seed for you, and ye shall sow the land. At the ingatherings ye shall give a fifth unto Pharaoh, and four parts shall be your own, for seed of the field, and for your food."

They said: "Thou hast saved our lives, and we will be Pharaoh's servants."

Jacob lived in the land of Egypt seventeen years; and the time drew near that he must die; and he called his son Joseph, and said unto him: "Bury me not, I pray thee, in Egypt, but when I die, thou shalt carry me out of Egypt, and bury me with my fathers in their burying-place."

Joseph said: "I will do as thou hast said."

It came to pass after these things, that Jacob was sick, and Joseph went to him. It was told Jacob: "Thy son Joseph cometh unto thee," and he strengthened himself, and sat up on the bed.

Israel said unto Joseph: "Behold, I die; but God shall be with you, and bring you again unto the land of your fathers;" and he called unto his other sons, and blessed them.

Then Jacob gathered up his feet into the bed, and yielded up the ghost. Joseph commanded the physicians to embalm his father, and he spake unto Pharaoh, saying: "My father made me swear to bury him in the land of Canaan. Now therefore let me go, I pray thee, and bury my father, and I will come again."

Pharaoh said: "Go and bury thy father, according as he made thee swear."

So Joseph went to bury his father; and with him went his brethren, and all the servants of Pharaoh, and all the elders of the land of Egypt. There went with him both chariots and horsemen; and it was a very great company. They came to the land of Canaan, and buried Jacob; and Joseph returned into Egypt, he, and his brethren, and all that went with him to bury his father.

Joseph dwelt in Egypt, he, and his father's house; and Joseph lived one hundred and ten years, and he said unto his brethren: "I die; but God will surely visit you, and bring you out of this land unto the land which he sware to Abraham, to Isaac, and to Jacob; and ye shall carry my bones hence."

So Joseph died, and they embalmed him, and he was put in a coffin in Egypt.

V

JOB AND HIS FRIENDS

THERE was a man in the land of Uz, whose name was Job; and that man was perfect and upright, and one that feared God. There were born unto him seven sons and three daughters. His substance was seven thousand sheep, and three thousand camels, and five hundred yoke of oxen, and five hundred she-asses, and a very great household, so that this man was the greatest of all the men of the east.

Now there was a day when the sons of God came to present themselves before the Lord, and Satan came also among them; and the Lord said unto Satan: "Whence comest thou?"

Then Satan answered and said: "From going to and fro on the earth."

The Lord said: "Hast thou considered My servant Job? for there is none like him, a perfect and an upright man."

Satan answered and said: "Doth Job fear God for nought? Thou hast blessed the work of his hands, and his substance is increased. But put forth Thine hand, and touch all that he hath, and he will curse Thee to Thy face."

The Lord said unto Satan: "Behold, all that he hath is in thy power."

So Satan went from the presence of the Lord; and on a day when Job's sons and daughters were eating and drinking in their eldest brother's house, there came a messenger unto Job, and said: "The oxen were plowing, and the asses feeding beside them, and the Sabeans took them away. Yea, they have slain the servants with the edge of the sword, and I only am escaped to tell thee."

While he was yet speaking, there came another, and said: "The fire of God is fallen from heaven, and hath burned up the sheep, and the servants. I only am escaped to tell thee."

While he was yet speaking, there came also another, and said: "The Chaldeans made a raid on the camels, and have taken them away, and slain the servants. I only am escaped to tell thee."

While he was yet speaking, there came also another, and said: "Thy sons and thy daughters were eating in their eldest brother's house; and there came a great wind from the wilderness, and smote the house, and it fell, and they are dead. I only am escaped to tell thee."

Then Job arose, and rent his mantle, and shaved his head, and fell down on the ground and worshipped. He said: "The Lord gave, and the Lord hath taken away. Blessed be the name of the Lord."

Again there was a day when the sons of God came to present themselves before the Lord, and Satan came also. The Lord said unto Satan: "My servant Job still holdeth fast his integrity, although thou movedst Me against him."

Satan answered: "All that a man hath will he give for his life. Put forth Thine hand, and touch his bone and his flesh, and he will curse Thee to Thy face."

The Lord said unto Satan: "Behold, he is in thine hand. Only spare his life."

So Satan went from the presence of the Lord, and smote Job with boils from the sole of his foot unto his crown; and he sat among the ashes. Then said his wife unto him: "Dost thou still hold fast thine integrity? Curse God, and die."

But he said unto her: "Thou speakest as one of the foolish women speaketh."

When Job's three friends, Eliphaz, and Bildad, and Zophar, heard of all this evil that was come on him, they came to comfort him. They lifted up their eyes afar off, and knew him not, and they wept, and rent every one his mantle, and sprinkled dust on their heads.* So they sat down with him on the ground seven days and seven nights, and none spake a word unto him; for they saw that his pain was very great. After this opened Job his mouth and said:

"Let the day perish wherein I was born.

Why died I not? for now should I have been quiet.

---

*To rend the clothes as a manifestation of great sorrow was a common custom in Bible times. The outer garment was a flowing mantle, and the rent was made more or less long according to the feelings of the afflicted one. To shave the head was another method of showing grief; and to sit among the ashes signified the deepest mourning and humility. Putting dust or earth on the head was likewise a conventional way of showing profound sorrow.

There the wicked cease from troubling;
And there the weary be at rest.
Wherefore is light given to him that is in misery,
And life unto the bitter in soul?"

Then Eliphaz said:
"Man is born unto trouble,
As the sparks fly upward.
But as for me, I would seek unto God,
And unto God would I commit my cause;
Who doeth great things and unsearchable,
Marvellous things without number.
Behold, happy is the man whom God correcteth.
Therefore despise not thou the chastening of the Almighty."

Then Job said:
"The arrows of the Almighty are within me,
The terrors of God do set themselves in array against me.
Oh that I might have my request!
Even that it would please God to destroy me.
When I lie down, I say:
'When shall I arise, and the night be gone?'
And I am full of tossings to and fro unto the dawning of the day.
I loathe my life. I would not live alway.
Let me alone; for my days are vanity."

Then Bildad said:
"If thou wouldest seek diligently unto God,
If thou wert pure and upright;

Surely now He would awake for thee,
And make the habitation of thy righteousness prosperous."

Then Job said:
"My soul is weary of my life.
I will give free course to my complaint.
I will say unto God: 'Do not condemn me.
Seest Thou as man seest,
That Thou inquirest after mine iniquity,
And searchest after my sin,
Although Thou knoweth that I am not wicked?
Are not my days few? Cease then,
And let me alone, that I may take comfort a little,
Before I go whence I shall not return.'"

Then Zophar said:
"Should thy boastings make men hold their peace?
Oh that God would speak,
And that He would show thee the secrets of wisdom.
But vain man is void of understanding.
Yea, man is born as a wild ass's colt."

Then Job said:
"I have understanding as well as you.
Ye are forgers of lies.
Ye are all physicians of no value.
Oh that ye would altogether hold your peace!
Your sayings are proverbs of ashes.
Your defences are defences of clay.

Behold now, I have set my cause in order,
I know that I am righteous."
Then Eliphaz said:
"Thou choosest the tongue of the crafty.
Thine own mouth condemneth thee, and not I.
Are the consolations of God too small for thee?
The wicked man behaveth himself proudly against the Almighty,
He shall not depart out of darkness."
Then Job said:
"I have heard many such things.
Miserable comforters are ye all.
God casteth me into the hands of the wicked.
I was at ease, and He dashed me to pieces."
Then Bildad said:
"The light of the wicked shall be put out.
He is cast into a net by his own feet.
Terrors shall make him afraid on every side.
His remembrance shall perish from the earth."
Then Job said:
"Have pity on me, have pity on me, O ye my friends;
For the hand of God hath touched me.
But I know that my Redeemer liveth,
And that He shall stand up at the last on the earth."
Then Zophar said:
"The triumphing of the wicked is short.
He shall fly away as a dream, and shall not be found.

Yea, he shall be chased away as a vision of the
  night.
The heavens shall reveal his iniquity,
And the earth shall rise up against him."
Then Job said:
"Shall any teach God knowledge?
One dieth in his full strength,
Being wholly at ease and quiet;
And another dieth in bitterness of soul,
And never tasteth of good.
They lie down alike in the dust."
Then Eliphaz said:
"Can a man be profitable unto God?
Surely he that is wise is profitable unto himself.
If thou return to the Almighty, thou shalt be built up,
And light shall shine on thy ways."
Then Job said:
"Oh that I knew where I might find Him!
My foot hath held fast to His steps.
His way have I kept, and turned not aside.
Till I die I will not put away mine integrity from me.
My righteousness I hold fast, and will not let it go.
For what is the hope of the godless, though he get
  him gain?
Will God hear his cry,
When trouble cometh on him?
Terrors overtake him like waters;
A tempest stealeth him away in the night.

Where shall wisdom be found?
The deep saith: 'It is not in me.'
It cannot be gotten for gold;
Yea, the price of wisdom is above rubies.
God understandeth the way thereof,
And unto man He said:
'Behold, the fear of the Lord, that is wisdom;
And to depart from evil is understanding.'
Oh that I were as in the months of old,
As in the days when God watched over me.
I caused the widow's heart to sing for joy.
I was eyes to the blind,
And feet was I to the lame.
I was a father to the needy.
Unto me men gave ear, and waited,
And kept silence for my counsel.
But my welfare is passed away as a cloud,
And the pains that gnaw me take no rest.
I am a brother to dragons,
And a companion to owls.
Therefore is my harp turned to mourning,
And my pipe into the voice of them that weep."
Then the Lord answered Job out of the whirlwind, and said:
"Where wast thou when I laid the foundations of the earth?
Who laid the corner stone thereof;
When the morning stars sang together,

And all the sons of God shouted for joy?
Hast thou walked in the recesses of the deep?
Have the gates of death been revealed unto thee?
Where is the way to the dwelling of light,
And as for darkness, where is the place thereof?
Canst thou lift up thy voice to the clouds,
That abundance of waters may cover thee?
Who provideth for the raven his food?
Hast thou given the horse his might?
Hast thou clothed his neck with the quivering mane?
Doth the hawk fly by thy wisdom?
Doth the eagle mount up at thy command
And make her nest on high?"
Then Job answered the Lord, and said:
"Behold, I am of small account. What shall I answer Thee?
I know that Thou canst do all things,
And that no purpose of Thine can be restrained.
I have uttered that which I understood not;
Wherefore I abhor myself, and repent
In dust and ashes."

The Lord said to Eliphaz: "My wrath is kindled against thee, and against thy two friends; for ye have not spoken of Me the thing that is right, as My servant Job hath. Now, therefore, take unto you seven bullocks and seven rams, and offer up for yourselves a burnt offering; and Job shall pray for you, that I deal not with you after your folly."

So Eliphaz and Bildad and Zophar did according as the Lord commanded them, and the Lord accepted Job; and the Lord gave Job twice as much as he had before. Then came there unto him all his brethren, and all his sisters, and all that had been of his acquaintance before, and did eat bread with him in his house, and they comforted him concerning all the evil that the Lord had brought on him.

The Lord blessed the latter end of Job more than his beginning; for he had fourteen thousand sheep, and six thousand camels, and a thousand yoke of oxen, and a thousand she-asses. He had also seven sons and three daughters, and in all the land were no women found so fair as the daughters of Job. After this Job lived a hundred and forty years, and saw his sons, and his sons' sons, even four generations. So Job died, being old and full of days.

VI

MOSES AND THE PLAGUES OF EGYPT

JOSEPH died, and all his brethren, and all that generation; and the children of Israel increased abundantly, and waxed exceeding mighty, and the land was filled with them.

Now there arose a king over Egypt, who remembered not Joseph; and he said unto his people: "Behold, the children of Israel are more than we. Come, let us deal with them, lest, when there falleth out any war, they join our enemies, and fight against us, and get out of the land."

Therefore the Egyptians set over the Israelites taskmasters to afflict them with burdens, and made their lives bitter with hard service in mortar and in brick, and in all manner of service in the field. Pharaoh also charged his people, saying: "Every son that is born among the Israelites ye shall cast into the river."

A man of the house of Levi took a wife, and the woman bare a son. When she saw that he was a goodly child, she hid him three months; and when she could not longer hide him, she took an ark of bulrushes, and daubed it with slime and with pitch; and she put the child therein, and laid the ark in the flags by the river's brink.

The child's sister stood afar off to know what would be done to him; and the daughter of Pharaoh came down to bathe in the river. She saw the ark among the flags and sent her maid to fetch it; and the maid opened it, and saw the child. The babe wept, and the maid had compassion on him, and said: "This is one of the Hebrews' children."

Then said the child's sister to Pharaoh's daughter: "Shall I go and call one of the Hebrew women, that she may nurse the child for thee?"

Pharaoh's daughter said to the child: "Go."

The maid went and called the child's mother; and Pharaoh's daughter said unto the woman: "Take this child away, and nurse it for me, and I will give thee thy wages."

The woman took the child and nursed it, and the child grew, and she brought him unto Pharaoh's daughter. He became a son to Pharaoh's daughter, and she called his name Moses.

It came to pass, when Moses was grown up, that he went out unto his brethren, and looked on their burdens; and he saw an Egyptian smiting a Hebrew. He looked this way and that way, and when he saw no one else, he slew the Egyptian and hid his body in the sand.

He went out the second day, and, behold, two men of the Hebrews strove together; and he said to him that did the wrong: "Wherefore smitest thou thy fellow?"

The man said: "Who made thee a prince and a judge over us? Intendest thou to kill me as thou killed the Egyptian?"

Then Moses feared, and said: "Surely the thing is known."

When Pharaoh heard it he sought to slay Moses; but Moses fled to the land of Midian; and he sat down by a well. The priest of Midian had seven daughters, and they came down and drew water, and filled the troughs to water their father's flock; and the shepherds came and drove them away; but Moses stood up and helped them, and watered their flock.

When they came to their father, he said: "How is it that ye are come so soon today?"

They said: "An Egyptian delivered us out of the hand of the shepherds, and drew water for us, and watered the flock."

He said unto his daughters: "And where is he? Why is it that ye have left the man? Call him that he may eat bread."

Moses was content to dwell there, and Jethro the priest of Midian gave Moses Zipporah his daughter for a wife.

In process of time the king of Egypt died, and the children of Israel sighed by reason of the bondage.

God heard their groaning, and God remembered his covenant with Abraham, with Isaac, and with Jacob.

Moses was keeping the flock of Jethro his father-in-law. He led the flock to the back of the wilderness, and came to the mountain of God, even to Horeb; and the angel of the Lord appeared unto him in a flame of fire out of the midst of a bush. He looked, and, behold; the bush burned with fire, and the bush was not consumed. Moses said: "I will turn aside, and see this great sight."

When the Lord saw that he turned aside to see, God called unto him out of the midst of the bush and said: "Moses, Moses."

Then Moses said: "Here am I."

God said: "Draw not nigh hither. Put off thy shoes from thy feet, for the place whereon thou standest is holy ground. I am the God of thy father, the God of Abraham, the God of Isaac, and the God of Jacob."

Moses hid his face; for he was afraid to look on God.

The Lord said: "I have seen the affliction of my people which are in Egypt, and have heard their cry by reason of their taskmasters. I know their sorrows, and I am come down to deliver them out of the hand of the Egyptians, and to bring them out of that land unto a land flowing with milk and honey—unto the place of the Canaanite, and the Amorite, and the Hivite, and the Jebusite. Now, therefore, I will send

Moses and the Plagues of Egypt

thee unto Pharaoh, that thou mayest bring forth My people out of Egypt."

Moses said unto God: "Who am I that I should go unto Pharaoh, and that I should bring forth the children of Israel out of Egypt? What shall I say unto them?"

God said unto Moses: "Go and gather the elders of Israel together, and say unto them: 'The Lord, the God of your fathers, has appeared unto me, saying: "I have seen that which is done to you, and I will bring you out of the affliction of Egypt unto a land flowing with milk and honey." They shall hearken to thy voice, and thou shalt come unto the king of Egypt and say unto him, 'Let us go, we beseech thee, three days' journey into the wilderness, that we may sacrifice to the Lord our God.' The king of Egypt will not give you leave to go; and I will stretch out My hand, and smite Egypt with all My wonders; and after that he will let you go."

Moses answered and said: "But, behold, they will not believe me, nor hearken unto my voice."

The Lord said unto him: "What is that in thine hand?"

Moses said: "A rod."

God said: "Cast it on the ground."

Moses cast it on the ground, and it became a serpent; and Moses fled from before it.

The Lord said unto Moses: "Put forth thine hand and take it by the tail."

Moses put forth his hand, and laid hold of it, and it became a rod.

The Lord said furthermore: "Put now thine hand into thy bosom."

Moses put his hand into his bosom, and when he took it out, behold, his hand was leprous, as white as snow.

God said: "Put thine hand into thy bosom again."

Moses put his hand into his bosom again, and when he took it out, it was turned as his other flesh.

God said: "If they will not believe thee, neither hearken to the voice of the first sign, they will believe the voice of the latter sign."

Moses said: "O Lord, I am slow of speech."

The Lord said unto him: "Who hath made man's mouth? or who maketh a man dumb, or deaf, or seeing, or blind? Is it not I, the Lord? Now therefore go, and I will be with thy mouth, and teach thee what thou shalt speak."

Moses said: "O Lord, send, I pray thee, by him whom Thou wilt send."

The anger of the Lord was kindled against Moses, and He said: "Aaron thy brother can speak well. Behold, he cometh to meet thee, and when he seeth thee he will be glad. Thou shalt speak unto him, and put the words in his mouth; and I will be with thy mouth, and with his mouth, and will teach you what ye shall do. He shall be thy spokesman unto the people;

Moses and the Plagues of Egypt

and thou shalt take in thine hand this rod, wherewith thou shalt do the signs."

The Lord said to Aaron: "Go into the wilderness to meet Moses."

He went, and met him in the mountain of God, and kissed him; and Moses told Aaron all the words of the Lord.

Moses returned to Jethro his father-in-law, and said: "Let me go, I pray thee, unto my brethren which are in Egypt, and see whether they be yet alive."

Jethro said to Moses: "Go in peace."

So Moses took his wife and his sons to the land of Egypt; and Moses and Aaron went and gathered together all the elders of the children of Israel; and Aaron spake all the words which the Lord had spoken unto Moses, and did the signs in the sight of the people. The people believed, and when they heard that the Lord had seen their affliction, they bowed their heads and worshipped.

Afterward Moses and Aaron went and told Pharaoh: "Thus saith the Lord, the God of Israel: 'Let my people go, that they may hold a feast unto me in the wilderness.'"

Pharaoh said: "Who is the Lord that I should obey His voice to let Israel go? I know not the Lord, and moreover I will not let Israel go. Wherefore do ye, Moses and Aaron, loose the people from their works?

Behold, the people are now many, and ye make them rest from their burdens."

The same day Pharaoh commanded the taskmasters of the people, saying: "Ye shall no more give the people straw* to make brick, as heretofore. Let them go and gather straw for themselves, and the tale of the bricks, which they did make heretofore, ye shall not diminish; for they be idle. Therefore they cry, saying: 'Let us go and sacrifice to our God.'"

The taskmasters went out, and spake to the people, saying: "Thus saith Pharaoh: 'I will not give you straw. Go, get you straw where ye can find it. Nought of your work shall be diminished.'"

So the people were scattered abroad throughout all the land of Egypt to gather stubble for straw, and the taskmasters were urgent, saying: "Fulfil your daily tasks."

The officers of the children of Israel that Pharaoh's taskmasters had set over them, were beaten, saying: "Wherefore have ye not fulfilled your task in making bricks as heretofore?"

Then the officers of the children of Israel came and cried unto Pharaoh, saying: "There is no straw given unto thy servants, and they say to us: 'Make brick;' and, behold, thy servants are beaten."

But he said: "Ye are idle, ye are idle. Go and work; for there shall no straw be given you."

---
*The bricks were sundried, and the straw was cut up and mixed with the clay to keep the bricks from cracking.

Moses and the Plagues of Egypt

The officers of the children of Israel met Moses and Aaron, as they came forth from Pharaoh, and Moses returned unto the Lord, and said: "Lord, wherefore hast Thou evil entreated this people? Why is it that Thou hast sent me?"

The Lord said unto Moses: "Now shalt thou see what I will do to Pharaoh. Say unto the children of Israel: 'I am the Lord, and I will bring you out from under the burdens of the Egyptians, and I will redeem you with a stretched out arm. I will take you to Me for a people, and I will be to you a God.'"

Moses spake so unto the children of Israel; but they hearkened not for anguish of spirit, and for cruel bondage.

The Lord spake unto Moses, saying: "Speak unto Pharaoh king of Egypt, that he let the children of Israel go out of his land; and I will harden Pharaoh's heart, and multiply My signs and My wonders in the land of Egypt, and the Egyptians shall know that I am the Lord."

Moses and Aaron did as the Lord commanded them; and Moses was fourscore years old, and Aaron was fourscore and three years old. They went in unto Pharaoh, and Aaron cast down his rod before Pharaoh, and before his servants, and it became a serpent. Then Pharaoh called for the wise men and the sorcerers; and they, the magicians of Egypt, cast down every man his rod, and the rods became serpents. But Aaron's rod swallowed up their rods.

Pharaoh's heart was hardened, and he hearkened not unto Moses and Aaron; and the Lord said unto Moses: "Get thee unto Pharaoh in the morning as he goeth out unto the water. Thou shalt stand by the river's brink to meet him; and the rod which was turned to a serpent shalt thou take in thine hand. Thou shalt say unto him: 'The Lord, the God of the Hebrews, hath sent me unto thee, saying: "Let My people go, that they may serve Me in the wilderness. Hitherto thou hast not hearkened. In this thou shalt know that I am the Lord: behold, the waters in the river, shall be turned to blood; and the fish that are in the river shall die, and the river shall stink, and the Egyptians shall loathe to drink the water from the river."

The Lord said unto Moses: "Say unto Aaron: 'Take thy rod, and stretch out thine hand over the waters of Egypt.'"

Moses and Aaron did as the Lord commanded, and Aaron lifted up the rod and smote the water that was in the river, and the water turned to blood; and the fish that were in the river died, and the river stank, and the Egyptians could not drink water from the river. Pharaoh's heart was hardened, and he turned and went into his house; and the Egyptians digged round about the river for water to drink.

Seven days were fulfilled after the Lord had smitten the river; and the Lord spake unto Moses: "Go to Pharaoh, and say: 'Thus saith the Lord: "Let My people go that they may serve Me. If thou refuse to let them go, behold, I will smite all thy borders with frogs. The river shall swarm with frogs, which shall come into thine house, and into thy bedchamber, and on thy bed, and into the houses of thy servants, and into thine ovens, and into thy kneading troughs. The frogs shall come up both on thee and on thy people."

The Lord said unto Moses: "Say unto Aaron: 'Stretch forth thine hand with thy rod over the streams and over the ponds.'"

Aaron stretched out his hand over the waters of Egypt; and the frogs came up, and covered the land. Then Pharaoh called for Moses and Aaron, and said: "Entreat the Lord, that He take away the frogs, and I will let your people go."

Moses said unto Pharaoh: "Be it according to thy word, that thou mayest know there is none like unto the Lord our God; and the frogs shall depart from thee and from thy people. They shall remain in the river only."

Moses and Aaron went out, and Moses cried unto the Lord concerning the frogs; and the frogs died out of the houses, out of the villages, and out of the fields; and the people gathered them together in heaps. But when

Pharaoh saw that there was respite, he hardened his heart.

The Lord said unto Moses: "Rise up early in the morning, and stand before Pharaoh, and say unto him: 'Thus saith the Lord: "Let My people go, that they may serve Me. Else, if thou wilt not let them go, behold, I will send swarms of flies on thee, and on thy servants, and the houses of the Egyptians shall be full of swarms of flies; and in the land of Goshen, in which My people dwell, no swarms of flies shall be there, to the end thou mayest know that I am the Lord. By tomorrow shall this sign be."

The Lord did so, and there came grievous swarms of flies into the house of Pharaoh, and in all Egypt the land was corrupted by reason of the swarms of flies.

Pharaoh called for Moses and for Aaron, and said: "Go ye, sacrifice to your God in the wilderness. Entreat for me."

Moses said: "Behold, I will entreat the Lord that the swarms of flies may depart from Pharaoh, and from his people; but let not Pharaoh deal deceitfully any more in not letting the people go."

Moses went out from Pharaoh, and entreated the Lord; and the Lord did according to the word of Moses. He removed the swarms of flies, and there remained not one.

Pharaoh hardened his heart this time also, and he did not let the people go. Then the Lord said unto

Moses and the Plagues of Egypt

Moses: "Go unto Pharaoh, and tell him: 'Thus saith the Lord: "Let My people go, that they may serve Me. If thou refuse, and wilt hold them still, behold, the hand of the Lord is on thy cattle which are in the field, on the horses, on the asses, on the camels, on the herds, and on the flocks. There shall be a very grievous murrain. Tomorrow the Lord shall do this thing."

The Lord did that thing on the morrow, and all the cattle of Egypt died; but of the cattle of the children of Israel died not one. But the heart of Pharaoh was stubborn, and he did not let the people go.

The Lord said unto Moses and unto Aaron: "Take to you handfuls of ashes, and let Moses sprinkle them toward heaven in the sight of Pharaoh; and the ashes shall become small dust over all the land of Egypt, and shall cause boils to break forth on man and on beast, throughout the land of Egypt."

They took ashes, and stood before Pharaoh; and Moses sprinkled them up toward heaven, and they caused boils to break forth on man and on beast. The magicians could not stand before Moses because of the boils; for the boils were on the magicians, and on all the Egyptians; and the Lord hardened Pharaoh's heart, and he hearkened not.

The Lord said unto Moses: "Rise up early in the morning, and stand before Pharaoh, and say unto him: 'Thus saith the Lord, the God of the Hebrews: "As yet exaltest thou thyself against My people that thou wilt not let them go? Behold, tomorrow about this time I will cause it to rain a very grievous hail, such as hath not been in Egypt since the day it was founded. Now therefore, hasten in thy cattle and all that thou hast in the field; for the hail shall come down on every man and beast not brought home, and they shall die."

He that feared the word of the Lord among the servants of Pharaoh made his servants and his cattle flee into the houses; and he that regarded not the word of the Lord left his servants and his cattle in the field. The Lord sent thunder and hail, and the fire ran down into the earth; and the hail smote throughout Egypt all that was in the field, both man and beast; and the hail smote every herb of the field, and brake every tree of the field. Only in the land of Goshen, where the children of Israel were, was there no hail.

Pharaoh sent, and called for Moses and Aaron, and said unto them: "I have sinned this time. The Lord is righteous, and I and my people are wicked. Entreat the Lord; for there hath been enough of these mighty thunderings and hail; and I will let you go."

Moses said unto him: "As soon as I am gone out of the city, I will spread abroad my hands unto the Lord. The thunders shall cease, neither shall there be any more hail. But as for thee and thy servants, I know that ye will not fear the Lord God."

Moses went out of the city, and spread abroad his hands unto the Lord; and the thunders and hail ceased.

Moses and the Plagues of Egypt

When Pharaoh saw that the hail and the thunders were ceased, he sinned yet more, and did not let the children of Israel go.

The Lord said unto Moses: "Go unto Pharaoh; for I have hardened his heart, and the heart of his servants, that I might show these my signs in the midst of them, and that thou mayest tell in the ears of thy son, and of thy son's son, what things I have wrought in Egypt, that ye may know I am the Lord."

Moses and Aaron went unto Pharaoh, and said: "Thus saith the Lord: 'How long wilt thou refuse to humble thyself before Me? Behold, tomorrow will I bring locusts, and they shall cover the face of the earth, and they shall eat the residue of that which is escaped from the hail, and shall eat every tree which groweth for you out of the field, and thy houses shall be filled.'"

Moses turned, and went out from Pharaoh; and Pharaoh's servants said unto Pharaoh: "How long shall this man be a snare unto us? Let the Hebrews go, that they may serve their God. Knowest thou not that Egypt is destroyed?"

Moses and Aaron were brought again unto Pharaoh; and he said to them: "Go serve the Lord your God; but who are they that shall go?"

Moses said: "We will go with our young and with our old, with our sons and with our daughters, with our flocks and with our herds; for we must hold a feast unto the Lord."

Pharaoh said: "Not so. Go ye that are men, and serve the Lord; for that is what ye desire;" and they were driven out from Pharaoh's presence.

The Lord said unto Moses: "Stretch out thine hand for the locusts."

Moses stretched forth his rod, and the Lord brought an east wind all that day, and all the night; and when it was morning, the east wind brought the locusts. They covered the face of the whole earth, so that the land was darkened; and they did eat every herb of the land, and all the fruit of the trees which the hail had left. There remained not any green thing, either tree or herb of the field, through all the land of Egypt.

Then Pharaoh called for Moses and Aaron in haste, and he said: "I have sinned against the Lord your God, and against you. Now therefore forgive my sin only this once, and entreat the Lord your God."

Moses went out from Pharaoh, and entreated the Lord; and the Lord turned an exceeding strong west wind, which took up the locusts, and drove them into the Red Sea. There remained not one locust in all Egypt. But the Lord hardened Pharaoh's heart, so that he would not let the children of Israel go.

The Lord said unto Moses: "Stretch out thine hand toward heaven that there may be darkness over the land of Egypt, even darkness which may be felt."

Moses stretched forth his hand toward heaven, and there was a thick darkness in all the land of Egypt three days. The people saw not one another, neither rose any from his place for three days; but all the children of Israel had light in their dwellings.

Pharaoh called unto Moses, and said: "Go ye, serve the Lord; only let your flocks and herds be stayed."

Moses said: "Our cattle shall go with us; for thereof must we take to serve the Lord our God."

But the Lord hardened Pharaoh's heart, and he would not let them go; and Pharaoh said unto Moses: "Get thee from me, take heed to thyself, see my face no more; for in the day thou seest my face thou shalt die."

Moses said: "Thou hast spoken well. I will see thy face no more."

The Lord said unto Moses: "Yet one more plague will I bring on Pharaoh, and on Egypt. Afterward he will let you go. Speak now in the ears of the people, and let them ask every man of his neighbor, and every woman of her neighbor, jewels of silver, and jewels of gold."

The children of Israel did according to the word of Moses, and they asked of the Egyptians jewels of silver, and jewels of gold; and the Lord gave the people favor in the sight of the Egyptians, so that they let them have what they asked.

The Lord spake unto Moses and Aaron, saying: "Speak ye unto all the congregation of Israel, saying: 'In the tenth day of this month they shall take to them every man a lamb for a household; and if the household be too little for a lamb, then shall he and his neighbor next unto his house take one. Your lamb shall ye keep until the fourteenth day of the month, and the whole assembly of the congregation of Israel shall kill it at even. They shall take of the blood and put it on the two side posts and lintel on the houses wherein they shall eat it. Ye shall eat the flesh that night, roast with fire, with your loins girded, your shoes on your feet, and your staff in your hand. It is the Lord's passover. For I will go through the land of Egypt in that night, and will smite all the firstborn in the land, both man and beast; and the blood shall be for a token on the houses where ye are. When I see the blood I will pass over you, and there shall no plague be on you to destroy you; and this day shall be unto you for a memorial. Ye shall keep it a feast to the Lord by an ordinance forever.'"

Then Moses called for all the elders of Israel, and said unto them: "Take you lambs according to your families, and kill the passover, and ye shall take a bunch of hyssop, and dip it in the blood, and strike the lintel and the two side posts with the blood; and none of you shall go out of the door of his house until the morning. For the Lord will pass through to smite the Egyptians; and when He seeth the blood, the Lord will pass over the door, and will not suffer the destroyer to come in."

The people bowed the head and worshipped, and went and did as the Lord had commanded.

It came to pass at midnight, that the Lord smote all the firstborn in the land of Egypt, from the firstborn of Pharaoh that sat on his throne unto the firstborn of the captive that was in the dungeon, and all the firstborn of cattle. Pharaoh rose up in the night, he, and all the Egyptians; and there was a great cry in Egypt; for there was not a house where there was not one dead; and he called for Moses and Aaron, and said: "Rise up, get you forth from among my people, both ye and the children of Israel, and go serve the Lord as ye have said. Take your flocks and herds, and be gone."

The children of Israel journeyed to Succoth, about six hundred thousand on foot that were men. A mixed multitude went also with them, and flocks and herds. God led them by the way of the wilderness by the Red Sea. The children of Israel went armed out of the land of Egypt; and Moses took the bones of Joseph with him; for Joseph had straitly sworn the children of Israel, saying: "God will surely visit you, and ye shall carry my bones away with you."

The Lord went before them by day in a pillar of cloud, to lead the way; and by night in a pillar of fire, to give them light, that they might go by day and by night.

The Lord spake unto Moses saying: "Speak unto the children of Israel, that they turn back and encamp between Migdol and the sea; and Pharaoh will say: 'They are entangled in the wilderness.' I will harden Pharaoh's heart, and he shall follow after them, and I will get me honor on Pharaoh, and the Egyptians shall know that I am the Lord."

The Israelites did so; and it was told the king of Egypt; and the heart of Pharaoh and of his servants was changed toward the people. They said: "What is this we have done, that we have let Israel go from serving us?"

Then Pharaoh made ready his chariot, and took his people with him, and all the chariots of Egypt. He pursued after the children of Israel, and overtook them encamping by the sea. When Pharaoh drew nigh, the children of Israel lifted up their eyes, and, behold, the Egyptians marched after them; and they were sore afraid, and cried out unto the Lord; and they said to Moses: "Hast thou taken us away to die in the wilderness? Wherefore hast thou dealt thus with us? Is not this the word we spake unto thee in Egypt, saying: 'Let us alone, that we may serve the Egyptians? For it were better for us to serve the Egyptians, than that we should die in the wilderness.'"

Moses said unto the people: "Fear ye not, stand still and see the salvation of the Lord, which He will work for you. The Egyptians whom ye have seen today, ye shall see again no more for ever. The Lord shall fight for you, and ye shall hold your peace."

Moses and the Plagues of Egypt

The angel of God which went before the camp of Israel, removed and went behind them, and the pillar of cloud came between the camp of Egypt and the camp of Israel, so that the one came not near the other all the night.

The Lord said unto Moses: "Speak unto the children of Israel, that they go forward. Lift thou up thy rod, and stretch out thine hand over the sea, and divide it; and the children of Israel shall go through the midst of the sea on dry ground."

Moses stretched out his hand over the sea, and the Lord caused the sea to go back by a strong east wind, and made the sea dry land. The waters were divided; and the children of Israel went into the midst of the sea on the dry ground, and the waters were a wall unto them on the right hand, and on their left.

The Egyptians pursued after them, all Pharaoh's chariots, and his horsemen; and it came to pass in the morning watch, that the Lord looked forth on the host of the Egyptians through the pillar of fire and of cloud, and discomfited them. He took off their chariot wheels, that they drave heavily; so that the Egyptians said: "Let us flee from Israel; for the Lord fighteth against the Egyptians."

The Lord said unto Moses: "Stretch out thine hand over the sea, that the waters may come on the Egyptians."

Moses stretched forth his hand over the sea, and the sea returned, and the waters covered the chariots, and the horsemen, even all the host of Pharaoh. There remained not so much as one of them. But the children of Israel walked on dry land in the midst of the sea. Thus the Lord saved Israel that day; and Israel saw the Egyptians dead on the sea shore; and the people feared the Lord, and they believed in the Lord, and in His servant Moses. Then sang Moses and the children of Israel a song unto the Lord, and Miriam the sister of Aaron took a timbrel in her hand, and all the women went out after her with timbrels and with dances.

VII

THE TEN COMMANDMENTS

MOSES led Israel onward from the Red Sea, and they went into the wilderness of Shur, three days, and found no water. When they came to Marah they could not drink of the waters, for they were bitter; and the people murmured against Moses, saying: "What shall we drink?"

He cried unto the Lord, and the Lord showed him a tree, and he cast it into the waters, and the waters were made sweet.

The children of Israel came unto the wilderness of Sin; and the whole congregation murmured against Moses and against Aaron, and said unto them: "Would that we had died in the land of Egypt, when we sat by the flesh pots, when we did eat bread to the full; for ye have brought us forth into this wilderness, to kill this whole assembly with hunger."

Then said the Lord unto Moses: "Behold, I will rain bread from heaven for you, and the people shall go out and gather a portion every day; and it shall come to pass on the sixth day, that which they bring in shall be twice as much as they gather daily. I have heard the murmurings of the children of Israel. Speak unto them saying: 'At even ye shall eat flesh, and in the morning ye shall be filled with bread; and ye shall know that I am the Lord your God.'"

It came to pass at even, that the quails came and covered the camp; and in the morning the dew lay round about the camp; and when the dew was gone, behold, on the face of the wilderness a small round thing, small as the hoar frost on the ground. The children of Israel said one to another: "What is it?" for they wist not what it was.

Moses said unto them: "This is the bread which the Lord hath given you to eat. Gather ye of it every man according to the number of persons that are in his tent."

The children of Israel did so; and Moses said unto them: "Let no man leave of it till the morning."

Notwithstanding some of them left of it until the morning, and it bred worms, and stank; and Moses was wroth with them.

They gathered it morning by morning, every man according to his eating; and when the sun waxed hot, it melted. On the sixth day they gathered twice as much bread, and Moses said: "Tomorrow is a holy Sabbath unto the Lord. Bake that which ye will bake, and all that remaineth over lay up to be kept until the morning."

They laid it up till the morning, as Moses bade, and it did not stink, neither was there any worm therein.

Moses said: "Eat that today, for ye shall not find it in the field. Six days ye shall gather it; but on the seventh day, which is the Sabbath, there shall be none."

It came to pass that there went out some of the people on the seventh day for to gather, and they found none; and the Lord said unto Moses: "How long refuse ye to keep my commandments? Let no man go out of his place on the seventh day."

So the people rested on the seventh day. They called the name of the bread, "Manna;" and it was like coriander seed, white; and the taste of it was like wafers made with honey. They ground it in mills, or beat it in mortars, and boiled it in pots, and made cakes; and they did eat the manna forty years, until they came unto the borders of the land of Canaan.

The children of Israel journeyed and encamped in Rephidim. Then came Amalek to fight with Israel; and Moses said unto Joshua: "Choose out men and fight with Amalek. Tomorrow I will stand on the top of the hill with the rod of God in mine hand."

Joshua did as Moses had said, and fought with Amalek; and Moses, Aaron, and Hur went up to the top of the hill. It came to pass when Moses held up his hand, that Israel prevailed, and when he let down his hand, Amalek prevailed. But Moses' hands were heavy; and they took a stone, and put it under him, and he sat thereon; and Aaron and Hur stayed up his hands, the one on the one side, and the other on the other side, and his hands were steady until the going down of the sun; and Joshua discomfited Amalek and his people with the edge of the sword.

Jethro, the priest of Midian, Moses' father-in-law, heard of all that God had done for Israel; and Jethro came unto Moses into the wilderness where he was encamped, at the mount of God. Moses went out to meet his father-in-law, and did obeisance, and kissed him. They asked each other of their welfare, and came into the tent; and Aaron came, and all the elders of Israel, to eat bread with Moses' father-in-law.

It came to pass on the morrow, that Moses sat to judge the people; and the people stood about Moses from the morning unto the evening. Moses' father-in-law said: "What is this thing that thou doest?"

Moses said: "The people come unto me, and I judge between one and another, and I make them know the statutes of God."

Moses' father-in-law said: "The thing that thou doest is not good. Thou wilt surely wear away, both thou, and this people that is with thee; for the thing is too heavy for thee. Thou art not able to perform it alone. Hearken now unto my voice. Provide out of all the people able men, such as fear God, men of truth, hating unjust gain, and place such to be rulers of thousands, rulers of hundreds, rulers of fifties, and rulers of tens. Let them judge the people, and every great matter they shall bring unto thee, but every small matter they shall judge themselves. So shall it be easier for thyself, and they shall bear the burden with thee."

Moses hearkened to the voice of his father-in-law and chose able men out of all Israel, and made them rulers of thousands, rulers of hundreds, rulers of fifties, and rulers of tens; and they judged the people. The hard causes they brought unto Moses, but every small matter they judged themselves.

In the third month after the children of Israel were gone forth out of the land of Egypt, came they into the wilderness of Sinai; and there camped before the mount. Moses went up unto God, and the Lord called unto him out of the mountain, saying: "Thus shalt thou say to the house of Jacob: 'Ye have seen what I did unto the Egyptians, and how I brought you unto myself. Now therefore, if ye will obey my voice, ye shall be unto me a holy nation.' Go unto the people, and let them wash their garments, and be ready against the third day; for the third day the Lord will come down in the sight of all the people on Mount Sinai. Thou shalt set bounds unto the people round about, saying: 'Take heed to yourselves that ye go not up into the mount, or touch the border of it. Whosoever toucheth the mount shall be surely put to death.'"

Moses went down unto the people, and said: "Be ready against the third day."

It came to pass on the third day in the morning, that there were thunders and lightnings, and a thick cloud on the mount, and the voice of a trumpet exceeding loud; and all the people trembled. Moses brought forth the people out of the camp to meet God, and they stood at the nether part of the mount; and Mount Sinai was altogether on smoke, because the Lord descended on it in fire, and the whole mount quaked greatly.

When the trumpet sounded louder and louder, Moses spake, and God answered him, and God said: "I am the Lord thy God.

"Thou shalt have no other gods before Me.

"Thou shalt not make unto thee any graven image, or any likeness of any thing that is in heaven above, or that is on the earth beneath, or that is in the water under the earth. Thou shalt not bow down thyself to them, nor serve them; for I the Lord thy God am a jealous God, visiting the iniquity of the fathers on the children, unto the third and fourth generation of them that hate Me; and showing mercy unto thousands of them that love Me and keep My commandments.

"Thou shalt not take the name of the Lord thy God in vain; for the Lord will not hold him guiltless that taketh His name in vain.

"Remember the Sabbath Day to keep it holy. Six days shalt thou labor and do all thy work; but the seventh day is the Sabbath of the Lord thy God. In it thou shalt not do any work, thou, nor thy son, nor thy daughter, thy manservant, nor thy maidservant, nor thy cattle, nor thy stranger that is within thy gates; for in six days the Lord made heaven and earth, the sea, and all that in them is, and rested the seventh day. Wherefore the Lord blessed the Sabbath Day, and hallowed it.

"Honor thy father and thy mother, that thy days may be long on the land which the Lord thy God giveth thee.

"Thou shalt not kill.

"Thou shalt not do anything which is immodest or unchaste.*

"Thou shalt not steal.

"Thou shalt not bear false witness against thy neighbor.

"Thou shalt not covet thy neighbor's house, thou shalt not covet thy neighbor's wife, nor his manservant, nor his maidservant, nor his ox, nor his ass, nor any thing that is thy neighbor's."

All the people saw the lightnings, and the mountain smoking; and they trembled, and stood afar off. They said unto Moses: "Speak thou with us, and we will hear; but let not God speak with us, lest we die."

Moses said unto the people: "Fear not;" and he drew near to the thick darkness where God was.

---

*This version of the seventh commandment is from an old catechism.

The Lord said unto Moses: "Thus shalt thou say unto the children of Israel: 'Behold, I send an angel before thee to bring thee to the place which I have prepared. Take ye heed of him, and hearken unto his voice. Then will I be an enemy unto thine enemies, and an adversary unto thine adversaries. I will deliver the inhabitants of the land into your hand, and thou shalt drive them out.'"

Moses came and told the people the words of the Lord, and the people with one voice said: "All the words which the Lord hath spoken will we do."

Moses rose up early in the morning, and builded an altar under the mount, and twelve pillars, according to the twelve tribes of Israel; and he sent young men who offered burnt offerings, and sacrificed peace offerings of oxen unto the Lord.

The Lord said unto Moses: "Come up to me into the mount, and I will give thee the law and the commandments, which I have written, that thou mayest teach them."

Moses rose up, and Joshua his minister, and went up into the mount, and the cloud covered the mount; and the glory of the Lord abode on Mount Sinai, and the cloud covered it six days. The seventh day God called to Moses out of the midst of the cloud. The appearance of the glory of the Lord was like devouring fire on the top of the mount in the eyes of the children of Israel. Moses entered into the cloud, and was in the mount forty days and forty nights.

The Lord spake unto Moses, saying: "Speak unto the children of Israel, that they make Me a sanctuary. They shall make an ark of acacia wood. Two cubits and a half shall be the length thereof, and a cubit and a half the breadth thereof, and a cubit and a half the height thereof. Thou shalt overlay it with pure gold, within and without; and thou shalt cast four rings of gold for it, and two rings shall be on the one side, and two rings on the other side of it. Thou shalt make staves of acacia wood and put the staves into the rings, to bear the ark withal. Thou shalt put into the ark the testimony which I shall give thee; and thou shalt make a mercy-seat, and two cherubim of gold, one cherub at the one end, and one cherub at the other end of the mercy-seat. The cherubim shall spread out their wings on high, covering the mercy-seat with their wings, with their faces one to another; and thou shalt put the mercy-seat on the ark. I will commune with thee from above the mercy-seat, from between the two cherubim, of all things which I will give thee in commandment unto the children of Israel.

"Thou shalt make a table of acacia wood; and thou shalt make the dishes thereof, and the spoons, the flagons, and the bowls thereof of pure gold; and thou shalt set on the table showbread before Me always.

"Thou shalt make a candlestick of pure gold, and there shall be six branches going out of the sides thereof.

"Moreover thou shalt make the tabernacle with ten curtains of fine linen, blue, purple, and scarlet; and thou shalt make curtains of goats' hair for a tent over the tabernacle. Thou shalt make a veil, and hang it on four pillars, and shalt bring within the veil the ark of the testimony; and the veil shall divide unto you the holy place and the most holy. Thou shalt set the table without the veil on the north side, and the candlestick over against the table on the side of the tabernacle toward the south.

"Thou shalt make the altar of acacia wood, five cubits long, and five cubits broad, and the height shall be three cubits, and thou shalt make the horns of it on the four corners thereof, and thou shalt overlay it with brass; and thou shalt make its pots, and its shovels, its basins, and its fleshhooks, and its firepans of brass.

"Thou shalt command the children of Israel, that they bring unto thee pure olive oil to cause a lamp to burn continually. In the tent of meeting, Aaron and his sons shall minister unto me in the priest's office. Thou shalt make holy garments for Aaron thy brother, for glory and for beauty.

"Thou shalt make an altar of acacia wood to burn incense on. A cubit shall be the length thereof, and a cubit the breadth thereof, and two cubits shall be the height thereof, and thou shalt overlay it with pure gold. Thou shalt put it before the veil that is by the ark of the testimony, and Aaron shall burn thereon incense of sweet spices every morning when he dresseth the lamps; and when Aaron lighteth the lamps at even, he shall burn it, a perpetual incense before the Lord throughout your generations.

"Appoint thou the Levites over the tabernacle and all that belongeth to it. They shall bear the tabernacle and all the furniture thereof, and they shall minister unto it, and shall encamp round about the tabernacle, and when the tabernacle setteth forward, the Levites shall take it down, and when the tabernacle is to be pitched, the Levites shall set it up."

God gave unto Moses, when He had made an end of communing with him, two tables of stone written with the finger of God.

When the people saw that Moses delayed to come down from the mount, they gathered themselves together unto Aaron, and said: "Up, make us gods, which shall go before us. As for this Moses, the man that brought us out of the land of Egypt, we know not what is become of him."

Aaron said unto them: "Break off the golden rings, which are in the ears of your wives, of your sons, and of your daughters, and bring them unto me."

All the people brake off the golden rings which were in their ears, and brought them unto Aaron. He received the rings, and made of them a molten calf; and the people said: "O Israel, this is thy god."

Then Aaron built an altar before it, and made proclamation, and said: "Tomorrow shall be a feast to the Lord."

They rose early on the morrow, and offered burnt offerings, and brought peace offerings; and the people sat down to eat and to drink, and rose up to play.

The Lord spake unto Moses: "Get thee down; for thy people have corrupted themselves. They have turned aside quickly out of the way which I commanded them. They have made a molten calf, and have worshipped it, and have sacrificed unto it. This is a stiffnecked people. Now therefore let Me alone, that My wrath may wax hot against them, and that I may consume them."

Moses besought the Lord his God and said: "Lord, why doth Thy wrath wax hot against Thy people, which Thou hast brought forth out of the land of Egypt with great power and with a mighty hand? Wherefore should the Egyptians speak, saying: 'For evil did He bring them forth to slay them in the mountains, and to consume them from the face of the earth?' Turn from Thy fierce wrath, and repent of this evil against Thy people. Remember Abraham, Isaac, and Israel, Thy servants, to whom Thou saidst: 'I will multiply your seed as the stars of heaven, and all this land that I have spoken of will I give unto your seed, and they shall inherit it for ever.'"

The Lord repented of the evil which He said He would do unto His people; and Moses turned, and went down from the mount, with the two tables of the testimony in his hands, tables that were written on both their sides, and the writing was the writing of God, graven on the tables. When Joshua heard the noise of the people as they shouted, he said unto Moses: "There is a noise of war in the camp."

Moses said: "It is not the voice of them that shout for mastery; neither is it the voice of them that cry for being overcome; but the noise of them that sing."

It came to pass, as soon as he came nigh unto the camp, that he saw the calf and the dancing; and Moses' anger waxed hot, and he cast the tables out of his hands, and brake them; and he took the calf which they had made, and burnt it with fire, and ground it to powder, and strewed it on the water, and made the children of Israel drink of it. Then Moses stood in the gate of the camp, and said: "Whoso is on the Lord's side, let him come unto me."

All the sons of Levi gathered themselves together unto him; and he said: "Thus saith the Lord: 'Put ye every man his sword on his thigh, and go to and fro from gate to gate throughout the camp, and slay every man his brother, and every man his companion, and every man his neighbor.'"

The sons of Levi did according to the word of Moses; and there fell of the people that day about three thousand men.

The Lord said unto Moses: "Hew two tables of stone like unto the first, and I will write on the tables the words that were on the tables which thou brakest. Come up unto Mount Sinai, and present thyself there to me on the top of the mount. No man shall come up with thee; neither let any man be seen throughout all the mount; neither let the flocks nor herds feed before the mount."

Moses hewed two tables of stone like unto the first, and went up unto Mount Sinai. The Lord descended in the cloud, and stood with him, and he was there with the Lord forty days and forty nights. He did neither eat bread, nor drink water; and God wrote on the tables the words of the ten commandments.

When Moses came down from Mount Sinai with the two tables of the testimony, the skin of his face shone by reason of his speaking with God, and Aaron and all the children of Israel were afraid to come nigh him. Moses called unto them, and he gave them in commandment all that the Lord had spoken with him in Mount Sinai; and the people made the tabernacle, and the ark, and the altars, and all things as God had ordered; and Moses blessed them.

Moses reared up the tabernacle, and put the testimony into the ark, and put the mercy-seat on the ark, and finished the work. Then the cloud covered the tent of meeting, and the glory of the Lord filled the tabernacle; and when the cloud was taken up from over the tabernacle, the children of Israel went onward; but if the cloud were not taken up, then they journeyed not till the day that it was taken up. For the cloud of the Lord was on the tabernacle by day, and there was fire therein by night, in the sight of all the house of Israel throughout all their journeys.

VIII

THE ISRAELITES IN THE WILDERNESS

IT came to pass in the second year, in the second month, that the cloud was taken up from off the tabernacle of the testimony. The children of Israel set forward out of the wilderness of Sinai, and the cloud abode in the wilderness of Paran.

The Lord spake unto Moses, saying: "Send thou men, that they may spy out the land of Canaan, which I give unto the children of Israel. Of every tribe of their fathers shall ye send a man."

Moses sent them according to the commandment of the Lord, and said unto them: "Go up into the mountains, and see the land, what it is; and the people that dwell therein, whether they be strong or weak, whether they be few or many. Be ye of good courage, and bring of the fruit of the land."

So they went, and spied out the land, and they came unto the valley of Eshcol, and cut down a branch with one cluster of grapes, and they bare it on a staff between two men. They brought also pomegranates, and figs. They returned from spying out the land at the end of forty days, and they came to Moses and to all the congregation of the children of Israel, unto the wilderness of Paran.

They said: "We came unto the land whither we were sent, and surely it floweth with milk and honey, and this is the fruit of it. Howbeit, the people that dwell in the land are strong, and the cities are fenced, and very great."

Caleb, one of the twelve who had spied out the land, said: "Let us go at once and possess it; for we are well able to overcome it."

But the men that went with him said: "We be not able to go against the people; for they are stronger than we. All the people that we saw are men of great stature, and we saw the sons of Anak, and we were as grasshoppers in their sight."

The children of Israel murmured against Moses and against Aaron, and said unto them: "Would God that we had died in the land of Egypt! Wherefore hath the Lord brought us unto this land to fall by the sword? Our wives and our little ones shall be a prey. Were it not better for us to return into Egypt?"

The Lord said unto Moses: "How long will this people despise Me? and how long will they not believe in Me, for all the signs which I have wrought among them? I will smite them with the pestilence and disinherit them."

Moses said unto the Lord: "I beseech Thee, let the power of the Lord be great, according as Thou hast spoken, saying: 'The Lord is slow to anger, and plentious in mercy, forgiving iniquity and transgression.' Pardon, I pray Thee, this people."

The Lord said: "I have pardoned according to thy word; but all those men who have not hearkened to My voice, surely they shall not see the land which I sware unto their fathers. How long shall I bear with this evil congregation? Say unto them: 'As I live,' saith the Lord, 'all twenty years old and upward shall not come into the land concerning which I lifted up My hand, save Caleb and Joshua. As for the rest of you, your carcasses shall fall in this wilderness."

Korah, and Dathan, and Abiram, and On, rose up, with two hundred and fifty princes of the congregation, and assembled together against Moses and against Aaron, and said unto them: "Ye take too much on you. All the congregation are holy, and the Lord is among them. Wherefore then lift ye up yourselves above the assembly of the Lord?"

Moses fell on his face, and he spake unto Korah, and unto all his company, saying: "In the morning the Lord will show who are His, and who is holy. This do; take you censers before the Lord tomorrow."

They took every man his censer, and put fire in them, and laid incense thereon, and stood at the door of the tent of meeting with Moses and Aaron and all the congregation, and the glory of the Lord appeared. The Lord spake unto Moses, saying: "Speak unto the congregation, saying: 'Get you up from about the tabernacle of Korah, Dathan, and Abiram.'"

Moses rose up, and he spake unto the congregation, saying: "Depart, I pray you, from the tents of these wicked men, and touch nothing of theirs, lest ye be consumed in their sins."

So they gat them up from the tabernacle of Korah, Dathan, and Abiram; and Dathan, and Abiram came out, and stood at the door of their tents, and their wives, and their sons, and their little ones. It came to pass that the ground clave asunder that was under them, and swallowed them up, and their households, and all the men that appertained unto Korah, and all their goods. They went down alive into the pit, and the earth closed on them, and they perished miserably. All Israel that were round about fled at the cry of them; and fire came down from the Lord, and consumed the two hundred and fifty men that offered incense.

But on the morrow the children of Israel murmured against Moses and against Aaron, saying: "Ye have killed the people of the Lord."

The Lord spake unto Moses saying: "Get you up from among this congregation, that I may consume them in a moment."

Moses said unto Aaron: "Take thy censer, and put fire therein from off the altar, and lay incense thereon, and carry it quickly unto the congregation, and make atonement for them; for there is wrath gone out from the Lord. The plague is begun."

Aaron did as Moses commanded, and ran into the midst of the assembly; and, behold, the plague was begun, and he made atonement for the people. He stood between the dead and the living, and the plague was stayed. They that died by the plague were fourteen thousand and seven hundred.

The Lord spake unto Moses, saying: "Speak unto the children of Israel, and take of them rods, one for each father's house, of all their princes, twelve rods. Write thou every man's name on his rod; and thou shalt write Aaron's name on the rod of Levi. Thou shalt lay them up in the tent where I meet with you. It shall come to pass, that the man whom I shall choose, his rod shall bud; and I will make to cease the murmurings of the children of Israel against you."

Moses spake unto the children of Israel, and all their princes gave him rods, for each prince one, even twelve rods; and the rod of Aaron was among their rods. Moses laid up the rods before the Lord in the tent of the testimony. On the morrow Moses went into the tent, and, behold, the rod of Aaron put forth buds, and bloomed blossoms, and bare ripe almonds. Moses brought out the rods unto the children of Israel, and they looked, and took every man his rod.

The Lord said unto Moses: "Put back the rod of Aaron before the testimony, to be kept for a token against the rebels."

Moses did as the Lord commanded him.

The children of Israel came into the wilderness of Zin and abode in Kadesh, and there was no water for the congregation, and they assembled together against Moses and against Aaron. The people strove with Moses, saying: "Wherefore have ye made us come out of Egypt, to bring us unto this evil place? It is no place of seed, or of figs, or of vines, or of pomegranates; neither is there any water to drink."

Moses and Aaron went from the presence of the assembly unto the door of the tent of meeting, and fell on their faces, and the glory of the Lord appeared unto them. The Lord spake unto Moses, saying: "Take the rod, and assemble the congregation, and speak ye unto the rock before their eyes, that it give forth water. So thou shalt give the congregation and their cattle drink."

Moses took the rod, and gathered the assembly together before the rock, and he said unto them: "Hear now, ye rebels; shall we bring you forth water out of this rock?"

Moses lifted up his hand, and smote the rock with his rod twice, and water came forth abundantly, and the congregation drank, and their beasts also.

They journeyed from Kadesh unto Mount Hor; and the Lord spake unto Moses and Aaron, saying: "Take Aaron and Eleazar his son, and bring them unto Mount Hor; and put Aaron's garments on Eleazar his son, and Aaron shall die there."

Moses did as the Lord commanded, and they went up into Mount Hor in the sight of all the congregation; and Moses put Aaron's garments on Eleazar, and Aaron died there on the top of the mount.

Israel journeyed from Mount Hor, and the soul of the people was much discouraged because of the way. They spake against God, and against Moses; and the Lord sent fiery serpents, and they bit the people, and much people died.

Therefore the people came to Moses, and said: "We have sinned, because we have spoken against the Lord, and against thee. Pray unto the Lord, that He take away the serpents from us."

Moses prayed for the people, and the Lord said unto Moses: "Make thee a serpent, and set it on a standard; and it shall come to pass, that everyone that is bitten, when he looketh on it, shall live."

Moses made a serpent of brass, and set it on the standard; and if a serpent had bitten any man, when he beheld the serpent of brass, he lived.

The children of Israel journeyed, and sent messengers unto Sihon king of the Amorites, saying: "Let us pass through thy land. We will not turn aside into

The Israelites in the Wilderness

field, or into vineyard; but we will go along by the king's highway, until we have passed thy border."

Sihon would not suffer Israel to pass through, but gathered all his people together and went out against Israel into the wilderness. He fought against Israel, and Israel smote him with the edge of the sword, and possessed his land, and Israel dwelt in all the cities of the Amorites.

Israel went up by the way of Bashan; and Og the king of Bashan went out against them, he and all his people. The Lord said unto Moses: "Fear him not; for I have delivered him into thy hand."

So they smote him, and his sons, and all his people, until there was none left alive, and they possessed his land.

The children of Israel set forward, and pitched in the plains of Moab, and Moab was sore afraid of the people, because they were many. Moab said unto the elders of Midian: "Now shall this multitude lick up all that is round about us, as the ox licketh up the grass of the field."

Balak was king of Moab at that time, and he sent messengers unto Balaam the son of Beor to call him, saying: "Behold, there is a people come out of Egypt. They cover the face of the earth. Come now therefore, I pray thee, curse me this people. Peradventure I shall prevail, that we may smite them, and drive them out of the land; for I know that he whom thou blessest is blessed, and he whom thou cursest is cursed."

The elders of Moab and the elders of Midian departed unto Balaam, and spake unto him the words of Balak.

Balaam said: "Lodge here this night, and I will bring you word, as the Lord shall speak unto me."

The princes of Moab abode with Balaam; and God came unto Balaam, and said: "What men are these with thee?"

Balaam said unto God: "Balak, king of Moab, hath sent unto me saying: 'Behold, the people that is come out of Egypt. Curse me them.'"

God said unto Balaam: "Thou shalt not go with these men. Thou shalt not curse the people; for they are blessed."

Balaam rose up in the morning, and said unto the princes of Balak: "Get you into your land; for the Lord refuseth to give me leave to go with you."

The princes of Moab went unto Balak, and said: "Balaam refuseth to come with us."

Balak sent yet again more princes, and they came to Balaam, and said to him: "Thus saith Balak: 'Let nothing hinder thee from coming unto me; for I will promote thee unto very great honor, and I will do whatsoever thou sayest unto me. Come therefore, I pray thee, curse me this people.'"

Balaam answered and said: "If Balak would give me his house full of silver and gold, I cannot go beyond the word of the Lord my God, to do less or more. Now therefore, tarry ye here this night, that I may know what the Lord will speak unto me."

God came unto Balaam at night, and said "If the men be come to call thee, go with them; but only the word which I speak unto thee, that shalt thou do."

Balaam rose up in the morning, and saddled his ass, and went with the princes of Moab. God's anger was kindled because he went; and the angel of the Lord placed himself in the way for an adversary against him. He was riding on his ass, and his two servants were with him; and the ass saw the angel of the Lord standing in the way, with his sword drawn in his hand. The ass turned aside out of the way, and went into the field; and Balaam smote the ass to turn her into the way. Then the angel of the Lord stood in a path between the vineyards, a wall being on this side, and a wall on that side. The ass saw the angel of the Lord, and she thrust herself unto the wall, and crushed Balaam's foot against the wall, and he smote her again. The angel of the Lord went farther, and stood in a narrow place, where there was no way to turn either to the right hand or to the left. The ass saw the angel of the Lord, and she lay down under Balaam; and Balaam's anger was kindled, and he smote the ass with his staff.

The Lord opened the mouth of the ass, and she said unto Balaam: "What have I done unto thee, that thou hast smitten me these three times?"

Balaam said unto the ass: "Because thou hast mocked me. I would there were a sword in mine hand, for now would I kill thee."

The ass said unto Balaam: "Am not I thine ass, on which thou hast ridden ever since I was thine until this day? Was I ever wont to do so unto thee?"

He said: "Nay."

Then the Lord opened the eyes of Balaam, and he saw the angel of the Lord standing in the way, with his sword drawn in his hand; and he bowed his head, and fell on his face. The angel of the Lord said unto him: "Wherefore hast thou smitten thine ass these three times? Behold, I am come forth for an adversary, because thy way is perverse before me; and the ass saw me, and turned aside from me these three times. Unless she had turned aside before, surely I had slain thee."

Balaam said unto the angel of the Lord: "I have sinned. I knew not that thou stoodest in the way. Now therefore, I will get me back."

The angel of the Lord said unto Balaam: "Go with the men; but only the word that I speak unto thee, that shalt thou speak."

So Balaam went with the princes of Balak. When Balak heard that Balaam was come, he went out to meet him. It came to pass in the morning, that Balak took Balaam up into the high places of Baal, and he saw thence the utmost part of the people. Balaam said unto Balak: "Build me here seven altars, and prepare me here seven bullocks and seven rams."

Balak did as Balaam had spoken; and Balak and Balaam offered on every altar a bullock and a ram. Balaam said unto Balak: "I will go. Peradventure the Lord will meet me; and whatsoever he showeth me I will tell thee."

He went to a bare height, and God met Balaam, and put a message in Balaam's mouth. Balaam returned, and, lo, Balak stood by his burnt offering, he, and all the princes of Moab; and Balaam said:

"How shall I curse, whom God hath not cursed?
And how shall I defy, whom the Lord hath not defied?
Who can count the children of Jacob
Or number the fourth part of Israel?
Let me die the death of the righteous,
And let my last end be like his."

Balak said unto Balaam: "What hast thou done unto me? I took thee to curse mine enemies, and, behold, thou hast blessed them."

Balaam answered and said: "Must I not take heed to speak that which the Lord putteth in my mouth?"

Balak's anger was kindled against Balaam, and he smote his hands together, and said: "I thought to promote thee unto great honor; but, lo, the Lord hath kept thee back from honor."

Balaam said unto Balak: "Spake I not to thy messengers thou sentest unto me, saying: 'If Balak would give me his house full of silver and gold, I cannot go beyond the word of the Lord, to do either good or bad of mine own mind? What the Lord saith that will I speak. Now, behold, I go unto my people."

Balaam returned to his place; and Balak also went his way.

The Lord spake unto Moses, saying: "Avenge the children of Israel of the Midianites."

Moses spake unto the people, saying: "Arm ye men from among you, that they may go against Midian, to execute the Lord's vengeance. Of every tribe a thousand shall ye send to the war."

So there were delivered twelve thousand armed for war; and Moses sent them, and Phinehas the son of Eleazar the priest, to the war, with the vessels of the sanctuary and the trumpets to blow in his hand. They warred against Midian, and they slew every male, and they slew the kings of Midian. Balaam also they slew with the sword. The children of Israel took captive the women of Midian and their little ones; and all their cattle, and all their flocks, and all their goods, they took for a prey. All their cities, and all their encampments, they burnt with fire; and they brought the captives, and the spoil, unto the camp by the Jordan.

The Israelites in the Wilderness

The children of Reuben and the children of Gad had a very great multitude of cattle; and when they saw the land of Jazer, and the land of Gilead, that the place was a place for cattle, they spake unto Moses, and to Eleazar the priest, and unto the princes of the congregation, saying: "If we have found grace in thy sight, let this land be given unto thy servants for a possession. Bring us not over Jordan."

Moses said unto the children of Gad and to the children of Reuben: "Shall your brethren go to the war, and shall ye sit here? Wherefore discourage ye the heart of the children of Israel from going over into the land which the Lord hath given them?"

They said: "We will build sheepfolds here for our cattle, and cities for our little ones; but we ourselves will be ready armed to go before the children of Israel, until we have brought them unto their place. We will not return to our houses, until the children of Israel have inherited every man his inheritance."

Moses said unto them: "If ye will arm yourselves, and every armed man of you will pass over Jordan before the Lord, until He hath driven out His enemies, and the land be subdued; then afterward ye shall return, and this land shall be your possession."

The Lord spake unto Moses, saying: "Get thee up unto Mount Nebo, which is in the land of Moab, that is over against Jericho, and behold the land of Canaan, which I give unto the children of Israel; and die in the mount, and be gathered unto thy people."

Moses went up from the plains of Moab unto Mount Nebo, to the top of Pisgah, and the Lord showed him all the land. The Lord said: "This is the land which I sware unto Abraham, unto Isaac, and unto Jacob, saying: 'I will give it unto thy seed.' I have caused thee to see it with thine eyes, but thou shalt not go over thither."

So Moses the servant of the Lord died there in the land of Moab, and God buried him; but no man knoweth of his sepulchre unto this day. Moses was a hundred and twenty years old when he died. His eye was not dim, nor his natural force abated; and the children of Israel wept for Moses in the plains of Moab thirty days. Joshua the son of Nun was full of the spirit of wisdom, for Moses had laid his hands on him; and the children of Israel hearkened unto him, and did as the Lord commanded Moses. There hath not arisen since in Israel a prophet like unto Moses, whom the Lord knew face to face, in all the signs and the wonders, which the Lord sent him to do in the land of Egypt, and in all the great terror, which Moses wrought in the sight of all Israel.

IX

GOD'S PEOPLE ENTER THE PROMISED LAND

IT came to pass after the death of Moses, that the Lord spake unto Joshua, saying: "Arise, go over this Jordan, thou, and all this people, unto the land which I do give to them. Every place that the sole of your foot shall tread on, to you have I given it. From the wilderness, even unto the great river Euphrates, and unto the great sea toward the going down of the sun, shall be your border. There shall not any man be able to stand before thee all the days of thy life. As I was with Moses, so I will be with thee. I will not fail thee, nor forsake thee. Thou shalt cause this people to inherit the land which I sware unto their fathers to give them. Only be strong and courageous, to observe all the law, which Moses My servant commanded thee. Turn not from it to the right hand or to the left, that thou mayest prosper whithersoever thou goest."

Then Joshua commanded the officers of the people, saying: "Pass through the midst of the camp, and command the people, saying: 'Prepare you victuals; for within three days ye are to pass over this Jordan, to possess the land, which the Lord your God giveth you."

To the Reubenites, and to the Gadites, and to the half tribe of Manasseh, spake Joshua, saying: "Your wives, your little ones, and your cattle, shall abide in the land which Moses gave you on this side Jordan; but ye shall pass over before your brethren armed, all the mighty men of valor, and shall help them, until the Lord hath given them rest."

They answered Joshua, saying: "All that thou hast commanded us we will do."

Joshua sent out two men as spies, saying: "Go view the land, and Jericho."

They went, and came into the house of a woman whose name was Rahab. It was told the king of Jericho, saying: "Behold, there came men in hither tonight of the children of Israel to search out the land."

The king of Jericho sent unto Rahab, saying: "Bring forth the men who are entered into thine house."

The woman took the two men, and hid them, and she said: "Yea, the men came unto me, but I wist not whence they were; and about the time of the shutting of the gate, when it was dark, the men went out. Whither they went I wot not. Pursue after them quickly; for ye shall overtake them."

But she had brought them up to the roof, and hid them with stalks of flax. The men of Jericho pursued after them to Jordan unto the fords; and as soon as they which pursued were gone, Rahab came up unto the men on the roof, and she said: "I know that the

God's People Enter the Promised Land

Lord hath given you the land, and that the fear of you is fallen on us. We have heard how the Lord dried up the water of the Red Sea before you, when you came out of Egypt; and what ye did unto the two kings of the Amorites, Sihon and Og, whom ye utterly destroyed. As soon as we had heard it, our hearts did melt, neither did there remain any more spirit in any man, because of you; for the Lord your God is God in heaven above, and on earth beneath. Now therefore, I pray you, swear unto me, since I have dealt kindly with you, that ye will deal kindly with my father's house. Give me a token, that ye will save alive my father, and my mother, and my brethren, and my sisters."

The men said unto her: "If ye utter not this our business, when the Lord giveth us the land, we will deal kindly and truly with thee."

Then she let them down by a cord through the window; for her house was on the town wall, and she said unto them: "Get you to the mountain, lest the pursuers light on you; and hide yourselves there three days, until the pursuers be returned. Afterward go your way."

The men said unto her: "Behold, when we come into the land, thou shalt bind in the window this line of scarlet cord which thou didst let us down by; and thou shalt gather unto thee into the house thy father, and thy mother, and thy brethren, and all thy father's household. Whosoever shall be with thee in the house, his blood shall be on our head, if any hand be on him."

She said: "According unto your words, so be it."

They departed, and she bound the scarlet line in the window. They went unto the mountain, and abode there three days, and the pursuers sought them throughout all the way, but found them not. Then the two men descended from the mountain, and came to Joshua; and they told him all that had befallen them.

Joshua rose early in the morning, and came to Jordan, he and all the children of Israel. After three days, Joshua said unto the people: "Sanctify yourselves; for tomorrow the Lord will do wonders among you. Hereby ye shall know that the living God is among you, and that He will without fail drive out from before you the Canaanite, and the Hittite, and the Perizzite, and the Jebusite. Behold, the ark of the covenant passeth over before you, and when the soles of the feet of the priests that bear the ark shall rest in the waters of Jordan, the waters shall be cut off, even the waters that come down from above; and they shall stand in a heap."

The people removed from their tents, and when they that bare the ark were come unto Jordan, and the feet of the priests that bare the ark were dipped in the brink of the water, the waters which came down from above rose up in a heap, a great way off. The priests that bare the ark stood firm on dry ground in the midst of Jordan, and all Israel passed over on dry ground.

The Lord spake unto Joshua, saying: "Take you twelve men out of the people, out of every tribe a man, and command ye them, saying: 'Take you out of the midst of Jordan, where the priests' feet stood firm, twelve stones, and carry them with you, and lay them down in the lodging place, where ye shall lodge this night.'"

Then Joshua called out of every tribe a man, and they took up twelve stones out of the midst of Jordan, and carried them unto the place where they lodged. On that day the Lord magnified Joshua in the sight of Israel; and they feared him, as they feared Moses, all the days of his life.

When the priests that bare the ark were come up out of Jordan, the waters returned, and flowed as they did before. The people encamped in Gilgal, on the east border of Jericho; and those twelve stones, which they took out of Jordan, did Joshua set up in Gilgal; and he spake unto the children of Israel, saying: "When your children shall ask their fathers in time to come, saying: 'What mean these stones?' then shall ye let your children know, saying: 'Israel came over Jordan on dry land. For the Lord your God dried up the waters from before you, until ye were gone over, that all the peoples of the earth may know the hand of the Lord, that it is mighty.'"

The children of Israel kept the passover in the plains of Jericho, and they did eat of the produce of the land on the morrow. The manna ceased on the morrow, after they had eaten of the produce of the land. Neither had the children of Israel manna any more; but they did eat of the fruit of the land of Canaan.

It came to pass, when Joshua was by Jericho, that he lifted up his eyes and looked, and, behold, there stood a man over against him with his sword in his hand; and Joshua went unto him, and said: "Art thou for us, or for our adversaries?"

He said: "As captain of the host of the Lord am I come."

Joshua fell on his face to the earth, and did worship, and the captain of the Lord's host said: "Put off thy shoes, for the place whereon thou standest is holy."

Joshua did so, and the Lord said: "I have given into thine hand Jericho. Ye shall compass the city, all the men of war going about the city once. Thus shalt thou do six days; and seven priests shall bear seven trumpets of rams' horns before the ark. The seventh day ye shall compass the city seven times, and the priests shall blow with the trumpets. When they make a long blast with the ram's horn, all the people shall shout with a great shout, and the wall of the city shall fall down flat, and the people shall go up every man straight before him."

God's People Enter the Promised Land 125

Joshua called the priests, and said unto them: "Take up the ark of the covenant, and let seven priests bear seven trumpets of rams' horns before the ark of the Lord."

He said unto the people: "Pass on, and compass the city, and let the armed men pass on before the ark of the Lord. Ye shall not shout, nor let your voice be heard, until the day I bid you shout."

So he caused the ark of the Lord to compass the city, going about it once; and they came into camp and lodged. Joshua rose early in the morning, and the priests took up the ark; and the seven priests bearing the seven trumpets went on continually, and blew with the trumpets; and the armed men went before them. The second day they compassed the city once, and returned into the camp. So they did six days.

It came to pass on the seventh day, that they rose about the dawning of the day, and compassed the city after the same manner seven times. At the seventh time, when the priests blew with the trumpets, Joshua said unto the people: "Shout; for the Lord hath given you the city."

So the people shouted with a great shout, and the wall fell flat. The people went into the city, every man straight before him, and they took the city. They utterly destroyed all that was in the city, except in the house of Rahab, both man and woman, young and old, and ox, and sheep, and ass, with the edge of the sword. They burnt the city with fire, and all that was therein; only the silver and the gold, and the vessels of brass and of iron, they put into the treasury of the Lord. But Rahab, and her father's household, and all that she had, did Joshua save; and she dwelt in the midst of Israel, because she hid the messengers, that Joshua sent to spy out Jericho. So the Lord was with Joshua; and his fame was in all the land.

When the inhabitants of Gibeon heard what Joshua had done unto Jericho, they did work wilily, and made as if they had been ambassadors, and took old sacks on their asses, and wine-skins, old and rent and bound up; and old shoes on their feet, and old garments on them; and all the bread of their provision was dry and was become mouldy. They went to Joshua, unto the camp at Gilgal, and said unto him, and to the men of Israel: "Make ye a convenant with us."

Joshua said unto them: "Whence come ye?"

They said unto him: "From a very far country thy servants are come because of the name of the Lord thy God; for we have heard the fame of Him, and all that He did in Egypt, and all that He did to Sihon king of Heshbon, and to Og king of Bashan. Our elders and all the inhabitants of our country spake to us, saying: 'Take provisions with you for the journey, and go to meet them, and say unto them: "We are your servants; therefore make ye a covenant with us." This our bread we took hot out of our houses on the day we came forth to go unto you; but now, behold, it is dry, and is become mouldy; and these wine-skins, which we filled, were new; and, behold, they be rent; and these our garments and our shoes are become old by reason of the very long journey."

Joshua made a covenant with them, to let them live: and the princes of the congregation sware unto them. It came to pass at the end of three days, that they heard they were neighbors. The children of Israel journeyed, and came unto their cities, and smote them not, because the princes of the congregation had sworn unto them by the God of Israel. Joshua called for them, and he spake unto them, saying: "Wherefore have ye beguiled us, saying: 'We are very far from you;' when ye dwell among us?"

They answered: "Because it was told thy servants, how that the Lord thy God commanded Moses to give you all the land, and to destroy all the inhabitants of the land from before you. Therefore we were sore afraid for our lives, and have done this thing. Now, behold, we are in thine hand. As it seemeth good and right unto thee to do unto us, do."

So Joshua made them hewers of wood and drawers of water for the congregation, and for the altar of the Lord.

It came to pass, when Adoni-zedec the Amorite king of Jerusalem heard how the inhabitants of Gibeon had made peace with Israel, he feared greatly, because Gibeon was a great city, and all the men thereof were mighty. Wherefore Adoni-zedec sent unto four other kings of the Amorites, saying: "Come unto me, and help me, and let us smite Gibeon; for it hath made peace with the children of Israel."

The five kings of the Amorites gathered themselves together, and they and all their hosts encamped before Gibeon, and made war against it.

The men of Gibeon sent unto Joshua, saying: "Slack not thy hand from thy servants. Come to us quickly, and save us; for all the kings of the Amorites that dwell in the hill country are gathered together against us."

So Joshua went from Gilgal, and all the people of war with him; and the Lord said unto Joshua: "Fear them not; for I have delivered them into thine hand. There shall not a man of them stand before thee."

Joshua came on them suddenly, and the Lord discomfited them before Israel, and slew them with a great slaughter. It came to pass, as they fled, that the Lord cast down great stones from heaven on them, and more died with the hailstones than they whom the children of Israel slew with the sword.

Then spake Joshua to the Lord, and he said in the sight of Israel:

"Sun, stand thou still on Gibeon;
And thou, Moon, in the valley of Ajalon."

And the sun stood still, and the moon stayed,
Until the people had avenged themselves on their enemies.

The sun stayed in the midst of heaven, and hasted not to go down about a whole day; and there was no day like that before or after it.

The five kings fled, and hid themselves in the cave at Makkedah; and Joshua said: "Roll great stones unto the mouth of the cave, and set men by for to keep it; but stay not ye. Pursue after your enemies."

When Joshua and the children of Israel had made an end of slaying them, and the remnant which remained had entered into the fenced cities, all the people returned to the camp at Makkedah. Then said Joshua: "Open the mouth of the cave, and bring out those five kings unto me."

They did so, and Joshua put the kings to death, and hanged them on five trees; and they were hanging on the trees until the evening. At the time of the going down of the sun, Joshua commanded, and they took them down off the trees, and cast them into the cave wherein they had hidden themselves.

Joshua made war a long time. There was not a city that made peace with the children of Israel, save Gibeon. For it was of the Lord to harden their hearts, to come against Israel in battle, that he might utterly destroy them. So Joshua took the whole land, and gave it for an inheritance unto Israel according to their divisions by tribes; and the land had rest from war.

It came to pass after many days, that Joshua called for all Israel, for their elders, and for their judges and for their officers, and said unto them: "I am old and well stricken in years; and ye have seen all that the Lord your God hath done. Behold, I have allotted unto you these nations that remain, to be an inheritance for your tribes, from Jordan even unto the great sea toward the going down of the sun. The Lord your God shall expel them from before you, and drive them out of your sight. One man of you shall chase a thousand; for the Lord your God fighteth for you. Take heed therefore unto yourselves, that ye love the Lord your God. Else if ye do in any wise cleave unto the remnant of these nations, and make marriages with them, the Lord your God will no more drive these nations from before you; but they shall be a snare unto you, and a scourge, until ye perish from off this good land which the Lord your God hath given you. Behold, I am going the way of all the earth, and ye know in your hearts, that not one thing hath failed of all the good things which the Lord your God spake concerning you."

The people said unto Joshua: "The Lord our God will we serve, and His voice will we obey."

After these things, Joshua, the servant of the Lord, died, being a hundred and ten years old; and they buried

God's People Enter the Promised Land

him. Israel served the Lord all the days of Joshua, and all the days of the elders that outlived Joshua, and had known all the work of the Lord, that He had wrought for Israel.

X

THE JUDGES

IT came to pass after the death of Joshua, that the children of Israel forsook the God of their fathers who brought them out of the land of Egypt, and followed the gods of the peoples that were round about them. The anger of the Lord was kindled against Israel, and he delivered them into the hands of spoilers that spoiled them, and he sold them into the hands of their enemies. Whithersoever they went, the hand of the Lord was against them, and they were greatly distressed. When the children of Israel cried unto the Lord, the Lord raised up a deliverer, who saved them, even Othniel. The spirit of the Lord came on him, and he judged Israel, and the land had rest forty years.

Othniel died, and the children of Israel again did that which was evil in the sight of the Lord, and the Lord strengthened Eglon the king of Moab against Israel. Eglon smote Israel, and the children of Israel served the king of Moab eighteen years. But when they cried unto the Lord, the Lord raised them up a deliverer, Ehud, a Benjamite. The children of Israel sent a present by him unto Eglon the king of Moab, and Ehud made a sword which had two edges, and he girded it under his raiment. When he had made an end of offering the present, he said: "I have a secret errand unto thee, O king."

The king said: "Keep silence."

All that stood by went out except Ehud. The king was sitting in his summer parlor; and Ehud said: "I have a message from God unto thee."

The king arose, and Ehud took the sword, and slew him. Then Ehud went forth into the porch, and shut the doors of the parlor, and locked them. When he was gone, the king's servants came, and they saw the doors of the parlor were locked, and they tarried till they were ashamed. The king opened not the doors. Therefore they took a key, and opened them; and, behold, their lord was fallen down dead.

Ehud escaped while they tarried, and it came to pass that he blew a trumpet in the hill country of Ephraim, and the children of Israel went down with him, and took the fords of Jordan. They slew of Moab about ten thousand men. So Moab was subdued that day, and the land had rest fourscore years.

The children of Israel again did that which was evil in the sight of the Lord, when Ehud was dead; and the Lord sold them into the hand of Jabin king of Canaan. Twenty years he mightily oppressed the children of Israel. Deborah, a prophetess, judged Israel at that time. She sent and called Barak the son of Abinoam, and said unto him: "Go unto Mount

Tabor, and take with thee ten thousand men, and I will draw unto thee Sisera, the captain of Jabin's army, with his chariots and his multitude, and I will deliver him into thine hand."

Deborah arose, and went with Barak to Kedesh, and Barak called together ten thousand men. Sisera gathered all his chariots, even nine hundred chariots of iron, and all the people that were with him, and Deborah said unto Barak: "Up; for this is the day in which the Lord hath delivered Sisera into thine hand."

So Barak went down from Mount Tabor, and ten thousand men after him; and the Lord discomfited Sisera, and all his chariots, and all his host, before Barak; and Sisera alighted from his chariot and fled away on his feet. Barak pursued after the chariots, and after the host; and all the host of Sisera fell by the edge of the sword. There was not a man left. Howbeit Sisera fled away on his feet to the tent of Jael the wife of Heber the Kenite, who had pitched a tent by Kedesh. Jael went out to meet Sisera, and said unto him: "Turn in, my lord, turn in to me. Fear not."

He turned in unto her into the tent, and she covered him with a rug. He said unto her: "Give me, I pray thee, a little water to drink; for I am thirsty."

She opened a bottle of milk, and gave him drink. He said: "Stand in the door of the tent, and when any man doth come, and say: 'Is there any man here?' thou shalt say: 'No.'"

While Sisera was in a deep sleep, Jael took a tent-pin and a hammer, and went softly unto him, and smote the pin into his temples. So he died. As Barak pursued Sisera, Jael came out to meet him, and said: "Come, and I will show thee the man whom thou seekest."

He came unto her, and, behold, Sisera lay dead.

So God subdued the king of Canaan before the children of Israel, and the land had rest forty years.

The children of Israel did that which was evil in the sight of the Lord, and the Lord delivered them into the hand of Midian, and they made dens in the mountains, and caves, and strongholds. When Israel had sown, the Midianites and the Amalekites and the children of the east came against them, and destroyed the increase of the earth, and left no sustenance in Israel, neither sheep, nor ox, nor ass. For they came as locusts for multitude. Both they and their camels were without number; and they came into the land to destroy it. Israel was greatly impoverished because of Midian; and the children of Israel cried unto the Lord.

The angel of the Lord came, and sat under an oak in Ophrah, and Gideon the son of Joash was beating out wheat. The angel of the Lord appeared unto him and said: "The Lord is with thee, thou mighty man of valor."

Gideon said: "If the Lord be with us, why then is all this befallen us? and where be all his wondrous works which our fathers told us of?"

The Lord looked on him, and said: "Go and save Israel from the hand of Midian."

Gideon said: "O Lord, wherewith shall I save Israel? Behold, my family is the poorest in Manasseh, and I am the least in my father's house."

The Lord said unto him: "Surely I will be with thee, and thou shalt smite the Midianites."

Gideon said: "If now I have found grace in thy sight, then show me a sign."

Gideon went in and made ready a kid and unleavened cakes. The flesh he put in a basket, and he put the broth in a pot, and brought it out under the oak.

The angel of God said: "Take the flesh and the unleavened cakes, and lay them on this rock, and pour out the broth."

Gideon did so. Then the angel of the Lord put forth the end of the staff that was in his hand, and touched the flesh and the unleavened cakes, and there went up fire out of the rock, and consumed the flesh and the unleavened cakes; and the angel of the Lord departed.

All the Midianites and the Amalekites and the children of the east assembled themselves together, and they passed over, and encamped in the valley of Jezreel. The spirit of the Lord came on Gideon, and he blew a trumpet, and sent messengers throughout all Manasseh, and unto Asher, and unto Zebulun, and unto Naphtali; and they came to meet him.

Gideon said unto God: "If Thou wilt save Israel by mine hand, behold, I will put a fleece of wool on the threshing-floor; if there be dew on the fleece only, and it be dry on all the ground, then shall I know that Thou wilt save Israel by mine hand."

He rose early on the morrow, and pressed the fleece together, and wringed the dew out of the fleece, a bowlful of water.

The Lord said unto Gideon: "The people that are with thee are too many for Me to give the Midianites into their hand, lest Israel vaunt themselves, saying: 'Mine own hand hath saved me.' Now therefore, proclaim in the ears of the people, saying: 'Whosoever is fearful and trembling, let him return.'"

There returned twenty and two thousand; and there remained ten thousand.

The Lord said unto Gideon: "The people are yet too many. Bring them down unto the water, and I will try them there."

So Gideon brought down the people unto the water, and the Lord said: "Everyone that lappeth of the water with his tongue, as a dog lappeth, him shalt thou set by himself. Likewise everyone that boweth down on his knees to drink."

The number of them that lapped, putting their hand to their mouth, was three hundred men; but all the rest of the people bowed down on their knees to drink.

The Lord said unto Gideon: "By the three hundred men that lapped will I deliver the Midianites into thine hand."

So Gideon sent all the rest of Israel every man unto his tent, but retained the three hundred men; and the camp of Midian was beneath him in the valley.

It came to pass the same night, that the Lord said unto Gideon: "Arise, get thee down against the camp. But if thou fear, go thou with Phurah thy servant to the camp, and thou shalt hear what they say; and afterward shall thine hands be strengthened."

Then Gideon went with Phurah his servant unto the outermost part of the camp; and, behold, a man told a dream unto his fellow, and said: "I dreamed, and, lo, a cake of barley bread tumbled into the camp of Midian, and came unto a tent, and smote it that it fell, and turned it upside down."

His fellow said: "This is nothing else save the sword of Gideon, a man of Israel. Into his hand God hath delivered Midian."

When Gideon heard the telling of the dream, and the interpretation thereof, he worshipped; and he returned into the camp of Israel, and said: "Arise, for the Lord hath delivered into your hand the host of Midian."

He divided the three hundred men into three companies, and he put into the hands of all of them trumpets, and empty pitchers, with torches in the pitchers. He said unto them: "Look on me, and do likewise;

and when I come to the outermost part of the camp and blow the trumpet, then blow ye the trumpets on every side of the camp, and say: 'The sword of the Lord and of Gideon.'"

So Gideon, and the hundred men that were with him, came unto the outermost part of the camp in the beginning of the middle watch; and they blew the trumpets, and brake in pieces the pitchers, and held the torches in their left hands, and the trumpets in their right hands to blow withal, and they cried: "The sword of the Lord and of Gideon."

They stood every man in his place round about the camp, and all the host ran, and the Lord set every man's sword against his fellow. The men of Israel pursued after Midian, and there fell a hundred and twenty thousand men. So Midian was subdued, and the land had rest forty years.

It came to pass, when Gideon was dead, that Abimelech his son was prince over Israel; and after Abimelech there arose Tola, a man of Issachar; and after him Jair, the Gileadite. Jair died, and the children of Israel again did that which was evil in the sight of the Lord, and the Lord sold them into the hand of the Philistines, and into the hand of the children of Ammon, who vexed and oppressed them eighteen years. The children of Israel cried unto the Lord, saying: "We have sinned against Thee."

The Lord said: "Ye have forsaken Me, and served other gods; wherefore I will save you no more. Go and cry unto the gods ye have chosen. Let them save you in the time of your tribulation."

The children of Israel said unto the Lord: "We have sinned. Do Thou unto us whatsoever seemeth good unto Thee; only deliver us, we pray Thee."

They put away the strange gods from among them, and served the Lord, and His soul was grieved for the misery of Israel.

The children of Ammon were gathered together, and encamped in Gilead; and the children of Israel assembled themselves, and encamped in Mizpeh. Now Jepthah the Gileadite was a mighty man of valor, and the elders of Gilead went to fetch Jepthah, and they said: "Come and be our chief, that we may fight with the children of Ammon."

Then Jepthah went, and the people made him chief over them. He fought against the children of Ammon, and the Lord delivered them into his hand. Jepthah smote them with a very great slaughter; and Jepthah judged Israel six years.

After him Ibzan of Beth-lehem judged Israel; and after him Elon the Zebulunite; and after him Abdon the son of Hillel.

The children of Israel again did that which was evil in the sight of the Lord; and the Lord delivered them into the hand of the Philistines forty years.

There was a certain man of the Danites, whose name was Manoah; and the angel of the Lord appeared unto his wife, and said: "Behold, thou shalt have a son. No razor shall come on his head; for he shall be a Nazarite* unto God; and he shall save Israel out of the hand of the Philistines."

Then the woman came and told her husband, saying: "A man of God came unto me, and his countenance was like the countenance of an angel of God, very terrible. He said: 'Thou shalt have a son, and the child shall be a Nazarite unto God from the day of his birth to the day of his death.'"

The woman had a son, and called his name Samson; and the child grew, and the Lord blessed him.

Samson went to Timnath, and he came, and told his father and his mother: "I have seen a woman in Timnath of the daughters of the Philistines. Now therefore get her for me to wife."

His father and his mother said: "Is there never a woman among all our people, that thou goest to take a wife of the Philistines?"

Samson said unto his father: "Get her for me; for she pleaseth me well."

Then went Samson, and his father and his mother, and came to the vineyards of Timnath, and, behold, a young lion roared against Samson. The spirit of the

---

*One whose life is consecrated to God. A Nazarite drank no wine or other spirituous liquor, and refrained from eating grapes.

Lord came mightily on him, and he rent the lion as he would have rent a kid, and he had nothing in his hand. He went and talked with the woman. After a time he returned to take her, and he turned aside to see the carcass of the lion. Behold, there was a swarm of bees in the body, and honey. He took the honey into his hands, and went on, eating as he went, and he came to his father and mother, and gave unto them, and they did eat; but he told them not that he had taken the honey out of the body of the lion.

His father went unto the woman, and Samson made there a feast. They brought thirty companions to be with him; and Samson said unto them: "Let me now put forth a riddle unto you. If ye can declare it within the seven days of the feast, then I will give you thirty linen garments and thirty changes of raiment; but if ye cannot declare it, then shall ye give me thirty linen garments and thirty changes of raiment."

They said unto him: "Put forth thy riddle, that we may hear it."

He said:

"Out of the eater came forth meat,
And out of the strong came forth sweetness."

They could not declare the riddle; and they said to Samson's wife: "Entice thy husband, that he may declare unto us the riddle, lest we burn thee and thy father's house with fire."

Samson slaying the lion

Samson's wife wept before him, and said: "Thou dost hate me, and lovest me not. Thou hast put forth a riddle unto the children of my people, and hast not told it me."

He said unto her: "Behold, I have not told it to my father nor my mother, and shall I tell it thee?"

She wept before him the seven days, while their feast lasted; and it came to pass on the seventh day, that he told her, because she pressed him sore; and she told the riddle to her people. The men of the city said unto him on the seventh day before the sun went down: "What is sweeter than honey? and what is stronger than a lion?"

The spirit of the Lord came mightily on him, and he went down to Ashkelon, and slew thirty men, and took their apparel, and gave the changes of raiment unto them that declared the riddle. His anger was kindled, and he went to his father's house.

It came to pass after a while, in the time of wheat harvest, that Samson visited his wife; but her father would not suffer him to go in, and said: "I verily thought that thou utterly hated her. Therefore I gave her to thy companion. Is not her younger sister fairer than she? Take her, I pray thee, instead."

Samson said: "This time shall I be blameless in regard of the Philistines, when I do them a mischief."

Samson went and caught three hundred foxes, and took firebrands, and turned tail to tail, and put a firebrand in the midst between every two tails. When he had set the brands on fire, he let the foxes go into the wheat of the Philistines, and burnt up both the shocks and the standing corn, and also the oliveyards. Then the Philistines said: "Who hath done this?"

They answered: "Samson, because his father-in-law hath taken his wife, and given her to his companion."

The Philistines came, and burnt her and her father with fire; and Samson said unto them: "Surely I will be avenged of you."

He smote them with a great slaughter, and he went and dwelt in the cleft of the rock of Etam. Then the Philistines went, and encamped in Judah, and the men of Judah said: "Why are ye come against us?"

They said: "To bind Samson are we come, to do to him as he hath done to us."

Then three thousand men of Judah went to the cleft of the rock of Etam, and said to Samson: "Knowest thou not that the Philistines are rulers over us? What then is this that thou hast done?"

He said: "As they did unto me, so have I done unto them."

They said unto him: "We come to bind thee, that we may deliver thee into the hand of the Philistines."

Samson said: "Swear unto me, that ye will not fall on me yourselves."

They spake, saying: "We will bind thee fast, and deliver thee into their hand; but we will not kill thee."

They bound him with two ropes, and brought him from the rock. The Philistines shouted as they met him; and the spirit of the Lord came mightily on him, and the ropes that were on his arms became as flax that was burnt with fire, and his bands dropped from off his hands. He found a jawbone of an ass, and took it, and smote a thousand men therewith.

Samson went to Gaza, and entered into a house, and it was told the Gazites, saying: "Samson is come hither."

They compassed him in, and laid wait for him all night in the gate of the city, saying: "Let be till morning light. Then we will kill him."

Samson lay till midnight, and arose, and laid hold of the doors of the gate of the city, and the two posts, and plucked them up, bar and all, and put them on his shoulders, and carried them up to the top of the mountain that is before Hebron.

It came to pass afterward, that he loved a woman in the valley of Sorek, whose name was Delilah; and the lords of the Philistines came, and said unto her: "Entice him, and see wherein his great strength lieth, and by what means we may prevail against him, that we may bind him to humble him; and we will give thee every one of us eleven hundred pieces of silver."

Delilah said to Samson: "Tell me, I pray thee, wherein thy great strength lieth, and wherewith thou mightest be bound."

Samson said unto her: "If they bind me with seven green withes that were never dried, then shall I become weak, and be as another man."

The lords of the Philistines brought to her seven green withes which had not been dried, and she bound him with them. She had liers in wait abiding in the inner chamber; and she said unto him: "The Philistines be upon thee, Samson."

He brake the withes, as a string of tow is broken when it toucheth the fire. So his strength was not known. Delilah said unto Samson: "Behold, thou hast mocked me, and told me lies. Tell me, I pray thee, wherewith thou mightest be bound."

He said unto her: "If they bind me with new ropes wherewith no work hath been done, then shall I become weak, and be as another man."

So Delilah took new ropes, and bound him therewith, and said unto him: "The Philistines be upon thee, Samson."

He brake the ropes from off his arms like a thread; and Delilah said unto Samson: "Hitherto thou hast told me lies. Tell me wherewith thou mightest be bound."

It came to pass, when she pressed him daily with her words, and urged him, that his soul was vexed unto death. So he told her all his heart, and said unto her: "There hath not come a razor on mine head.

If I be shaven, then my strength will go from me, and I shall become weak, and be like any other man."

Delilah sent for the lords of the Philistines, saying: "Come this once, for he hath told me all his heart."

The lords of the Philistines came unto her, and brought the money in their hands. She made him sleep on her knees; and she called for a man who shaved off the seven locks of his head; and his strength went from him. She said: "The Philistines be upon thee, Samson."

He awoke out of his sleep, and said: "I will go out as at other times, and shake myself."

He wist not that the Lord was departed from him; and the Philistines laid hold on him, and put out his eyes; and they brought him to Gaza, and bound him with fetters of brass; and he did grind in the prison house. Howbeit the hair of his head began to grow after he was shaven.

The lords of the Philistines gathered together to offer a great sacrifice unto Dagon their god, and to rejoice; for they said: "Our god hath delivered Samson our enemy into our hand."

The people praised their god, and it came to pass, when their hearts were merry, that they said: "Call Samson, that he may make us sport."

They called Samson out of the prison house; and he made sport before them, and they set him between the pillars.

Samson said unto the lad that held him by the hand: "Suffer me that I may feel the pillars whereon the house resteth, that I may lean on them."

Now the house was full of men and women, and all the lords of the Philistines were there; and there were on the roof about three thousand men and women, that beheld while Samson made sport. Samson called unto the Lord, and said: "O Lord God, remember me, I pray Thee, and strengthen me, that I may be avenged of the Philistines for my two eyes."

Samson took hold of the two middle pillars on which the house rested, and leaned on the one with his right hand, and on the other with his left; and Samson said: "Let me die with the Philistines."

He bowed himself with all his might, and the house fell on the lords, and on all the people that were therein. So the Philistines that he slew at his death were more than they that he slew in his life. Then his brethren and all the house of his father came, and took him, and buried him in the buryingplace of Manoah his father.

XI

RUTH

IT came to pass in the days when the judges ruled, that there was a famine in the land; and a certain man of Beth-lehem went to sojourn in the country of Moab, he, and his wife, and his two sons. The name of the man was Elimelech, and the name of his wife Naomi, and the name of his sons Mahlon and Chilion.

They came into the country of Moab, and continued there, and Elimelech died. The two sons took wives of the women of Moab; and the name of one was Orpah, and the name of the other Ruth. After about ten years Mahlon and Chilion died, and Naomi arose that she might return unto Beth-lehem, and she said unto her daughters-in-law: "Go, each of you, to her mother's house. The Lord deal kindly with you, as ye have dealt with the dead, and with me."

They said unto her: "Nay, but we will return with thee unto thy people."

Naomi said: "My daughters, why will ye go with me? The hand of the Lord is gone forth against me."

They lifted up their voices, and wept, and Orpah kissed her mother-in-law, and returned; but Ruth clave unto her.

Naomi said: "Behold, thy sister-in-law is gone back unto her people. Return thou after her."

Ruth said: "Entreat me not to leave thee; for whither thou goest, I will go, and where thou lodgest, I will lodge. Thy people shall be my people, and thy God my God. Where thou diest, will I die, and there will I be buried."

When Naomi saw that Ruth was steadfastly minded to go with her, she left speaking unto her. So they two went until they came to Beth-lehem; and all the city was moved about them, and the women of the city said: "Is this Naomi?"

She said unto them: "The Almighty hath dealt very bitterly with me. I went out full, and the Lord hath brought me home empty."

Naomi and Ruth the Moabitess came to Beth-lehem in the beginning of the barley harvest. Naomi had a kinsman of her husband's, a mighty man of wealth, and his name was Boaz. Ruth said unto Naomi: "Let me go to glean among the ears of corn after him in whose sight I shall find grace."

Naomi said: "Go, my daughter."

She went, and gleaned after the reapers, and her hap was to light on the field belonging unto Boaz. Behold, Boaz came from Beth-lehem, and said unto the reapers: "The Lord be with you."

They answered him: "The Lord bless thee."

Then said Boaz unto his servant that was set over the reapers: "Whose damsel is this?"

The servant answered: "It is the Moabitish damsel that came back with Naomi; and she said: 'Let me, I pray you, gather after the reapers among the sheaves.' So she came, and hath continued even from the morning until now, save that she tarried a little in the house."

Then said Boaz unto Ruth: "Go not to glean in another field; but abide here by my maidens. Let thine eyes be on the field that they do reap, and go thou after them. When thou art athirst, go unto the vessels, and drink of that which the young men have drawn."

She bowed herself to the ground, and said unto him: "Why have I found grace in thine eyes, seeing I am a stranger?"

Boaz answered: "It hath fully been showed me, all that thou hast done unto thy mother-in-law since the death of thine husband, and how thou hast left thy father and thy mother, and the land of thy nativity, and art come unto a people which thou knewest not. The Lord recompense thy work, and a full reward be given thee of the God of Israel, under whose wings thou art come to take refuge."

Then she said: "My lord, thou hast comforted me; for thou hast spoken kindly unto thine handmaid."

At meal-time Boaz said unto her: "Come hither, and eat of the bread, and dip thy morsel in the vinegar."

She sat beside the reapers, and they reached her parched corn, and she did eat, and was sufficed. When she was risen up to glean, Boaz commanded his young men, saying: "Let her glean even among the sheaves. Also let fall some of the handfuls for her, that she may glean them, and rebuke her not."

So she gleaned in the field until even; and she beat out what she had gleaned, and it was about an ephah of barley. She took it up, and went into the city; and her mother-in-law saw what she had gleaned, and said unto her: "Where hast thou gleaned today?"

Ruth said: "The man's name with whom I wrought is Boaz."

Naomi said unto her daughter-in-law: "Blessed be he of the Lord, who hath not left off his kindness to the living and to the dead. The man is near of kin unto us. It is good, my daughter, that thou go out with his maidens."

So Ruth kept fast by the maidens of Boaz to glean unto the end of harvest. She dwelt with her mother-in-law, and Naomi said unto her: "Behold, Boaz winnoweth barley tonight. Wash thyself therefore, and put thy raiment on thee, and get thee down to the threshing-floor; but make not thyself known unto the man, until he shall have done eating and drinking. When he lieth down, mark the place where he shall lie, and go in, and lay thee down at his feet, and he will tell thee what thou shalt do."

Ruth said: "All that thou sayest I will do."

She went unto the threshing-floor, and when Boaz had eaten and drunk, and his heart was merry, he went to lie down at the end of the heap of barley; and she came softly, and laid her down. At midnight the man turned himself, and, behold, a woman lay at his feet; and he said: "Who art thou?"

She answered: "I am Ruth, thine handmaid. Spread therefore thy skirt over thine handmaid; for thou art a near kinsman."

He said: "Blessed be thou of the Lord, my daughter. It is true that I am a near kinsman; howbeit there is a kinsman nearer than I. Let him do the kinsman's part; but if he will not, then will I, as the Lord liveth. Lie down until the morning."

She lay at his feet until the morning, and she rose up, and he said: "Bring the mantle that is on thee, and hold it."

She held it, and he measured six measures of barley, and laid it on her. When she came to her mother-in-law, Naomi said: "How hast thou fared, my daughter?"

Ruth told all that the man had done to her, and said: "These six measures of barley gave he me."

Then Naomi said: "My daughter, the man will not rest, until he have finished the thing."

Boaz went up to the gate, and sat down there; and, behold, the near kinsman of whom Boaz spake came by; unto whom he said: "Ho! turn aside, sit down here."

He turned aside, and sat down; and Boaz took ten men of the elders of the city, and said: "Sit ye down here."

They sat down, and he said unto the near kinsman: "Naomi, that is come out of the country of Moab, selleth the parcel of land, which was our brother Elimelech's. Buy it before them that sit here; but if thou wilt not redeem it, then tell me, for I am after thee; and thou must buy it also of Ruth the Moabitess."

The near kinsman said: "I cannot redeem it."

In former times concerning redeeming and exchanging, to confirm all things, a man drew off his shoe, and gave it to his neighbor. So the near kinsman said unto Boaz: "Buy it for thyself;" and he drew off his shoe.

Boaz said unto the elders, and unto all the people: "Ye are witnesses this day, that I have bought all that was Elimelech's, and all that was Chilion's and Mahlon's. Moreover Ruth the Moabitess, the wife of Mahlon, have I purchased to be my wife."

All the people that were in the gate said: "We are witnesses."

So Boaz took Ruth, and she became his wife, and she bare a son; and the women said unto Naomi: "Blessed be the Lord, which hath not left thee without a near kinsman. The child shall be unto thee a nourisher of thine old age."

Naomi took the child, and became nurse unto it, and the women, her neighbors, called his name Obed, and from him was descended David king of Israel.

XII

SAMUEL AND THE FIRST OF THE KINGS

THERE was a certain man of the hill country of Ephraim, and his name was Elkanah, and he had a wife named Hannah; but Hannah had no children. This man went from year to year to worship and to sacrifice unto the Lord in Shiloh. At one time, when Elkanah sacrificed, Eli the priest sat by the doorpost of the temple of the Lord; and Hannah was in bitterness of soul, and prayed and wept. She vowed a vow, and said: "O Lord of hosts, if Thou wilt look on the affliction of thine handmaid, and wilt give unto thine handmaid a man child, then I will give him unto the Lord all the days of his life."

It came to pass as she continued praying that Eli said: "Go in peace, and the God of Israel grant thy petition."

So the woman went her way, and her countenance was no more sad, and she and Elkanah returned to their house to Ramah. The Lord remembered her, and it came to pass that Hannah bare a son; and she called his name Samuel. When she had weaned him, she took him unto the house of the Lord in Shiloh, and they brought the child to Eli. She said: "I am the woman that stood by thee here, praying unto the Lord.

For this child I prayed; and the Lord hath given me my petition. Therefore I have granted the child to the Lord."

They worshipped, and went to Ramah, and the child did minister unto the Lord before Eli the priest, girded with a linen ephod. Moreover his mother made him a little robe, and brought it to him from year to year, when she came with her husband to offer the yearly sacrifice; and the child Samuel grew, and was in favor with the Lord, and also with men.

Now the sons of Eli knew not the Lord, and the sin of the young men was very great. Eli heard all that his sons did, and he said unto them: "Why do ye such things? Ye make the Lord's people to transgress."

Notwithstanding they hearkened not unto the voice of their father; and there came a man of God unto Eli, and said unto him: "Thus saith the Lord: 'Them that honor Me will I honor, and they that despise Me shall be lightly esteemed. Behold, in one day thy two sons shall die both of them; and I will raise Me up a faithful priest. Everyone that is left in thine house shall come and bow down to him for a piece of silver and a morsel of bread."

The child Samuel ministered unto the Lord before Eli, and when Samuel was laid down to sleep, in the temple of the Lord, where the ark of God was, the Lord called Samuel.

He ran unto Eli, and said: "Here am I; for thou calledst me."

Eli said: "I called not. Lie down again."

Samuel went and lay down, and the Lord called yet again: "Samuel."

Samuel arose and went to Eli, and said: "Here am I; for thou calledst me."

Eli answered: "I called not, my son. Lie down again."

The Lord called Samuel the third time. He arose and went to Eli and said: "Here am I; for thou didst call me."

Eli perceived that the Lord had called the child. Therefore Eli said unto Samuel: "Go, lie down; and it shall be, if He call thee, that thou shalt say: 'Speak, Lord; for thy servant heareth.'"

So Samuel went and lay down in his place; and the Lord came, and stood, and called as at other times: "Samuel, Samuel."

Then Samuel said: "Speak; for thy servant heareth."

The Lord said: "Behold, I will perform against Eli all that I have spoken concerning his house, because his sons made themselves vile, and he restrained them not."

Samuel lay until the morning, and opened the doors of the house of the Lord; and Samuel feared to show Eli the vision. Then Eli called Samuel, and said: "What is the thing that the Lord hath spoken unto thee?"

Samuel told him, and Eli said: "It is the Lord. Let Him do what seemeth good."

Samuel grew, and the Lord was with him, and all Israel from Dan even to Beer-sheba* knew that Samuel was established to be a prophet of the Lord.

Israel went out against the Philistines to battle, and Israel was smitten before the Philistines. When the people were come into the camp, the elders of Israel said: "Wherefore hath the Lord smitten us today before the Philistines? Let us fetch the ark of the covenant unto us, that it may save us out of the hand of our enemies."

So the people sent to Shiloh, and brought thence the ark of the covenant of the Lord; and the two sons of Eli were with the ark of the covenant. When it came into the camp, all Israel shouted with a great shout. The Philistines heard the noise of the shout, and said: "What meaneth this great shout in the camp of the Hebrews?"

They understood that the ark of the Lord was come into the camp; and the Philistines were afraid, for they said: "God is come into the camp. Woe unto us! This is the God that smote the Egyptians with all manner of plagues. Be strong, O ye Philistines, that ye be not servants unto the Hebrews. Quit yourselves like men, and fight."

---

*Dan was a city recognized as the most northern landmark of Palestine, and Beer-sheba was at the southern limit of the country.

Samuel and the First of the Kings 159

The Philistines fought, and there fell of Israel thirty thousand men; and the ark of God was taken, and the two sons of Eli were slain. There ran a man out of the army, and came to Shiloh with his clothes rent, and with earth on his head; and, lo, Eli sat by the wayside watching. When the man came into the city, all the city cried out, and Eli said: "What meaneth this tumult?"

The man hasted, and came and told Eli: "Israel is fled before the Philistines, and there hath been a great slaughter among the people, and thy two sons are dead, and the ark of God is taken."

It came to pass, when he made mention of the ark of God, that Eli fell off his seat backward by the side of the gate, and his neck brake, and he died; for he was an old man, and heavy.

The Philistines had taken the ark of God, and they brought it unto Ashdod into the house* of Dagon, and set it by Dagon. When they of Ashdod arose early on the morrow, behold, Dagon was fallen on his face to the ground before the ark of the Lord. They took Dagon and set him in his place; and when they arose on the morrow, Dagon was fallen on his face before the ark of the Lord; and the head of Dagon and both of his hands lay cut off on the threshold.

---

*This was a place of worship, and contained an image of Dagon the god of the Philistines. Dagon was represented to have a human head and arms; but the lower portion of the body was that of a fish.

The hand of the Lord was heavy on them of Ashdod, and he destroyed them, and smote them with tumors; and they said: "The ark of the God of Israel shall not abide with us; for His hand is sore on us, and on Dagon our god."

They sent therefore and gathered all the lords of the Philistines unto them, and said: "What shall we do with the ark of the God of Israel?"

They answered: "Let it be carried unto Gath."

They carried the ark thither, and the Lord smote the men of the city. So they sent it to Ekron; and the Ekronites cried out, saying: "They have brought the ark of the God of Israel to slay our people. Let it go to its own place."

There was a deadly discomfiture throughout all the city; and the Philistines called for the priests and diviners who said: "Make a new cart, and take two milch kine, and tie the kine to the cart, and lay. the ark on the cart, and send it away."

The men did so, and the kine took the straight way to Beth-shemesh, lowing as they went, and turned not aside to the right hand or to the left; and the lords of the Philistines went after them unto the border of Beth-shemesh. They of Beth-shemesh were reaping their wheat, and they lifted up their eyes, and saw the ark, and rejoiced. The cart came into a field, and stood there; and they clave the wood of the cart, and offered up the kine for a burnt offering unto the Lord.

The Lord smote the men of Beth-shemesh, because they looked into the ark; and they sent messengers to the inhabitants of Kirjath-jearim, saying: "The Philistines have brought the ark of the Lord. Come ye, and fetch it to you."

The men of Kirjath-jearim came, and brought it into the house of Abinadab in Gibeah, and the ark abode there twenty years.

Israel lamented after the Lord, and Samuel spake, saying: "If ye do return unto the Lord with all your heart, put away the strange gods from among you, and the Lord will deliver you out of the hand of the Philistines."

Then the children of Israel served the Lord only, and Samuel said: "Gather all Israel to Mizpeh, and I will pray for you."

They gathered together to Mizpeh, and fasted. When the Philistines heard that the children of Israel were gathered together, they went against Israel; and the children of Israel were afraid, and said to Samuel: "Cease not to cry unto the Lord our God for us, that He will save us out of the hand of the Philistines."

Samuel cried unto the Lord, and the Philistines drew near to battle against Israel; but the Lord thundered with a great thunder on the Philistines, and they were smitten before Israel. So the Philistines were subdued, and the cities which they had taken from Israel were restored.

Samuel judged Israel all the days of his life; and it came to pass, when Samuel was old, that he made his sons judges over Israel; and his sons walked not in his ways, but took bribes, and perverted judgment. Then all the elders of Israel came to Samuel, and said: "Behold, thou art old, and thy sons walk not in thy ways. Now make us a king to judge us."

The thing displeased Samuel, and he prayed unto the Lord. The Lord said: "Hearken unto the voice of the people in all that they say unto thee. Howbeit protest solemnly unto them, and show them the manner of the king that shall reign over them."

Samuel told all the words of the Lord unto the people, and said: "The king that shall reign over you will take your sons, and appoint them to be his horsemen, and he will set some to plow his ground, and to reap his harvest, and to make his instruments of war. He will take your daughters to be cooks, and to be bakers. He will take your fields and your vineyards, even the best of them, and give them to his servants, and he will take the tenth of your seed. He will take your menservants, and your maidservants, and your asses, and put them to his work. Ye shall cry out in that day because of your king, and the Lord will not answer you."

But the people refused to hearken unto the voice of Samuel; and they said: "Nay, but we will have a king over us, that we may be like all the nations, and that our king may judge us, and fight our battles."

Samuel heard all the words of the people, and said: "Go ye every man unto his city."

There was a man of Benjamin, whose name was Kish; and he had a son, whose name was Saul. There was not among the children of Israel a goodlier person than Saul. From his shoulders and upward he was higher than any of the people.

The asses of Kish were lost, and Kish said to Saul: "Take one of the servants, and go seek the asses."

Saul passed through the country till he was come to the land of Zuph, but he found them not; and he said to his servant: "Let us return."

The servant said: "Behold, there is in this city a man of God, and all that he saith cometh surely to pass. Peradventure he can tell us concerning our journey."

Then said Saul to his servant: "But if we go, what shall we bring the man?"

The servant answered: "I have in my hand the fourth part of a shekel of silver.* That will I give to the man of God, to tell us our way."

So they went unto the city where the man of God was; and as they came within the city, behold, Samuel came out. Now the Lord had told Samuel a day before Saul came: "Tomorrow about this time I will send

---

*The ordinary shekel of gold had a value of about eleven dollars. The silver shekel was worth about seventy-five cents.

thee a man out of the land of Benjamin, and thou shalt anoint him to be prince over My people Israel, that he may save My people out of the hand of the Philistines."

When Samuel saw Saul, the Lord said unto him: "Behold the man of whom I spake to thee. This same shall reign over My people."

Then Saul drew near to Samuel in the gate, and said: "Tell me I pray thee, where the seer's house is."

Samuel answered: "I am the seer. Ye shall eat with me today, and tomorrow I will let thee go. As for thine asses that were lost three days ago, they are found."

Samuel took Saul and his servant, and brought them into the guest-chamber, and made them sit in the chiefest place among them that were bidden, who were about thirty persons. So Saul did eat with Samuel that day, and they spread a couch for Saul on the housetop, and he lay down. About the spring of the day Samuel called to Saul, saying: "Up, that I may send thee away."

Saul arose, and they went out. At the end of the city, Samuel said to Saul: "Bid the servant pass on before us."

Then Samuel took a vial of oil, and poured it on Saul's head, and kissed him, and said: "The Lord hath anointed thee to be prince over His inheritance. God is with thee."

Saul returned to his father's house, and Saul's uncle said unto him and to his servant: "Whither went ye?"

Saul said: "To seek the asses; and when they were not found, we came to Samuel."

Saul's uncle said: "Tell me, I pray thee, what Samuel said unto you."

Saul said: "He told us plainly that the asses were found." But concerning the matter of the kingdom, whereof Samuel spake, he told him not.

Samuel called the people together, and said: "Thus saith the Lord: 'I delivered you out of the hand of the Egyptians, and out of the hand of all the kingdoms that oppressed you; but ye have rejected your God, who saveth you out of all your adversities and your distresses, and ye have said unto Him: "Set a king over us." Now therefore present yourselves before the Lord by your tribes, and by your thousands.'"

But Saul the son of Kish could not be found; and the Lord said: "Behold he hath hid himself among the baggage."

They ran and fetched him, and when he stood among the people, he was higher than any from his shoulders and upward. Samuel said to the people: "See ye him whom the Lord hath chosen, that there is none like him."

All the people shouted, and said: "God save the king."

Then Samuel sent the people away, and Saul went home to Gibeah.

Nahash the Ammonite came and encamped against Jabesh-gilead; and the men of Jabesh said unto Nahash: "Make a covenant with us, and we will serve thee."

Nahash said unto them: "On this condition will I make it, that all your right eyes be put out."

The elders of Jabesh said unto him: "Give us seven days' respite, that we may send messengers unto all the borders of Israel; and then, if there be no man to save us, we will come to thee."

The messengers came to Gibeah, and the people lifted up their voices, and wept. Saul came following the oxen out of the field, and Saul said: "What aileth the people that they weep?"

They told him the words of the men of Jabesh; and the spirit of God came mightily on Saul, and his anger was kindled greatly. He sent messengers throughout Israel, and the people came as one man. Saul put the people in three companies, and they came in the morning watch, and smote the Ammonites until the heat of the day; and the Ammonites which remained were scattered, so that two of them were not left together.

Then said Samuel to the people: "Let us go to Gilgal, and renew the kingdom."

All the people went to Gilgal, and there they made Saul king; and the Philistines assembled to fight with Israel, thirty thousand chariots, and six thousand horsemen, and people as the sand which is on the seashore in multitude. Then the people of Israel did hide themselves in caves, and in thickets and in pits. Saul was yet in Gilgal, and Saul numbered the people that were present with him, about six hundred men. Jonathan, the son of Saul, said unto the young man that bare his armor: "Come and let us go to the Philistines' garrison;" but he told not his father.

Between the passes by which Jonathan sought to go unto the Philistines' garrison, there was a rocky crag on the one side, and a rocky crag on the other side. Jonathan climbed up on his hands and on his feet, and his armorbearer after him, and the Philistines fell before Jonathan. That first slaughter, which Jonathan and his armorbearer made, was about twenty men, within as it were half a furrow's length in an acre of land;' and there was a trembling in the camp among all the people.

The watchmen of Saul looked, and, behold, the multitude melted away, and went hither and thither; and Saul and the people that were with him came to the battle, and there was a very great discomfiture. All the men of Israel that had hid themselves in the hill country of Ephraim, when they heard that the Philistines fled, followed hard after them in the battle. So the Lord saved Israel, and the Philistines went to their own place.

Samuel said unto Saul: "Thus saith the Lord: 'Go and smite Amalek, and utterly destroy all that they have. Spare them not; but slay man, woman and infant, ox and sheep, camel and ass.'"

Saul summoned the people, and smote the Amalekites, and he took Agag their king alive, and utterly destroyed all the people with the edge of the sword. But Saul spared the best of the sheep, and of the oxen, and the lambs. Then came the word of the Lord unto Samuel, saying: "It repenteth Me that I have set up Saul to be king; for he is turned back from following Me."

Samuel rose early to meet Saul in the morning, and Saul said unto him: "I have performed the commandment of the Lord."

Samuel said: "What meaneth then this bleating of the sheep in mine ears, and the lowing of the oxen which I hear?"

Saul said: "The people spared the best of the sheep and of the oxen, to sacrifice unto the Lord."

Samuel said unto Saul: "The Lord sent thee on a journey, and said: 'Go and utterly destroy the sinners, the Amalekites, and fight against them until they be consumed.' Hath the Lord as great delight in burnt offerings and sacrifices, as in obeying the voice of the Lord? Behold, to obey is better than sacrifice, and to hearken than the fat of rams. Because thou hast rejected the word of the Lord, He hath also rejected thee from being king."

Saul said: "I have transgressed the commandment of the Lord, and thy words. I pray thee, pardon my sin, and turn again with me, that I may worship the Lord."

Samuel turned after Saul, and Saul worshipped the Lord. Then said Samuel: "Bring ye hither to me Agag the king of the Amalekites."

Agag came and said: "Surely the bitterness of death is past."

Samuel said: "As thy sword hath made women childless, so shall thy mother be childless;" and Samuel hewed Agag in pieces before the Lord in Gilgal.

Then Samuel went to Ramah, and Saul went to his house to Gibeah. Samuel came no more to see Saul, but Samuel mourned for Saul; and the Lord said unto Samuel: "How long wilt thou mourn for Saul, seeing I have rejected him? Fill thine horn with oil, and I will send thee to Jesse the Beth-lehemite; for I have provided Me a king among his sons."

Samuel said: "How can I go? If Saul hear it, he will kill me."

The Lord said: "Take a heifer with thee, and say: 'I am come to sacrifice to the Lord.' Call Jesse to the sacrifice, and thou shalt anoint him whom I name unto thee."

Samuel did that which the Lord spake, and came to Beth-lehem; and he sanctified Jesse and his sons, and called them to the sacrifice. When they were come, he looked on Eliab, and said: "Surely the Lord's anointed is before Him."

But the Lord said unto Samuel: "I have rejected him. The Lord seeth not as man seeth; for man looketh on the outward appearance, but the Lord looketh on the heart."

Jesse made seven of his sons pass before Samuel, and Samuel said: "The Lord hath not chosen these. Are here all thy children?"

Jesse said: "There remaineth yet the youngest, and, behold, he keepeth the sheep."

Samuel said: "Send and fetch him."

Jesse sent, and brought him in. Now he was ruddy, and withal of a beautiful countenance, and goodly to look on. The Lord said: "Arise, anoint him; for this is he."

Then Samuel took the horn of oil, and anointed him in the midst of his brethren; and the spirit of the Lord came mightily on David from that day forward.

The spirit of the Lord had departed from Saul, and an evil spirit troubled him; and Saul's servants said unto him: "Let our lord command thy servants to seek out a man who is a cunning player on the harp; and it shall come to pass, when the evil spirit is on thee, that he shall play, and thou shalt be well."

Saul said: "Provide me a man that can play well, and bring him to me."

Then answered one of the servants: "Behold, I have seen a son of Jesse the Beth-lehemite, that is cunning in playing, and prudent in speech, and a comely person, and the Lord is with him."

Wherefore Saul sent messengers unto Jesse, and said: "Send me David thy son."

David came to Saul, and stood before him, and became his armorbearer. When the evil spirit was on Saul, David took the harp, and played. So Saul was refreshed, and the evil spirit departed from him.

The Philistines gathered together their armies, and Saul and the men of Israel set the battle in array against the Philistines. The Philistines stood on a mountain on the one side, and Israel stood on the mountain on the other side, and there was a valley between them. A champion went out of the camp of the Philistines, named Goliath, whose height was six cubits and a span. He had a helmet of brass on his head, and he was clad with a coat of mail, and the staff of his spear was like a weaver's beam. He stood and cried unto the ranks of Israel, and said: "Choose you a man, and let him come down to me. If he be able to fight with me, and kill me, then will we be your servants; but if I prevail against him, and kill him, then shall ye serve us."

When Saul and all Israel heard those words of the Philistine, they were dismayed, and greatly afraid; and the Philistine drew near morning and evening, and presented himself forty days

The three eldest sons of Jesse had gone after Saul to the battle. But David returned to feed his father's sheep at Beth-lehem. Jesse said unto David: "Take this parched corn, and these ten loaves, and carry them quickly to the camp to thy brethren, and look how thy brethren fare."

David left the sheep with a keeper, and went, as Jesse commanded him, and he came to the place of the wagons, as the host was going forth to the fight. Israel and the Philistines put the battle in array, army against army; and David left his baggage, and ran into the army, and saluted his brethren. As he talked with them, behold, there came the champion Goliath out of the ranks of the Philistines, and spake according to the same words.

David spake to the men that stood by him, saying: "What shall be done to the man that killeth this Philistine? for who is this Philistine, that he should defy the armies of the living God?"

The people answered: "The man who killeth him, the king will enrich with great riches, and will give him his daughter."

Eliab his eldest brother heard when he spake unto the men; and Eliab's anger was kindled against David, and he said: "Why art thou come, and with whom hast thou left those few sheep in the wilderness? I know thy pride, and the naughtiness of thine heart; for thou art come that thou mightest see the battle."

David turned toward another, and spake after the same manner, and the words David spake were rehearsed before Saul; and Saul sent for him. David said to Saul: "Thy servant will go and fight with this Philistine."

Saul said: "Thou art but a youth, and he a man of war."

David said unto Saul: "Thy servant kept his father's sheep, and when there came a lion, and took a lamb out of the flocks, I went after him and smote him, and delivered it out of his mouth; and when he arose against me, I caught him by his beard, and slew him. The Lord that delivered me out of the paw of the lion, will deliver me out of the hand of this Philistine."

Saul said unto David: "Go, and the Lord shall be with thee."

Saul clad David with his apparel, and he put a helmet of brass on his head, and he clad him with a coat of mail. David said: "I cannot go with these, for I have not proved them;" and David put them off him.

He took his staff in his hand, and chose five smooth stones out of the brook, and put them in the shepherd's bag which he had; and his sling was in his hand, and he drew near to the Philistine. When the Philistine looked about, and saw David, he disdained him; for he was but a youth. The Philistine said unto David: "Am I a dog that thou comest to me with staves?" And the Philistine cursed David by his gods.

The Philistine said to David: "Come to me, and I will give thy flesh unto the fowls of the air, and to the beasts of the field."

Then said David: "Thou comest to me with a sword, and with a spear; but I come to thee in the name of the God of the armies of Israel. This day will the Lord deliver thee into mine hand."

It came to pass, when the Philistine drew nigh to meet David, that David hastened, and ran to meet the Philistine. David put his hand in his bag, and took thence a stone, and slang it, and smote the Philistine in his forehead, and he fell on his face to the earth. So David prevailed over the Philistine with a sling and with a stone; but there was no sword in the hand of David. Then David stood over the Philistine, and took his sword out of the sheath, and cut off his head.

When the Philistines saw that their champion was dead, they fled; and the men of Israel shouted, and pursued the Philistines to the gates of Ekron.

The captain of the host brought David before Saul with the head of the Philistine in his hand; and Saul would let him go no more to his father's house. David went out whithersoever Saul sent him, and behaved himself wisely; and Saul set him over the men of war.

As they returned from the slaughter of the Philistines, the women came out of all the cities of Israel, to meet King Saul, singing and dancing, and with instruments of music. The women sang to one another in their play, and said:

"Saul hath slain his thousands,
And David his ten thousands."

Saul was very wroth, and this saying displeased him. Michal Saul's daughter loved David; and they told Saul, and Saul said: "I will give him her, that she may be a snare to him."

Saul commanded his servants, saying: "Commune with David secretly, and say: 'Behold, the king hath delight in thee. Now therefore be the king's son-in-law. The king desireth not any dowry, but that thou should kill a hundred of the Philistines.'"

When his servants told David these words, David arose and went, he and his men, and slew of the Philistines two hundred men; and Saul gave him Michal his daughter to wife. Saul saw that the Lord was with David, and Saul was David's enemy, and spake to Jonathan his son, and to all his servants, that they should kill David. But Jonathan delighted much in David, and Jonathan spake good of David unto Saul, and said: "Let not the king sin against David. He put his life in his hand, and slew the Philistine, and the Lord wrought a great victory for all Israel. Thou sawest it and didst rejoice. Wherefore then wilt thou slay David without a cause?"

Saul hearkened unto the voice of Jonathan, and Jonathan brought David to Saul, and he was in his presence, as beforetime.

There was war again; and David fought with the Philistines, and they fled before him. An evil spirit was on Saul, as he sat in his house with his spear in his hand. David played, and Saul sought to smite David with the spear; but David slipped away out of Saul's presence, and Saul smote the spear into the wall.

David escaped, and came and said before Jonathan: "What is mine iniquity, that thy father seeketh my life? There is but a step between me and death."

Then said Jonathan: "Whatsoever thy soul desireth, I will even do it for thee."

David said: "Tomorrow is the new moon, and I should not fail to sit with the king at meat; but let me go, that I may hide myself. If thy father miss me, then say: 'David earnestly asked leave of me that he might run to Beth-lehem his city; for it is the yearly sacrifice there for all the family.' If he say: 'It is well,' thy servant shall have peace; but if he be wroth, evil is determined by him."

Jonathan said: "When thou hast stayed three days thou shalt come to the stone Ezel. I will shoot three arrows on the side thereof, as though I shot at a mark; and I will send a lad, saying: 'Go, find the arrows.' If I say unto the lad: 'Behold, the arrows are on this side of thee;' come, for there is peace to thee. But if I say unto the boy: 'Behold the arrows are beyond thee,' go thy way."

So David hid himself, and when the new moon was come the king sat down to eat; but David's place was empty. Nevertheless Saul spake not anything that day; for he thought: "Something hath befallen him."

On the morrow Saul said unto Jonathan: "Wherefore cometh not the son of Jesse to meat?"

Jonathan answered: "David earnestly asked leave of me to go to Beth-lehem; and he said: 'Let me go, I pray thee; for our family hath a sacrifice in the city.'"

Then Saul's anger was kindled against Jonathan, and he said: "Do not I know that thou hast chosen the son of Jesse to thine own shame? for as long as the son of Jesse liveth thou shalt not be established, nor thy kingdom. Send and fetch him unto me, for he shall surely die."

Jonathan answered: "Wherefore shall he be slain? What hath he done?"

Saul cast his spear at him to smite him. So Jonathan arose from the table in fierce anger.

In the morning Jonathan went out into the field at the time appointed, and a little lad with him. He said unto his lad: "Run, find now the arrows which I shoot."

As the lad ran, Jonathan shot an arrow beyond him, and cried after the lad: "Is not the arrow beyond thee? Make speed. Stay not."

Jonathan's lad gathered up the arrows, and came to his master; and Jonathan gave his weapons unto his lad, and said: "Carry them to the city."

As soon as the lad was gone, David arose, and they kissed one another, and wept with one another, and Jonathan said to David: "Go in peace."

David departed, and Jonathan went into the city.

Then came David to Nob to Ahimelech the priest, and Ahimelech said: "Why art thou alone?"

David said: "The king hath said unto me: 'Let no man know anything of the business whereabout I send thee.' Now therefore, give me five loaves of bread."

The priest said: "There is no common bread under mine hand, but there is holy bread."

So the priest gave him the showbread, that was taken from before the Lord.

David said unto Ahimelech: "Is there not here spear or sword? for I have neither brought my sword nor any weapons, because the king's business required haste."

The priest said: "The sword of Goliath the Philistine, whom thou slewest, is here wrapped in a cloth. If thou wilt take that, take it; for there is no other."

David said: "Give it me."

David fled that day to Achish the king of Gath; and the servants of Achish said: "Is not this David?

Did they not sing one to another of him in dances, saying:

'Saul hath slain his thousands,
And David his ten thousands?'"

David laid up these words in his heart, and was sore afraid; and he changed his behavior, and feigned himself mad, and scrabbled on the doors of the gate, and let his spittle fall down on his beard. Then said Achish unto his servants: "Lo, ye see the man is mad. Have I need of mad men, that ye have brought this fellow to play the mad man in my presence?"

David therefore departed, and escaped to the cave of Adullam; and his brethren and all his father's house went down thither to him; and everyone that was in distress, and everyone that was in debt, and everyone that was discontented, gathered themselves unto him. He became captain over them, and there were with him about four hundred men.

David went and dwelt in the strongholds of En-gedi. Saul took three thousand chosen men and went to seek David on the rocks of the wild goats; and he came to a cave, and Saul went in. David and his men were abiding in the innermost parts of the cave; and David cut off the skirt of Saul's robe privily. Saul rose up out of the cave, and went on his way. David also went out of the cave, and he cried after Saul, saying: "My lord the king."

When Saul looked behind him, David bowed with his face to the earth, and said: "Wherefore hearkenest thou to men's words, saying: 'Behold, David seeketh thy hurt?' This day thine eyes have seen how the Lord had delivered thee into mine hand in the cave. Some bade me kill thee, but I said: 'I will not put forth mine hand against my lord.' Moreover, see the skirt of thy robe in my hand; for in that I cut off the skirt of thy robe and killed thee not, know thou that there is neither evil nor transgression in mine hand, and I have not sinned against thee. The Lord judge between me and thee, and deliver me out of thine hand."

When David had made an end of speaking these words, Saul lifted up his voice, and wept; and he said to David: "Thou art more righteous than I; for thou hast rendered unto me good, whereas I have rendered unto thee evil. Now, behold, I know that thou shalt surely be king, and that the kingdom of Israel shall be established in thine hand."

Saul went home; but David and his men gat them up unto the stronghold.

Samuel died, and all Israel gathered together, and lamented him, and buried him.

There was a man whose possessions were in Carmel, and he had three thousand sheep, and a thousand goats. The name of the man was Nabal, and the name of his wife Abigail; and the woman was of good understanding, and of a beautiful countenance; but the man was churlish and evil in his doings. David heard in the wilderness that Nabal did shear his sheep; and David sent ten young men, and said: "Go to Nabal, and greet him in my name, and thus ye shall say to him: 'Peace be to thee, and to thine house. Thy shepherds have been with us, and we did them no hurt, neither was there aught missing unto them. Wherefore let the young men find favor in thine eyes. Give, I pray thee, whatsoever cometh to thine hand, unto thy servants.'"

David's young men spake to Nabal according to all those words, and Nabal answered: "Who is David? Shall I take my bread, and my flesh that I have killed for my shearers, and give it unto men of whom I know not whence they be?"

So David's young men went back, and told him all those sayings.

David said unto his men: "Gird ye on every man his sword."

They girded on every man his sword, and there went up after David about four hundred men. But one of the servants told Abigail, Nabal's wife, saying: "Behold, David sent messengers out of the wilderness to salute our master; and he railed on them. The men were very good unto us, and we were not hurt, neither missed we anything, as long as we were conversant with them. They were a wall unto us both by night and by day, all the while we were with them keeping the sheep. Now therefore consider what thou wilt do; for evil is determined against our master, and against all his household."

Then Abigail made haste, and took two hundred loaves, and two bottles of wine, and five sheep ready dressed, and five measures of parched grain, and a hundred clusters of raisins, and two hundred cakes of figs, and laid them on asses. She said unto her servants: "Go on before me. I come after you;" but she told not her husband.

As she rode by the covert of the mountain, David and his men came down against her. When Abigail saw David, she alighted, and bowed herself to the ground, and said: "Hear thou the words of thine handmaid. Let not my lord, I pray thee, regard this man Nabal; for folly is with him. Now therefore, this present which thine handmaiden hath brought, let it be given unto the young men that follow my lord."

David said to Abigail: "Blessed be the God of Israel who sent thee this day to meet me. Except thou hadst come, surely there had not been left unto Nabal by the morning light so much as one man child."

So David received of her hand that which she had brought him; and he said unto her: "Go in peace to thine house."

It came to pass about ten days after, that the Lord smote Nabal, that he died; and when David heard that Nabal was dead he sent and spake concerning

Abigail, to take her to wife. Abigail hasted, and rode after the messengers of David, and became his wife.

In those days the Philistines gathered to fight with Israel; and Saul gathered all Israel together, and they encamped in Gilboa. When Saul saw the host of the Philistines, he was afraid, and his heart trembled greatly; and when Saul inquired of the Lord, the Lord answered him not, neither by dreams, nor by prophets. The Philistines fought against Israel, and the men of Israel fled; and the Philistines followed hard on Saul and on his sons, and the Philistines slew Jonathan, and Abinadab, and Malchishua, the sons of Saul. The battle went sore against Saul, and the archers wounded him, and he was greatly distressed. Then said Saul to his armorbearer: "Draw thy sword, and thrust me through therewith."

But his armorbearer would not. Therefore Saul took his sword and fell on it; and when his armorbearer saw that Saul was dead, he likewise fell on his sword, and died with him.

XIII

KING DAVID

AFTER the death of Saul, behold, a man came out of the camp from Saul with his clothes rent, and earth on his head, and came to David, and did obeisance. David said unto him: "Whence comest thou?"

The man said: "Out of the camp of Israel am I escaped. The people are fled from the battle, and many of the people are fallen; and Saul and Jonathan his son are dead."

Then David took hold on his clothes, and rent them; and likewise all the men that were with him; and they mourned, and wept, and fasted until even, for Saul, and for Jonathan, because they were fallen by the sword.

It came to pass after this, that David inquired of the Lord, saying: "Shall I go into any of the cities of Judah?"

The Lord said: "Go."

David said: "Whither shall I go?"

The Lord said: "Unto Hebron."

So David went thither, and the men of Judah came, and there they anointed David king over Judah.

Abner, captain of Saul's host, had taken Ish-bosheth the son of Saul, and made him king over all Israel;

King David

but the house of Judah followed David. There was a long war between the house of Saul and the house of David; and David waxed stronger and stronger; but the house of Saul waxed weaker and weaker.

Ish-bosheth had two men that were captains of bands, who went about the heat of the day to his house, as he took his rest at noon, and they slew him, and beheaded him. They brought the head of Ish-bosheth unto David to Hebron, and said: "The Lord hath avenged the king this day of Saul."

David answered and said unto them: "When wicked men have slain a righteous person in his own house, shall I not require his blood of their hand?"

David commanded his young men, and they slew them. All the tribes of Israel came to David and spake, saying: "Behold, in times past, when Saul was king over us, it was thou that leddest out and broughtest in Israel; and the Lord said to thee: 'Thou shalt be prince over Israel.' "

So they anointed David king over Israel. David was thirty years old when he began to reign, and he reigned forty years. In Hebron he reigned over Judah seven years and six months; and in Jerusalem he reigned thirty and three years over all Israel. The king and his men went to Jerusalem against the Jebusites, the inhabitants of the land. David took the stronghold of Zion; and David dwelt in the stronghold, and called it the city of David.

Hiram king of Tyre sent messengers to David, and cedar trees, and carpenters, and masons, and they built David a house; and David took more wives, and there were sons and daughters born to David.

David gathered together all the chosen men of Israel, thirty thousand, and went to bring the ark of God. They set the ark of God on a new cart, and brought it out of the house of Abinadab that was in Gibeah, and Uzzah and Ahio, the sons of Abinadab, drave the cart; and David and all the house of Israel played before the Lord with harps, and with psalteries, and with castanets, and with cymbals. Uzzah put forth his hand to the ark of God, and took hold of it; for the oxen stumbled. The anger of the Lord was kindled against Uzzah, and God smote him, and there he died by the ark of God.

David was displeased, because the Lord had broken forth on Uzzah, and he would not remove the ark of the Lord to the city of David; but carried it aside into the house of Obed-edom, the Gittite. The ark of the Lord continued in the house of Obed-edom three months; and it was told David, saying: "The Lord hath blessed Obed-edom, and all that pertaineth to him, because of the ark of God." So David went and brought the ark of God into the city of David with gladness.

It came to pass, when the king dwelt in his house, and the Lord had given him rest from all his enemies round about, that the king said unto Nathan the prophet: "See now, I dwell in a house of cedar, but the ark of God dwelleth within curtains."

The same night the word of the Lord came unto Nathan, saying: "Go and tell my servant David: 'Thus saith the Lord: "I took thee from following the sheep, that thou shouldest be ruler over My people, and I have been with thee whithersoever thou wentest, and have cut off all thine enemies from before thee. When thy days be fulfilled, and thou shalt sleep with thy fathers, I will set up thy seed after thee. He shall build a house for My name, and I will establish the throne of his kingdom for ever."

According to these words, so did Nathan speak unto David.

David reigned over all Israel; and executed judgment and justice unto all his people; and Joab was over the host. David said: "Is there yet any that is left of the house of Saul, that I may show him kindness for Jonathan's sake?"

There was of the house of Saul a servant whose name was Ziba, and they called him unto David. Ziba said: "Jonathan hath a son, who is lame on his feet."

The king said: "Where is he?"

Ziba said: "Behold, he is in the house of Machir, in Lo-debar."

David sent, and fetched him. Mephibosheth the son of Jonathan came unto David, and fell on his face, and did obeisance. David said unto him: "Fear not; for I will surely show thee kindness for Jonathan thy father's sake, and will restore thee all the land of Saul, and thou shalt eat bread at my table continually."

Then the king called to Ziba, and said: "All that pertained to Saul have I given unto thy master's son. Thou and thy sons shalt till the land for him."

Then said Ziba: "According to all that my lord the king commandeth his servant, so shall thy servant do."

It came to pass that David sent Joab and all Israel, and they destroyed the children of Ammon, and besieged Rabbah.

David tarried at Jerusalem, and at eventide David walked on the roof of the king's house. From the roof he saw a woman, and the woman was very beautiful. David sent and inquired after the woman; and one said: "Is not this Bath-sheba, the wife of Uriah the Hittite?"

David sent to Joab saying: "Send me Uriah the Hittite."

When Uriah was come, David asked how Joab did, and how the people fared, and how the war prospered; and David wrote a letter to Joab, and sent it by the hand of Uriah. He wrote saying: "Set ye Uriah in the forefront of the hottest battle, and retire ye from him, that he may be smitten, and die."

It came to pass, when Joab kept watch on the city, that he assigned Uriah unto a place where he knew

King David

that valiant men were; and the men of the city went out, and fought with Joab, and there fell some of the servants of David, and Uriah the Hittite died also. Then Joab sent and told David all the things concerning the war. The messenger said unto David: "The men prevailed against us, and came out into the field, and we were on them even to the entering of the gate; and the shooters shot at thy servants from off the wall, and some of the king's servants be dead, and Uriah the Hittite is dead also."

David said: "Thus shalt thou say unto Joab: 'Let not this thing displease thee, for the sword devoureth one as well as another. Make thy battle more strong against the city, and overthrow it;' and encourage thou him."

When the wife of Uriah heard that her husband was dead, she made lamentation for him; and after the mourning was past, David sent and fetched her to his house. She became his wife, and bare him a son; but the thing that David had done displeased the Lord.

The Lord sent Nathan unto David; and Nathan said: "There were two men in one city, the one rich, and the other poor. The rich man had exceeding many flocks and herds; but the poor man had nothing save one little ewe lamb, which he had bought and nourished. It grew up with him and with his children. It did eat of his own morsel, and drank of his own cup, and lay in his bosom, and was unto him as a daughter. There came a traveller unto the rich man, and he spared to take of his own flock and of his own herd, to dress for the wayfaring man, but took the poor man's lamb, and dressed it for the traveller."

David's anger was greatly kindled, and he said to Nathan: "As the Lord liveth, the man that hath done this shall die, and he shall restore the lamb fourfold, because he did this thing, and because he had no pity."

Nathan said to David: "Thou art the man. Thus saith the Lord: 'I anointed thee king over Israel, and delivered thee out of the hand of Saul. Wherefore hast thou despised the word of the Lord, to do that which is evil in His sight? Thou hast killed Uriah the Hittite with the sword, and hast taken his wife to be thy wife. Because by this deed thou hast given great occasion to the enemies of the Lord to blaspheme, the child that is born unto thee shall surely die.'"

Nathan departed unto his house; and the Lord struck the child, and it was very sick. David therefore besought God for the child; and David fasted. On the seventh day the child died, and the servants of David feared to tell him that the child was dead. But when David saw that his servants whispered together, David perceived that the child was dead, and David arose and washed, and changed his apparel; and he came into the house of the Lord, and worshipped. Then he came to his own house, and he did eat. He said: "While the child was yet alive, I fasted and wept.

But now he is dead, wherefore should I fast? Can I bring him back? I shall go to him, but he shall not return to me."

David comforted Bath-sheba his wife, and she bare a son, and he called his name Solomon; and the Lord loved him.

Absalom the son of David had a fair sister, whose name was Tamar; and Amnon the son of David mistreated her. It came to pass that Absalom had sheepshearers in Baal-hazor; and Absalom came to the king, and said: "Behold, thy servant hath sheepshearers. Let the king, I beseech thee, and his servants go with thy servant."

The king said to Absalom: "Nay, my son, lest we be burdensome to thee."

But Absalom pressed him, that he let Amnon and all the king's sons go with him. Absalom commanded his servants, saying: "Mark ye now, when Amnon's heart is merry with wine, and when I say unto you: 'Smite Amnon;' then kill him."

The servants did unto Amnon as Absalom had commanded. Then all the rest of the king's sons arose, and every man gat him on his mule, and fled. Tidings came to David, saying: "Absalom hath slain all the king's sons, and there is not one of them left."

The king arose, and tare his garments, and lay on the earth, and all his servants stood by with their clothes rent. Jonadab, the son of David's brother, said: "Let not my lord suppose that they have slain all the king's sons. Amnon only is dead; for by the appointment of Absalom this hath been determined from the day that he mistreated Absalom's sister Tamar."

As soon as he had made an end of speaking, behold, the king's sons came; but Absalom fled to Geshur, and was there three years; and the soul of King David longed to go forth unto Absalom. The king said unto Joab: "Go, bring the young man Absalom to his own house; but let him not see my face."

So Joab arose, and went to Geshur, and brought Absalom to Jerusalem. In all Israel there was none to be so much praised as Absalom for his beauty. From the sole of his foot even to the crown of his head there was no blemish in him. Absalom dwelt two full years in Jerusalem, and saw not the king's face. Then Absalom sent for Joab to send him to the king; but Joab would not come. Therefore Absalom said unto his servants: "See, Joab's field is near mine, and he hath barley there. Go and set it on fire."

Absalom's servants set the field on fire. Then Joab arose, and came to Absalom, and said: "Wherefore have thy servants set my field on fire?"

Absalom answered: "Behold, I sent unto thee, saying: 'Come hither, that I may send thee to the king to say: "Wherefore am I come from Geshur? It were better for me to be there still. Let me see the king's face; and if there be iniquity in me, let him kill me."

So Joab told the king, and when the king called for Absalom, he came and bowed himself on his face to the ground, and the king kissed him.

After this Absalom prepared him a chariot and horses, and fifty men to run before him. Absalom rose up early, and stood beside the way of the gate; and when any man had a suit which should come to the king for judgment, then Absalom called unto him, and said: "There is no man deputed to hear thee. Oh that I were made judge in the land, that every man who hath any suit or cause might come unto me, and I would do him justice!"

When any man came nigh to do him obeisance, he put forth his hand, and took hold of him, and kissed him. So Absalom stole the hearts of the men of Israel.

It came to pass that Absalom went to Hebron; and he sent spies throughout all the tribes of Israel, saying: "As soon as ye hear the sound of the trumpet, then ye shall say: 'Absalom reigneth in Hebron.'"

Absalom sent for Ahithophel, David's counsellor, and the conspiracy was strong; for the people increased continually with Absalom.

There came a messenger to David, saying: "The hearts of the men of Israel are after Absalom."

David said unto his servants that were with him at Jerusalem: "Arise, and let us flee, lest he bring evil on us and smite the city with the edge of the sword."

The king's servants said: "Behold, thy servants are ready to do whatsoever my lord the king shall choose."

The king went forth, and all his household after him. David went up by the ascent of the mount of Olives; and wept as he went up. He had his head covered, and went barefoot; and all the people that were with him covered every man his head, and they went up weeping. One told David, saying: "Ahithophel is among the conspirators with Absalom."

David said: "O Lord, I pray Thee, turn the counsel of Ahithophel into foolishness."

When David was come to the top of the mount, behold, Hushai the Archite came to meet him with his clothes rent, and earth on his head. David said unto him: "Return to the city, and say unto Absalom: 'I will be thy servant, O king.' Then shalt thou defeat for me the counsel of Ahithophel. Hast thou not there with thee Zadok and Abiathar the priests? Therefore it shall be, that what thing soever thou shalt hear out of the king's house, thou shalt tell it to Zadok and Abiathar. Behold, they have with them their two sons, Ahimaaz and Jonathan; and by them ye shall send unto me everything that ye hear."

So Hushai, David's friend, came into the city.

When King David came to Bahurim, there came out thence a man, whose name was Shimei. He cursed as he came, and he cast stones at David, and at all the servants of King David. Thus said Shimei: "Begone, begone, thou man of blood! The Lord hath delivered the kingdom into the hand of Absalom, and thou art taken in thine own mischief."

Then said Abishai the son of Zeruiah unto the king: "Why should this dead dog curse my lord the king? Let me go and take off his head."

The king said: "Let him curse; for the Lord hath bidden him."

So David and his men went by the way; and Shimei went along on the hillside over against them, and cursed, and threw stones, and cast dust.

Absalom came to Jerusalem, and when Hushai, David's friend, was come, he said unto Absalom: "God save the king, whom the Lord and all the men of Israel have chosen. With him will I abide."

Ahithophel said unto Absalom: "Let me choose twelve thousand men, and I will arise and pursue after David this night, and I will come on him while he is weary and weak handed, and will make him afraid. All the people that are with him shall flee, and I will smite the king, and bring back the people unto thee."

The saying pleased Absalom well, and all the elders of Israel. Then said Absalom: "Call now Hushai the Archite, and let us hear what he saith."

Hushai said to Absalom: "The counsel that Ahithophel hath given this time is not good. Thou knowest thy father and his men be mighty men, and they be chafed in their minds, as a bear robbed of her whelps. I counsel that all Israel be gathered together unto thee, and that thou go to battle in thine own person. So shall we light on him as the dew falleth on the ground; and of him and of all the men that are with him we will not leave so much as one."

Absalom and the men of Israel said: "The counsel of Hushai is better than the counsel of Ahithophel;" for the Lord had ordained to defeat the good counsel of Ahithophel, to the intent that the Lord might bring evil on Absalom.

Then said Hushai unto Zadok and to Abiathar the priests: "Send quickly, and tell David, saying: 'Lodge not this night at the fords of the wilderness, but pass over, lest the king be swallowed up, and all the people that are with him.'"

Jonathan and Ahimaaz went, but a lad saw them, and told Absalom. They came to the house of a man in Bahurim, who had a well in his court, and they went down thither. The woman spread a covering over the well's mouth, and strewed bruised grain thereon. Absalom's servants came to the woman, and they said: "Where are Ahimaaz and Jonathan?"

The woman said: "They be gone over the brook."

When they had sought and could not find them, they returned to Jerusalem, and Jonathan and Ahimaaz came up out of the well, and went and told King David. Then David arose, and all the people that were with

King David

him, and they passed over Jordan. By the morning light there lacked not one of them that was not gone over Jordan.

David came to Mahanaim; and Absalom passed over Jordan, he and all the men of Israel. David numbered the people that were with him, and set captains of thousands and captains of hundreds over them; and David sent forth the people, a third part unto Joab, a third part under Abishai, and a third part under Ittai the Gittite. The king stood by the gate, and all the people went out; and the king commanded Joab and Abishai and Ittai, saying: "Deal gently for my sake with the young man, even with Absalom."

All the people heard when the king gave the captains charge concerning Absalom. So the people went out against Israel. The battle was in the forest of Ephraim, and the people of Israel were smitten before the servants of David, and there was a great slaughter. Absalom rode on his mule, and the mule went under the thick boughs of a great oak, and his head caught hold of the oak, and he was taken up between the heaven and the earth; and the mule that was under him went on. A certain man saw it, and told Joab: "Behold, I saw Absalom hanging in an oak."

Joab said unto the man: "Why didst thou not smite him to the ground? I would have given thee ten pieces of silver, and a girdle."

The man said: "Though I should receive a thousand pieces of silver, yet would I not put forth mine hand against the king's son; for in our hearing the king charged thee saying: 'Beware that none touch the young man Absalom.'"

Then said Joab: "I may not tarry thus with thee;" and he took three darts in his hand, and thrust them through the heart of Absalom, while he was yet in the midst of the oak.

Joab blew the trumpet, and the people returned from pursuing after Israel; and they took Absalom, and cast him into a pit in the forest, and raised over him a very great heap of stones.

Then said Ahimaaz: "Let me now run, and bear the king tidings, how that the Lord hath avenged him of his enemies."

Joab said: "Thou shalt not be the bearer of tidings this day."

Then said Joab to the Cushite*: "Go tell the king what thou hast seen."

The Cushite bowed himself unto Joab, and ran.

Then said Ahimaaz yet again to Joab: "But come what may, I will run."

Joab said unto him: "Run."

David sat between the two gates, and the watchman went up to the roof over the gate, and lifted up his eyes,

---

*Or Ethiopian, probably one of Joab's servants.

and, behold, a man running alone. The watchman cried, and told the king; and the king said: "If he be alone, there is tidings in his mouth."

He came apace, and drew near; and the watchman called unto the porter, and said: "Behold, another man running alone."

The king said: "He also bringeth tidings."

The watchman said: "Me thinketh the running of the foremost is like the running of Ahimaaz."

The king said: "He is a good man, and cometh with good tidings."

Ahimaaz bowed himself before the king with his face to the earth, and said: "Blessed be the Lord thy God, which hath delivered up the men that lifted their hands against the king."

The king said: "Is the young man Absalom safe?"

Ahimaaz answered: "When Joab sent me, I saw a great tumult, but I knew not what it was."

The king said: "Turn aside, and stand here."

He turned aside, and the Cushite came, and the king said: "Is the young man Absalom safe?"

The Cushite answered: "The enemies of my lord the king, and all that rise against thee, be as that young man is."

The king was much moved, and went up to the chamber over the gate, and wept; and as he went, thus he said: "O my son Absalom, my son, my son Absalom!

Would God I had died for thee, O Absalom, my son, my son!"

King David was old and stricken in years, and Adonijah his son exalted himself, saying: "I will be king."

He conferred with Joab, and with Abiathar, and they helped him. But Zadok, and Nathan, and the mighty men who belonged to David, were not with Adonijah. Then Nathan spake unto Bath-sheba the mother of Solomon, saying: "Hast thou not heard that Adonijah doth reign, and David knoweth it not? Now therefore, let me give thee counsel, that thou mayest save thine own life, and the life of thy son Solomon. Get thee in unto King David, and say: 'Didst not thou, my lord, swear unto thine handmaid, saying: "Assuredly Solomon thy son shall reign after me, and he shall sit on my throne?" Why then doth Adonijah reign?'"

Bath-sheba went in unto the king and did obeisance, and the king said: "What wouldest thou?"

She said unto him: "My lord, thou swearest unto thine handmaid, saying: 'Assuredly Solomon thy son shall sit on my throne.' Now, behold, Adonijah reigneth, and he hath sacrificed oxen and fatlings and sheep in abundance, and hath called all the sons of the king, and Abiathar the priest, and Joab the captain of the host, but Solomon hath he not called. The eyes of all Israel are on thee, that thou shouldest tell them who shall sit on the throne of my lord the king. Otherwise it shall come to pass, when my lord the king shall sleep with his fathers, that I and my son Solomon shall be counted offenders."

The king said: "As the Lord liveth, I sware unto thee saying: 'Assuredly Solomon shall reign after me.'"

King David said: "Call Zadok the priest, and Nathan the prophet."

They came before the king, and the king said unto them: "Take with you the servants of your lord, and cause Solomon my son to ride on mine own mule, and bring him to Gihon. Let Zadok and Nathan anoint him there king over Israel, and blow ye with the trumpet, and say: 'God save King Solomon.' Then he shall come and sit on my throne; for he shall be king in my stead. I have appointed him to be ruler over Israel."

So Zadok and Nathan went, and caused Solomon to ride on King David's mule, and brought him to Gihon; and Zadok the priest took the horn of oil out of the tabernacle, and anointed Solomon. They blew the trumpet, and the people said: "God save King Solomon."

All the people came after him, and piped with pipes, and rejoiced with great joy. Adonijah and the guests that were with him heard the sound as they made an end of eating, and Joab said: "Wherefore is this noise of the city being in an uproar?"

While he yet spake, Jonathan the son of Abiathar came, and said to Adonijah: "Verily David hath made Solomon king, and Zadok and Nathan have anointed him king in Gihon; and they are come thence rejoicing. This is the noise that ye have heard."

The guests of Adonijah were afraid, and rose up, and went every man his way. Solomon sent for Adonijah; and he came and did obeisance, and Solomon said: "Go to thine house."

David charged Solomon, saying: "I go the way of all the earth. Be thou strong, and show thyself a man; and keep the charge of the Lord thy God, to walk in His ways, that thou mayest prosper in all that thou doest;" and David slept with his fathers, and was buried in the city of David.

XIV

SOLOMON THE WISE

SOLOMON sat on the throne, and his kingdom was established greatly. Solomon thrust out Abiathar from being priest, and the tidings came to Joab; and Joab fled unto the tabernacle of the Lord, and caught hold on the horns of the altar. Then Solomon sent Benaiah the son of Jehoiada, saying: "Go, fall on him."

Benaiah came to the tabernacle, and said: "Come forth."

Joab said: "Nay, but I will die here."

Benaiah brought the king word, and the king said: "Do as he hath said."

Then Benaiah went, and slew Joab, and the king put Benaiah over the host.

Solomon made affinity with Pharaoh king of Egypt, and took Pharaoh's daughter, and brought her into the city of David. Solomon loved the Lord, and he went to Gibeon to sacrifice there. In Gibeon the Lord appeared to Solomon in a dream by night, and God said: "Ask what I shall give thee."

Solomon said: "O Lord my God, Thou hast made Thy servant king, and I know not how to go out or come in. Give Thy servant therefore an understanding heart to judge Thy people, that I may discern between good and evil."

The speech pleased the Lord, and God said: "Because thou hast not asked for thyself long life; neither hast asked riches, nor the life of thine enemies, I have done according to thy words. I have also given thee that which thou hast not asked, both riches and honor, so that there shall not be any among the kings like unto thee all thy days."

Solomon awoke, and, behold, it was a dream, and he came to Jerusalem. There came two women unto the king, and stood before him, and one woman said: "Oh my lord, I and this woman dwell in one house; and I had a child; and it came to pass the third day after, that this woman also had a child. We were together, and there was no stranger with us in the house. This woman's child died in the night, because she overlaid it; and she arose and took my son from beside me, while thine handmaid slept, and laid it in her bosom, and laid her dead child in my bosom. When I rose in the morning, my child was dead; but when I had considered, behold, it was not my son."

The other woman said: "Nay, but the living is my son, and the dead is thy son."

Thus they spake before the king. Then said the king: "Bring me a sword."

They brought a sword, and the king said: "Divide the living child in two, and give half to one, and half to the other."

Then spake the woman whose the living child was: "Oh my lord, give her the child, and in no wise slay it."

But the other said: "It shall be neither mine nor thine. Divide it."

Then the king said: "Give her the child who would not have it slain. She is the mother thereof."

All Israel heard of the judgment, and they feared the king; for they saw that the wisdom of God was in him.

Solomon ruled over all the kingdoms from the river Euphrates unto the border of Egypt; and Judah and Israel dwelt safely, every man under his vine and under his fig tree, from Dan even to Beer-sheba, all the days of Solomon. Solomon's wisdom excelled the wisdom of all the children of the east, and all the wisdom of Egypt. His fame was in all the nations round about, and he spake three thousand proverbs, and his songs were a thousand and five.

Solomon sent to Hiram, king of Tyre, saying: "Thou knowest that David, my father, could not build a house for the Lord his God for the wars which were about him on every side. But now the Lord hath given me rest; and, behold, I purpose to build a house for the Lord. Therefore command thou that they hew me cedar trees out of Lebanon; and my servants shall be with thy servants, and I will give thee hire for thy servants according to all that thou shalt say."

Hiram sent to Solomon, saying: "I will do all thy desire concerning timber of cedar, and concerning timber of fir. My servants shall bring the timbers down from Lebanon unto the sea, and I will make them into rafts to go by sea unto the place that thou shalt appoint me."

King Solomon raised a levy out of all Israel, thirty thousand men; and he sent them to Lebanon, ten thousand a month by courses. A month were they in Lebanon, and two months at home. Solomon had threescore and ten thousand that bare burdens, and fourscore thousand that were hewers in the mountains, besides officers that were over the work. The king commanded, and they hewed out great stones to lay the foundation of the house. The house was built of stone made ready at the quarry, and there was neither hammer, nor ax, nor any tool of iron heard in the house while it was building. There was cedar on the house within; and Solomon prepared an oracle in the midst of the house to set there the ark of the covenant, and he drew chains of gold across before the oracle. The whole altar that belonged to the oracle he overlaid with gold; and in the oracle he made two cherubim of olive wood, each ten cubits high, and he carved all the walls of the house round about with figures. He was seven years in building the house, and Solomon was building his own house thirteen years.

All the work that King Solomon wrought in the house of the Lord was finished, and Solomon brought in the silver and the gold, and the vessels, and put them among the treasures of the house of the Lord. Then Solomon assembled the elders of Israel, and the heads of the tribes; and the priests brought the ark of the Lord into the oracle of the house, to the most holy place, even under the wings of the cherubim. When the priests were come out of the holy place, the glory of the Lord filled the house, and the king blessed all the congregation of Israel, and he offered for the sacrifice of peace offerings two and twenty thousand oxen, and a hundred and twenty thousand sheep.

When the queen of Sheba heard of the fame of Solomon, she came to prove him with hard questions. She came with a very great train, with camels that bare spices, and very much gold, and precious stones; and when she was come to Solomon, she communed with him of all that was in her heart. Solomon told her all her questions, and when the queen of Sheba had seen all the wisdom of Solomon, and the house that he had built, and his ministers, and their apparel, there was no more spirit in her. She said to the king: "It was a true report that I heard of thine acts, and of thy wisdom. Howbeit I believed not until I came; and, behold, the half was not told me. Happy are thy servants, which stand continually before thee, and hear thy wisdom. Blessed be the Lord thy God which set thee on the throne of Israel."

She gave the king a hundred and twenty talents of gold, and of spices a very great store, and precious stones; and King Solomon gave to the queen of Sheba all her desire, whatsoever she asked.

The king made a great throne of ivory, and overlaid it with the finest gold; and all King Solomon's drinking vessels were of gold. The king had at sea a navy. Once in three years came the navy bringing gold, and silver, ivory, and apes, and peacocks. So King Solomon exceeded all the kings of the earth in riches and in wisdom; and the king made silver to be in Jerusalem as stones.

But King Solomon loved many strange women of the nations concerning which the Lord said unto the children of Israel: "Ye shall not go among them, neither shall they come among you."

Solomon had seven hundred wives, and it came to pass, when Solomon was old, that his wives turned away his heart after other gods; and the Lord was angry with Solomon.

Jeroboam, an Ephraimite, was a mighty man of valor, and Solomon saw the young man that he was industrious, and he gave him charge over all the labor of the house of Joseph. It came to pass, when Jeroboam went out of Jerusalem, that the prophet Ahijah found him. They two were alone in the field; and Ahijah laid hold of the garment that was on him, and rent it in twelve pieces, and he said: "Take thee ten pieces; for thus saith the Lord: 'Behold, I will rend the kingdom out of the hand of Solomon's son, and will give ten tribes to thee; and unto his son will I give one tribe, that David my servant may have a light always before me in Jerusalem, the city which I have chosen. Thou shalt reign over Israel."

Solomon sought therefore to kill Jeroboam, but Jeroboam fled into Egypt. The time that Solomon reigned in Jerusalem was forty years; and Solomon slept with his fathers, and was buried in the city of David, and Rehoboam his son reigned in his stead.

XV

THE LATER KINGS

REHOBOAM went to Shechem, where all Israel were come to make him king; and Jeroboam and the congregation of Israel spake unto Rehoboam, saying: "Thy father made our yoke grievous. Now therefore make thou the service which he put on us lighter, and we will serve thee."

King Rehoboam consulted with the old men that had stood before Solomon his father, and they spake, saying: "Speak good words unto this people. Then will they be thy servants forever."

But he forsook the counsel of the old men, and consulted with the young men that were grown up with him. They said: "Thus shalt thou say unto this people: 'Whereas my father did lade you with a heavy yoke, I will add to your yoke. My father chastised you with whips, but I will chastise you with scorpions.'"

So the king answered the people roughly, and when they saw that the king hearkened not unto them, they made Jeroboam king. There was none that followed the house of David but the tribe of Judah. Jeroboam said in his heart: "If this people go to offer sacrifices in the house of the Lord at Jerusalem, then shall they turn again unto Rehoboam, and they shall kill me."

Whereupon the king made two calves of gold; and he said: "It is too much to go to Jerusalem. Behold thy gods, O Israel, which brought thee out of Egypt."

He set one in Bethel, and the other put he in Dan. The people went to worship before them, and he made houses of high places, and made priests from among the people, that were not of the sons of Levi.

Abijah the son of Jeroboam fell sick, and Jeroboam said to his wife: "Arise, I pray thee, and disguise thyself, that thou be not known to be the wife of Jeroboam; and get thee to Shiloh to Ahijah the prophet. He shall tell thee what shall become of the child."

Jeroboam's wife arose, and went to Shiloh. Ahijah could not see by reason of his age; and the Lord said unto Ahijah: "Behold, the wife of Jeroboam cometh to inquire of thee concerning her son. Thus and thus shalt thou say unto her; for she shall feign to be another woman."

When Ahijah heard the sound of her feet, he said: "Come in, thou wife of Jeroboam. Why feignest thou thyself to be another? Go tell Jeroboam: 'Thus saith the Lord: "Forasmuch as thou hast made thee other gods, and molten images, and hast cast Me behind thy back, therefore I will utterly sweep away the house of Jeroboam. Arise, get thee to thine house, and when thy feet enter into the city, the child shall die."

Jeroboam's wife departed, and as she came to the threshold of the house, the child died; and all Israel mourned for him.

Jeroboam reigned two and twenty years, and he slept with his fathers, and Nadab his son reigned in his stead.

Rehoboam reigned in Judah, and Judah did that which was evil in the sight of the Lord; and Shishak king of Egypt came against Jerusalem. He took away the treasures of the house of the Lord, and the treasures of the king's house; and he took away all the shields of gold which Solomon had made, and King Rehoboam made in their stead shields of brass.

There was war between Rehoboam and Jeroboam continually; and Rehoboam slept with his fathers, and was buried, and Abijam his son reigned in his stead.

Abijam walked in all the sins of his fathers; and Abijam died, and Asa his son reigned.

Asa did that which was right in the eyes of the Lord, and removed all the idols that his fathers had made; and Asa died, and Jehoshaphat his son reigned.

Nadab the son of Jeroboam reigned over Israel two years, and he did that which was evil. Baasha, of the house of Issachar, conspired against him, and smote him, and reigned in his stead. As soon as Baasha was king, he smote all the house of Jeroboam. He left not to Jeroboam any that breathed. Baasha did that which was evil, and made Israel to sin; and Baasha slept with his fathers.

Elah his son reigned in his stead, and Zimri, captain of half the chariots, conspired against Elah, and killed him, and reigned in his stead. Zimri slew all the house of Baasha, and left not a single man child, neither of his kinsfolks, nor of his friends. Zimri reigned seven days in Tirzah; and the people were encamped against Gibbethon, which belonged to the Philistines; and the people heard say: "Zimri hath conspired and slain the king;" wherefore they made Omri, the captain of the host, king over Israel. Omri besieged Tirzah; and when Zimri saw that the city was taken, he went into the king's house, and burnt the king's house over him, and died. Omri reigned twelve years, and Omri slept with his fathers and Ahab his son reigned in his stead.

Ahab reigned over Israel in Samaria twenty and two years. He took to wife Jezebel the daughter of the king of the Zidonians; and he reared up an altar for Baal in Samaria, and did more to provoke the Lord to anger than all the kings of Israel that were before him.

Elijah the Tishbite said unto Ahab: "As the Lord liveth, there shall not be dew nor rain, but according to my word."

The word of the Lord came unto Elijah, saying: "Get thee hence, and hide thyself by the brook Cherith. I have commanded the ravens to feed thee there."

So he went and dwelt by the brook Cherith; and the ravens brought him bread and flesh in the morning, and bread and flesh in the evening; and he drank of the brook. After a while the brook dried up, because there was no rain in the land; and the word of the Lord came, saying: "Arise, get thee to Zarephath. I have commanded a widow woman there to sustain thee."

So he arose and went to Zarephath; and when he came to the gate of the city, behold, a widow woman was there gathering sticks. He called to her and said: "Fetch me, I pray thee, a little water that I may drink."

As she was going to fetch it, he said: "Bring me, I pray thee, a morsel of bread."

She said: "I have not a cake, but a handful of meal in the jar, and a little oil in the cruse; and I am gathering sticks, that I may prepare a cake for me and my son, that we may eat it, and die."

Elijah said unto her: "Fear not; but make me a little cake first, and bring it forth unto me. Afterward make for thee and for thy son. For thus saith the Lord: 'The jar of meal shall not waste, neither shall the cruse of oil fail, until the day that the Lord sendeth rain on the earth.'"

She went and did according to the saying of Elijah; and she, and he, and her household, did eat many days. The jar of meal wasted not, neither did the cruse of oil fail.

It came to pass that the son of the woman fell sick; and his sickness was so sore that there was no breath left in him. Elijah said unto her: "Give me thy son."

He took him and carried him up into the chamber, where he abode, and laid him on his own bed; and he cried unto the Lord, and said: "O Lord, my God, hast Thou brought evil on the widow with whom I sojourn, by slaying her son?"

He stretched himself on the child three times, and cried unto the Lord: "O Lord, let this child's soul come into him again."

The Lord hearkened unto the voice of Elijah, and the child revived, and Elijah brought him down out of the chamber, and delivered him unto his mother.

The word of the Lord came to Elijah, in the third year, saying: "Go, show thyself unto Ahab; and I will send rain on the earth."

The famine was sore in Samaria; and Ahab called Obadiah, who was over the household, and said: "Go through the land, unto all the fountains of water, and unto all the brooks. Peradventure we may find grass to save the horses and mules alive."

They divided the land between them to pass throughout it. Ahab went one way, and Obadiah went another way. Elijah met Obadiah, and said: "Go, tell thy lord: 'Elijah is here.'"

So Obadiah went to Ahab, and told him, and Ahab went to meet Elijah. When Ahab saw Elijah he said: "Art thou he that troubleth Israel?"

Elijah answered: "I have not troubled Israel; but thou, and thy father's house, in that ye have forsaken the commandments of the Lord. Now therefore send, and gather to me all Israel unto Mount Carmel, and the prophets of Baal, four hundred and fifty, who eat at Jezebel's table."

So Ahab sent unto all the children of Israel, and gathered the prophets together unto Mount Carmel. Elijah came near unto the people, and said: "How long halt ye between two opinions? If the Lord be God, follow Him; but if Baal, then follow him. I, even I only, am left a prophet of the Lord; but Baal's prophets are four hundred and fifty men. Give us two bullocks, and let them choose one bullock, and cut it in pieces, and lay it on the wood, and put no fire under. I will dress the other bullock, and lay it on the wood, and put no fire under. Call ye on the name of your god, and I will call on the name of the Lord; and the God that answereth by fire, let him be God."

All the people answered and said: "It is well spoken."

The prophets of Baal took the bullock which was given them, and dressed it, and called on the name of Baal from morning until noon, saying: "O Baal, hear us."

But there was no voice, nor any that answered, and they leaped about the altar which was made. Elijah mocked them, and said: "Cry aloud; for either he is talking, or he is on a journey, or peradventure he sleepeth, and must be awaked."

They cried aloud, and cut themselves after their manner with knives and lances, till the blood gushed out on them.

Elijah took twelve stones, according to the number of the tribes of the sons of Jacob, and with the stones he built an altar. He made a trench about the altar, and he put the wood in order, and cut the bullock in pieces, and laid it on the wood, and said: "Fill four jars with water, and pour it on the burnt offering, and on the wood."

He said: "Do it the second time;" and they did it the second time.

He said: "Do it the third time;" and they did it the third time.

The water ran about the altar, and he filled the trench also with water; and Elijah said: "O Lord, let it be known this day that Thou art God in Israel, and that I am Thy servant, and that I have done all these things at Thy word. Hear me, O Lord, hear me."

Then the fire of the Lord fell, and consumed the burnt offering, and the wood, and the stones, and the dust, and licked up the water that was in the trench. When the people saw it, they fell on their faces, and they said: "The Lord is God."

Elijah said unto them: "Take the prophets of Baal. Let not one of them escape."

They took them, and Elijah slew them. Elijah said unto Ahab: "Eat and drink; for there is the sound of abundance of rain."

Ahab went to eat and to drink; and Elijah went to the top of Carmel, and bowed himself down on the earth, and put his face between his knees. He said to his servant: "Go now, look toward the sea."

The servant looked, and said: "There is nothing."

Elijah said: "Go again," seven times.

It came to pass at the seventh time, that the servant said: "Behold, there ariseth a cloud out of the sea, as small as a man's hand."

Elijah said: "Go, say unto Ahab: 'Prepare thy chariot, and get thee down, that the rain stop thee not.'"

In a little while the heaven grew black with clouds and wind, and there was a great rain. Ahab rode, and Elijah girded up his loins, and ran before Ahab to the entrance of Jezreel.

Ahab told Jezebel all that Elijah had done, and how he had slain all the prophets. Then Jezebel sent a messenger unto Elijah, saying: "So let the gods do to me, and more also, if I make not thy life as the life of one of them by tomorrow about this time."

Then he went for his life to Beer-sheba, and left his servant there. But he himself went a day's journey into the wilderness, and sat down under a juniper tree;

and he requested that he might die. He lay down and slept, and, behold, an angel touched him, and said: "Arise and eat."

He looked, and there was at his head a cake baken on the coals, and a cruse of water. He did eat and drink, and lay down again; and the angel of the Lord came the second time, and touched him, and said: "Arise and eat."

He arose, and did eat and drink, and went in the strength of that meat forty days and forty nights unto Horeb the mount of God. He came thither unto a cave, and lodged there; and, behold, the Lord passed by, and a great and strong wind rent the mountains, and brake in pieces the rocks; but the Lord was not in the wind. After the wind there was an earthquake; but the Lord was not in the earthquake. After the earthquake there was a fire; but the Lord was not in the fire. After the fire there was a still small voice. When Elijah heard it, he wrapped his face in his mantle, and went out, and stood in the entering in of the cave; and there came a voice unto him, and said: "What doest thou here, Elijah?"

He said: "The children of Israel have forsaken Thy covenant, thrown down Thine altars, and slain Thy prophets with the sword. I only am left, and they seek my life to take it away."

The Lord said: "Return, and Elisha the son of Shaphat shalt thou anoint to be prophet in thy room."

So Elijah departed thence, and found Elisha plowing, with twelve yoke of oxen before him. Elijah cast his mantle on him, and Elisha went after Elijah, and ministered unto him.

It came to pass after these things, that Naboth the Jezreelite had a vineyard, which was hard by the palace of Ahab king of Samaria. Ahab spake unto Naboth, saying: "Give me thy vineyard, that I may have it for a garden of herbs, and I will give thee for it a better vineyard, or I will give thee the worth of it in money."

Naboth said to Ahab: "The Lord forbid that I should give the inheritance of my fathers unto thee."

Ahab came into his house heavy and displeased, and he lay down on his bed, and turned away his face, and would eat no bread. Jezebel his wife came to him, and said: "Why is thy spirit so sad?"

He said: "Because I spake unto Naboth, and said: 'Give me thy vineyard for money, or I will give thee another vineyard for it;' and he answered: 'I will not give thee my vineyard.'"

Jezebel said: "Arise, and eat bread, and let thine heart be merry. I will give thee the vineyard of Naboth."

So she wrote letters in Ahab's name, and sealed them with his seal, and sent them unto the nobles that were in his city. She wrote, saying: "Proclaim a fast, and set Naboth on high among the people; and set two men before him, and let them bare witness against him saying: 'Thou didst curse God and the king.' Then carry him out, and stone him, that he die."

The elders and the nobles did according as it was written in the letters. They proclaimed a fast, and set Naboth on high among the people. Two men came and bare witness against him. Then they carried him forth out of the city, and stoned him with stones, that he died. When Jezebel heard that Naboth was stoned, she said to Ahab: "Arise, take possession of the vineyard of Naboth; for Naboth is dead."

Ahab rose to go to the vineyard; and the word of the Lord came to Elijah, saying: "Go to meet Ahab king of Israel. Behold, he is in the vineyard of Naboth; and thou shalt say: 'Thus saith the Lord: "In the place where the dogs licked the blood of Naboth shall dogs lick thy blood."

Ahab said to Elijah: 'Hast thou found me, O mine enemy?'"

Elijah answered: "I have found thee. Behold, I will bring evil on thee; and I will make thine house like the house of Jeroboam, and like the house of Baasha. Him that dieth of Ahab in the city the dogs shall eat; and him that dieth in the field shall the fowls of the air eat."

It came to pass, that Jehoshaphat the king of Judah came to the king of Israel; and the king of Israel said unto his servants: "Know ye that Ramoth-gilead is ours, and we take it not out of the hand of the king of Syria?" and he said unto Jehoshaphat: "Wilt thou go with me to battle to Ramoth-gilead?"

Jehoshaphat said: "I am as thou art, my people as thy people, my horses as thy horses."

So the king of Israel and the king of Judah went to Ramoth-gilead, and the king of Israel said unto Jehoshaphat: "I will disguise myself, and go into the battle; but put thou on thy robes."

The king of Syria had commanded the captains of his chariots, saying: "Fight neither with small nor great, save only with the king of Israel."

The captains saw Jehoshaphat, and they turned aside to fight against him; and Jehoshaphat cried out. When the captains of the chariots saw that it was not the king of Israel, they turned back from pursuing him. A certain man drew his bow at a venture, and smote the king of Israel between the joints of his armor, wherefore the king said unto the driver of his chariot: "Carry me out of the host; for I am sore wounded."

The battle increased, and the king died at even, and there went a cry throughout the host, saying: "Every man to his city, and every man to his country."

The king was brought to Samaria, and buried.

Jehoshaphat reigned twenty and five years in Jerusalem, doing that which was right in the eyes of the Lord; and Jehoshaphat slept with his fathers, and Jehoram his son reigned in his stead.

Ahaziah fell down through the lattice that was in his chamber, and he died, and Joram his brother began to reign in his stead.

It came to pass, that Elijah went with Elisha from Gilgal; and Elijah said unto Elisha: "Tarry here, I pray thee; for the Lord hath sent me to Beth-el."

Elisha said: "As the Lord liveth, I will not leave thee."

So they went to Beth-el, and Elijah said: "Tarry here, I pray thee; for the Lord hath sent me to Jericho."

Elisha said: "As the Lord liveth, I will not leave thee."

So they came to Jericho, and Elijah said: "Tarry here, I pray thee; for the Lord hath sent me to Jordan."

Elisha said: "As the Lord liveth, I will not leave thee."

They went on, and stood by Jordan. Elijah took his mantle, and wrapped it together, and smote the waters, and they were divided hither and thither, so that they two went over on dry ground. As they still went on, and talked, behold, there appeared a chariot of fire, and horses of fire, and Elijah went up by a whirlwind into heaven.

Elisha cried: "My father, my father!" and he saw him no more.

He took up the mantle of Elijah that fell from him, and went back, and stood by the bank of Jordan; and he took the mantle of Elijah, and smote the waters, and said: "Where is the Lord, the God of Elijah?" and the waters were divided, and Elisha went over.

He went thence unto Beth-el, and there came forth young lads out of the city, and mocked him, and said: "Go up,* thou bald head! Go up, thou bald head!"

He looked behind him, and cursed them in the name of the Lord; and there came two she-bears out of the wood, and tare forty and two lads of them; and he went to Samaria.

There cried a certain woman unto Elisha, saying: "My husband is dead, and the creditor is come to take my two sons to the bondmen."

Elisha said: "Tell me; what hast thou in the house?"

She said: "Thine handmaid hath not anything in the house, save a pot of oil."

Then he said: "Go, borrow vessels of all thy neighbors, even empty vessels. Borrow not a few, and thou shalt go in, and shut the door, and pour out into all those vessels."

So she went from him, and her sons brought the vessels to her, and she poured out. When the vessels were full, the oil stayed. Then she came and told the man of God; and he said: "Go, sell the oil, and pay thy debt, and live thou and thy sons of the rest."

Naaman, captain of the host of the king of Syria, was a great man, and honorable, but he was a leper. The Syrians had brought away captive out of the land of Israel a little maid; and she waited on Naaman's

---

*They had heard with disbelief that Elijah was "gone up" to heaven, and they insultingly bade Elisha to follow him.

wife. She said unto her mistress: "Would God my lord were with the prophet that is in Samaria. Then would he recover of his leprosy."

Naaman went and told the king: "Thus and thus said the maid that is of the land of Israel."

The king said: "Go, and I will send a letter unto the king of Israel, saying: 'Behold, I have sent Naaman, my servant, to thee, that thou mayest recover him of his leprosy.'"

He departed and brought the letter to the king of Israel. When the king of Israel had read the letter, he rent his clothes, and said: "Am I God, to kill and to make alive, that this man doth send unto me to recover a man of his leprosy? He seeketh a quarrel against me."

When Elisha heard that the king had rent his clothes, he sent to the king, saying: "Let Naaman come to me."

So Naaman came with his horses and with his chariots, and stood at the door of the house of Elisha. Elisha sent a messenger unto him, saying: "Go and wash in Jordan seven times, and thy flesh shall come again to thee."

But Naaman was wroth, and said: "I thought: 'He will surely come out to me, and stand and call on his God, and wave his hand, and recover the leper.' Are not the rivers of Damascus better than all the waters of Israel? May I not wash in them, and be clean?"

So he turned and went away in a rage; and his servants spake unto him, and said: "If the prophet had bid thee do some great thing, wouldest thou not have done it? How much rather then, when he saith to thee: 'Wash, and be clean?'"

Then went he, and dipped seven times in Jordan; and his flesh came again like unto the flesh of a little child. He returned to the man of God, he and all his company, and stood before him; and he said: "Now I know that there is no God in all the earth, but in Israel. Therefore, I pray thee, take a present of thy servant."

Elisha said: "As the Lord liveth, I will receive none."

So Naaman departed; but Gehazi, the servant of Elisha said: "I will run after him, and take somewhat of him."

When Naaman saw Gehazi running after him, he alighted from the chariot to meet him, and said: "Is all well?"

Gehazi said: "All is well. My master hath sent me, saying: 'Behold, there be come to me two young men of the sons of the prophets. Give them, I pray thee, a talent* of silver, and two changes of raiment.'"

Naaman said: "Take two talents;" and he bound two talents of silver in two bags, with two changes of raiment, and laid them on two of his servants.

They bare the bags before Gehazi, and he bestowed them in the house, and let the men go. He went and

---

*A talent of silver was equal to about three thousand shekels, or expressed in American money, to about two thousand dollars.

stood before his master, and Elisha said: "Whence comest thou, Gehazi?"

He said: "Thy servant went no whither."

Elisha said unto him: "Went not mine heart with thee, when the man turned from his chariot to meet thee? Is it a time to receive money, and to receive garments? The leprosy therefore of Naaman shall cleave unto thee;" and Gehazi went out from Elisha's presence a leper as white as snow.

The sons of the prophets said unto Elisha: "The place where we dwell is too strait for us. Let us go and take every man a beam, and make us a place where we may dwell."

He answered: "Go ye."

One said: "I pray thee, go with thy servants."

He answered: "I will go."

When they came to Jordan, they cut down wood; but as one was felling a beam, the ax-head fell into the water, and he cried: "Alas! it was borrowed."

The man of God said: "Where fell it?"

He showed him the place; and Elisha cut a stick, and cast it in thither, and the iron did swim; and he said: "Take it up to thee."

So he put out his hand, and took it.

The king of Syria warred against Israel; and he took counsel with his servants, saying: "In such and such a place shall be my camp."

The man of God sent unto the king of Israel, saying: "Beware that thou pass not such a place; for thither the Syrians are coming."

The king of Syria was sore troubled for this thing; and he called his servants, and said: "Will ye not show me which of us is for the king of Israel?"

One of his servants said: "My lord, Elisha the prophet telleth the king of Israel the words that thou speakest in thy bedchamber."

The king said: "Go and see where he is, that I may send and fetch him."

It was told the king, saying: "Behold, he is in Dothan."

Therefore sent he thither horses, and chariots, and a great host; and they came by night and compassed the city about. When the servant of the man of God was risen early, and gone forth, behold, a host with horses and chariots was round about the city. The servant said: "My master! how shall we do?"

Elisha answered: "Fear not; for they that be with us are more than they that be with them."

Elisha prayed, and said: "Lord, open his eyes, that he may see."

The Lord opened the eyes of the young man; and he saw the mountain was full of horses and chariots round about Elisha.

Elisha prayed, and said: "Smite this people with blindness."

God smote them with blindness, and Elisha said unto them: "This is not the city. Follow me, and I will bring you to the man whom ye seek."

He led them to Samaria, and the Lord opened their eyes, and, behold, they were in the midst of Samaria. The king of Israel said unto Elisha: "Shall I smite them?"

Elisha answered: "Thou shalt not smite them. Set bread and water before them, that they may eat and drink, and go to their master."

The king prepared great provision for them; and when they had eaten and drunk, he sent them away.

After this, Ben-hadad king of Syria gathered all his host, and besieged Samaria, and there was a great famine in Samaria, until an ass's head sold for fourscore pieces of silver. Elisha sat in his house, and the king sent a messenger to him. The messenger came, and Elisha said: "Thus saith the Lord: 'Tomorrow about this time shall a measure of flour be sold for a shekel, and two measures of barley for a shekel, in the gate of Samaria.'"

There were four leprous men at the entering in of the gate; and they said one to another: "Why sit we here until we die? Let us fall unto the host of the Syrians. If they kill us, we shall but die."

They rose up in the twilight, and when they were come to the outermost part of the camp of the Syrians, behold, there was no man there. For the Lord had made the Syrians to hear a noise of chariots, and a noise of horses, even the noise of a great host; and they said one to another: "Lo, the king of Israel hath hired against us the kings of the Hittites, and the kings of the Egyptians."

Wherefore, they arose, and left their tents, and their horses, and their asses, and fled for their life.

When the lepers came to the camp, they went into one tent, and did eat and drink, and carried thence silver, and gold, and raiment, and went and hid it; and they came back, and entered into another tent, and carried thence also, and went and hid it. Then said one to another: "We do not well. This day is a day of good tidings, and we hold our peace. If we tarry till the morning light, punishment will overtake us. Now, therefore, let us go and tell the king's household."

So they came and called unto the porters of the city, and told them, saying: "We came to the camp of the Syrians, and there was no man there, but the horses tied, and the asses tied, and the tents as they were."

The porters told the king's household, and the king said unto his servants: "The Syrians know that we be hungry. Therefore are they gone out of the camp to hide themselves, saying: 'When they come out of the city, we shall take them alive, and get into the city.'"

One of his servants answered and said: "Let some take five of the horses which are left in the city, and let us send and see."

They took therefore two chariots with horses, and they went unto Jordan; and, lo, all the way was full of garments and vessels, which the Syrians had cast away in their haste. The messengers returned, and told the king, and the people went out, and spoiled the camp of the Syrians. So a measure of fine flour was sold for a shekel, and two measures of barley for a shekel, according to the word of the Lord.

Jehoram reigned eight years in Jerusalem, and died, and Ahaziah his son reigned in his stead.

Joram the son of Ahab went to war against the king of Syria at Ramoth-gilead; and the Syrians wounded him. King Joram returned to be healed in Jezreel, and Ahaziah went to see Joram because he was sick.

Elisha the prophet called one of the sons of the prophets, and said unto him: "Take this vial of oil, and go to Ramoth-gilead. When thou comest thither, look out Jehu the son of Nimshi, and carry him to an inner chamber. Then take the vial of oil, and pour it on his head, and say: 'Thus saith the Lord: "I have anointed thee king over Israel."

So the young man went to Ramoth-gilead, and, behold, the captains of the hosts were sitting; and he said to Jehu: "I have an errand to thee, O captain."

Jehu arose, and went into the house, and the young man poured the oil on his head, and said: "Thus saith the Lord: 'I have anointed thee king over Israel; and thou shalt smite the house of Ahab thy master, that I may avenge the blood of My servants the prophets, and the blood of all the servants of the Lord, at the hand of Jezebel.'"

Then Jehu came forth to the servants of his lord, and one said unto him: "Wherefore came this mad fellow to thee?"

Jehu said: "He spake to me, saying: 'Thus saith the Lord: "I have anointed thee king over Israel."

Then they hasted, and blew with trumpets, saying: "Jehu is king."

So Jehu conspired against Joram, and rode in a chariot to Jezreel. A watchman stood on the tower in Jezreel, and he spied the company of Jehu as he came, and said: "I see a company, and the driving is like the driving of Jehu; for he driveth furiously."

Joram king of Israel, and Ahaziah king of Judah, went out, each in his chariot, and met Jehu, and Joram said: "Is it peace, Jehu?"

Jehu answered: "What peace, so long as the witchcrafts of thy mother Jezebel are so many?"

Joram said to Ahaziah: "There is treachery."

Jehu drew his bow with his full strength, and smote Joram, and Joram sunk down in his chariot.

Ahaziah fled, and Jehu followed after him, and said: "Smite him also." They did so, and he died.

When Jehu was come to Jezreel, Jezebel heard of it, and she looked out at the window; and as Jehu entered in at the gate he lifted up his face to the window, and there looked out to him two or three officers, and he said: "Throw her down."

So they threw her down, and he trode her underfoot. Jehu slew all that remained of the house of Ahab, all his great men, and his familiar friends, and his priests, until he left him none remaining.

Jehu gathered all the people together, and said unto them: "Ahab served Baal a little; but Jehu shall serve him much. Now therefore call unto me all the prophets of Baal, all his worshippers, and all his priests; for I have a great sacrifice to do to Baal."

Jehu sent through all Israel, and all the worshippers of Baal came, and the house of Baal was filled from one end to another. Jehu had appointed fourscore men without, and as soon as he had made an end of offering the burnt offering, Jehu said to the guard: "Go in, and slay them. Let none come forth."

They smote them with the edge of the sword, and thus Jehu destroyed Baal out of Israel. But Jehu took no heed to walk in the law of the Lord with all his heart; and Jehu slept with his fathers, and they buried him, and Jehoahaz his son reigned.

When Athaliah the mother of Ahaziah saw that her son was dead, she arose and destroyed all the seed royal. But Jehosheba, sister of Ahaziah, took Joash the son of Ahaziah, and stole him away, so that he was not slain. He was with her hid in the house of the Lord six years; and Athaliah reigned over the land. In the seventh year. Johoida the priest fetched the captains of the guard into the house of the Lord, and made a covenant with them. Then he brought out the king's son, and put the crown on him, and they clapped their hands, and said: "God save the king."

When Athaliah heard the noise, she came into the temple of the Lord; and she looked, and, behold, the captains by the king, and all the people of the land rejoiced, and blew with trumpets. Then Athaliah cried: "Treason, treason!" and she went to the king's house, and there she was slain.

Joash reigned forty years; and his servants made a conspiracy, and smote Joash, and he died, and Amaziah his son reigned in his stead.

Jehoahaz the son of Jehu reigned over Israel seventeen years; and Jehoahaz slept with his fathers, and Jehoash his son reigned in his stead.

Now Elisha was fallen sick, and Jehoash came, and wept over him. Elisha said: "Take bow and arrows."

He took unto him bow and arrows, and Elisha said: "Open the window eastward."

He opened it. Then Elisha said: "Shoot;" and he shot.

Elisha said: "The Lord's arrow of victory, even the arrow of victory over Syria;" and he said: "Take the arrows, and smite on the ground."

The king smote thrice, and stayed; and the man of God was wroth with him, and said: "Thou shouldest

The Later Kings

have smitten five or six times. Then hadst thou smitten Syria till thou hadst consumed it. Whereas now thou shalt smite Syria but thrice."

Jehoash took out of the hand of the king of Syria the cities of Israel which he had taken. Three times did Jehoash smite him, and Jehoash died, and Jeroboam his son reigned in his stead.

Amaziah reigned in Jerusalem, and they made a conspiracy against him, and slew him. The people took Azariah, and made him king in the room of his father.

Jeroboam reigned in Samaria forty and one years, and Jeroboam slept with his fathers, and Zachariah his son reigned in his stead.

Azariah reigned in Jerusalem, and he did that which was right. Howbeit the people still sacrificed and burnt incense on the high places; and the Lord smote the king, so that he was a leper unto the day of his death, and Azariah slept with his fathers, and Jotham his son reigned in his stead.

Zachariah reigned in Samaria six months, and Shallum the son of Jabesh slew him, and reigned in his stead. Shallum reigned the space of a month, and Menahem the son of Gadi slew him and reigned in his stead. Menahem did that which was evil in the sight of the Lord, and Menahem died. Pekahiah his son reigned two years, and Pekah his captain conspired against him, and slew him, and reigned in his stead. Pekah reigned twenty years, and Hoshea the son of Elah slew him, and reigned in his stead.

Jotham reigned sixteen years in Jerusalem, and Jotham slept with his fathers, and Ahaz his son reigned. Ahaz did that which was right, and Ahaz slept with his fathers, and Hezekiah his son reigned.

Hoshea reigned over Israel. Against him came the king of Assyria, and took Samaria, and carried Israel away into Assyria, and he brought men from Babylon, and from Cuthah, and from Hamath, and placed them in the cities of Samaria.

Hezekiah reigned in Jerusalem, and he did that which was right, according to all that David his father had done. He removed the high places, and he brake in pieces the brazen serpent that Moses had made; for the children of Israel did burn incense to it. He clave to the Lord, and the Lord was with him. Whithersoever he went forth he prospered; and he rebelled against the king of Assyria, and served him not.

In the fourteenth year of King Hezekiah did Sennacherib king of Assyria come against all the fortified cities of Judah, and took them, and sent a great host against Jerusalem. When the host was come, one of the captains stood, and cried with a loud voice: "Hear ye the word of the king of Assyria. Thus saith the king: 'Make your peace with me, that ye may live, and not die. Hearken not unto Hezekiah, when he persuadeth you, saying: "The Lord will deliver us." Hath any of the gods of the nations ever delivered his land out of the hand of the king of Assyria?'"

King Hezekiah rent his clothes, and covered himself with sackcloth,* and he sent Eliakim, who was over the household, and the elders of the priests to Isaiah the prophet. They said unto him: "Thus saith Hezekiah: 'This is a day of trouble. Wherefore lift up thy prayer.'"

Isaiah said: "Say to your master: 'Thus saith the Lord: "Be not afraid of the words that thou hast heard, wherewith the servants of the king of Assyria have blasphemed Me. Behold, he shall hear tidings, and shall return to his own land."

It came to pass, that the angel of the Lord went forth, and smote in the camp of the Assyrians a hundred fourscore and five thousand. So Sennacherib king of Assyria returned, and dwelt at Nineveh.

In those days was Hezekiah sick unto death; and Isaiah the prophet came to him and said: "Thus saith the Lord: 'Set thine house in order; for thou shalt die.'"

Then Hezekiah turned his face to the wall, and prayed, saying: "Remember now, O Lord, I beseech Thee, how I have walked before Thee in truth and with

---

*A coarse, dark, goat-hair cloth used for making sacks. Garments of this material were worn by mourners to manifest their grief. They were usually put on over the ordinary clothing, but in extreme cases next to the skin.

a perfect heart, and have done that which is good in Thy sight."

Hezekiah wept sore, and before Isaiah was gone out of the middle court, the word of the Lord came to him, saying: "Turn again, and tell Hezekiah: 'Thus saith the Lord: "I have heard thy prayer, I have seen thy tears. Behold, I will heal thee. On the third day thou shalt go up unto the house of the Lord, and I will add unto thy days fifteen years."

Hezekiah said unto Isaiah: "What shall be the sign that the Lord will heal me?"

Isaiah said: "This shall be the sign;" and he cried unto the Lord, and the Lord brought the shadow ten degrees backward, by which it had gone down on the dial.

The son of the king of Babylon sent letters and a present unto Hezekiah, and Hezekiah showed the messengers all the house of his precious things, the silver, and the gold, and the spices, and all that was in his treasures. Then came Isaiah the prophet unto King Hezekiah, and said: "Behold, the days come, that all that is in thine house, and that which thy fathers have laid up in store unto this day, shall be carried to Babylon. Nothing shall be left."

Hezekiah slept with his fathers, and Manasseh his son reigned in his stead. Manasseh did that which was evil, and he died; and Amon his son reigned. The servants of Amon conspired against him, and put

The Later Kings

the king to death. But the people made Josiah his son king. Josiah walked in all the way of David. Notwithstanding the Lord turned not from the fierceness of his great wrath, wherewith his anger was kindled against Judah, because of all the provocations that Manasseh had provoked him withal; and the Lord said: "I will remove Judah out of my sight, as I have removed Israel, and I will cast off this city which I have chosen."

The king of Egypt went against the king of Assyria, and King Josiah went against him, and was slain. His servants carried him in a chariot dead to Jerusalem, and buried him in his own sepulchre; and the people took Jehoahaz the son of Josiah, and made him king in his father's stead.

Jehoahaz reigned three months, and Pharaoh put him in bonds, and made Jehoiakim the son of Josiah king. Jehoiakim reigned eleven years. In his days Nebuchadnezzar king of Babylon came, and Jehoiakim became his servant three years. Then he rebelled against him. Jehoiakim died, and Jehoiachin his son reigned. At that time Nebuchadnezzar came against Jerusalem, and the city was besieged; and Jehoiachin went out to the king of Babylon, he, and his mother, and his servants, and his officers; and the king of Babylon carried thence all the treasures of the house of the Lord, and the treasures of the king's house, and all the princes, and all the mighty men of valor, and all the craftsmen. None remained, save the poorest sort of the people.

Nebuchadnezzar made Zedekiah, Jehoiachin's brother, king over Judah. Zedekiah did that which was evil. He humbled not himself before Jeremiah the prophet, and he rebelled against King Nebuchadnezzar. Moreover all the chiefs of the priests, and the people, transgressed very greatly, until the wrath of the Lord arose against His people. Therefore He brought on them the king of the Chaldeans, who slew their young men, burnt the house of God, and brake down the wall of Jerusalem, and burnt all the palaces thereof with fire. Them that escaped from the sword the king of the Chaldeans carried away to Babylon, and they were servants to him and his sons.

XVI

THE STORY OF JONAH

THE word of the Lord came unto Jonah, saying: "Go to Nineveh, that great city, and cry against it; for its wickedness is come up before Me."

But Jonah rose up to flee from the presence of the Lord; and he went to Joppa, and found a ship going to Tarshish. So he paid the fare, and went into it; but the Lord sent a great wind, and there was a mighty tempest, so that the ship was like to be broken. Then the mariners were afraid, and cried every man unto his god; and they cast forth the wares that were in the ship into the sea, to lighten it.

Jonah was gone down into the innermost parts of the ship, and he lay fast asleep. The shipmaster came to him, and said: "What meanest thou, O sleeper? Arise, call on thy God, that we perish not."

They said every one to his fellow: "Let us cast lots, that we may know for whose cause this evil is on us."

So they cast lots, and the lot fell on Jonah. Then said they unto him: "Tell us, we pray thee, what is thine occupation? and whence comest thou?"

He said: "I am a Hebrew; and I fear the Lord, who hath made the sea and the dry land."

Then the men said unto him: "What is this thou hast done?" For the men knew that he had fled from the presence of the Lord, because he had told them.

Then said they unto him: "What shall we do, that the sea may be calm?"

He said: "Take me up, and cast me forth into the sea. So shall the sea be calm. For I know that for my sake this great tempest is on you."

Nevertheless the men rowed hard to get to the land; but they could not. Wherefore they cried unto the Lord, and said: "We beseech Thee, O Lord, let us not perish for this man's sake."

So they took up Jonah, and cast him forth into the sea; and the sea ceased from its raging. Then the men feared the Lord exceedingly, and they offered a sacrifice unto the Lord, and made vows.

The Lord had prepared a great fish to swallow Jonah; and Jonah was in the belly of the fish three days and three nights. Then Jonah prayed unto his God out of the fish's belly; and the Lord spake unto the fish, and it vomited out Jonah on the dry land.

The word of the Lord came unto Jonah the second time, saying: "Arise, go unto Nineveh, that great city, and preach unto it the preaching that I bid thee."

So Jonah arose, and went unto Nineveh, and he cried, and said: "Yet forty days, and Nineveh shall be overthrown."

Jonah at Nineveh

The Story of Jonah

The people of Nineveh believed God, and they proclaimed a fast, and put on sackcloth, from the greatest of them even to the least of them; and the king of Nineveh made proclamation, saying: "Let neither man nor beast taste anything—let them not feed, nor drink water; but let them cry mightily unto God; yea, let them turn every one from his evil way. Who knoweth whether God will not repent, that we perish not?"

God saw that they turned from their evil way; and God repented of the evil, which He said He would do unto them; and He did it not. But this displeased Jonah exceedingly, and he was angry. Then Jonah went out of the city, and made him a booth, and sat under it, till he might see what would become of the city; and the Lord prepared a gourd, and made it to come up over Jonah, that it might be a shadow over his head. Jonah was exceeding glad because of the gourd. But God prepared a worm when the morning rose the next day, and it smote the gourd, that it withered. It came to pass when the sun arose, that God prepared a sultry east wind, and the sun beat on the head of Jonah, that he fainted, and wished in himself to die.

God said to Jonah: "Doest thou well to be angry for the gourd?"

He said: "I do well to be angry even unto death."

The Lord said: "Thou hast had pity on the gourd, for the which thou hast not labored, neither madest it grow, which came up in a night, and perished in a night; and should not I have pity on Nineveh, that great city?"

XVII

DANIEL IN BABYLON

IN the reign of Jehoiakim king of Judah came Nebuchadnezzar king of Babylon unto Jerusalem, and besieged it; and the Lord gave Jehoiakim into his hand. Nebuchadnezzar spake unto the master of his officers, that he should bring in certain of the children of Israel, youths in whom was no blemish, and skilful in wisdom, and that he should teach them the learning of the Chaldeans. The king appointed for them a daily portion of the king's meat, and of the wine which he drank, and that they should be nourished three years. Among these youths were Daniel, Hananiah, Mishael, and Azariah; and the prince of the officers gave names unto them. Unto Daniel he gave the name of Belteshazzar; and to Hananiah, of Shadrach; and to Mishael, of Meshach; and to Azariah, of Abed-nego.* Daniel requested that he might not defile himself with the king's meat, nor with the wine which the king drank.

---

*Their original names all had a meaning connected with God. Daniel, for instance, meant, "God my Judge." Their new names were compounded from the names of the idols of Babylon, and intimated that a change was desired and expected in the young men's religion.

The prince of the officers said unto Daniel: "I fear the king, who hath appointed your meat and your drink; for why should he see your faces worse liking than the youths which are of your own age? So shall ye endanger my head with the king."

Then said Daniel: "Prove thy servants, I beseech thee, ten days; and give us pulse* to eat, and water to drink. Then let our countenances be looked on before thee; and as thou seest, deal with thy servants."

He consented to them in this matter, and proved them ten days. At the end of ten days their countenances appeared fairer, and they were fatter in flesh, than all the youths that did eat of the king's meat. So the steward took away their meat, and the wine, and gave them pulse. As for these four youths, God gave them skill in all learning and wisdom; and Daniel had understanding in visions and dreams. At the end of the days which the king had appointed, the prince of the officers brought them in before Nebuchadnezzar, and the king communed with them.

Nebuchadnezzar dreamed, and his spirit was troubled. Then the king commanded to call the magicians, and the sorcerers, and the Chaldeans;† and the king said unto them: "I have dreamed a dream, and my spirit is troubled."

---

*Daniel asked for vegetable instead of animal food. Pulse means leguminous seeds such as peas and beans.

†The Chaldeans were much addicted to the study of the stars, and the word Chaldeans is here equivalent to astrologers.

Then spake the Chaldeans: "O king, live forever. Tell thy servants the dream, and we will show the interpretation."

The king answered: "The thing is gone from me. If ye make not known unto me the dream and the interpretation thereof, ye shall be cut in pieces. But if ye show the dream and the interpretation, ye shall receive gifts and great honor."

The Chaldeans said: "There is not a man on the earth that can show the king's matter."

For this cause the king was very furious, and commanded to destroy all the wise men of Babylon.

Then was the secret revealed unto Daniel in a vision of the night. Therefore Daniel went unto Arioch, whom the king had appointed to destroy the wise men of Babylon, and said: "Bring me in before the king, and I will show the interpretation."

Arioch brought Daniel before the king in haste, and the king said to Daniel: "Art thou able to make known unto me the dream which I have seen?"

Daniel answered: "The secret which the king hath demanded cannot wise men, enchanters, magicians, nor soothsayers, show unto the king; but there is a God in heaven that revealeth secrets, and He hath made known to the king what shall be in the latter days. Thou, O king, sawest a great image. This image stood before thee, and the aspect thereof was terrible. His head was of fine gold, his breast and his arms of silver, his body and his thighs of brass, his legs of iron, his feet part of iron, and part of clay. Thou sawest a stone, which smote the image on his feet, and brake them in pieces. Then was the iron, the clay, the brass, the silver, and the gold, broken in pieces, and became like chaff, and the wind carried them away; and the stone that smote the image became a great mountain, and filled the whole earth.

"This is the dream; and we will tell the interpretation. Thou, O king, art king of kings. Thou art the head of gold. After thee shall arise another kingdom inferior to thee; and another third kingdom of brass, which shall bear rule over all the earth. The fourth kingdom shall be strong as iron. Whereas thou sawest the feet and toes, part of clay, and part of iron, it shall be a divided kingdom; and in the days of those kings shall the God of heaven set up a kingdom, which shall never be destroyed; but it shall break in pieces and consume all these kingdoms, and it shall stand for ever."

Then the king fell on his face, and worshipped Daniel, and commanded that they should offer an oblation and sweet odors unto him. The king made Daniel great, and gave him many gifts, and made him chief governor over all the wise men of Babylon; and he appointed Shadrach, Meshach, and Abed-nego, over the affairs of the province of Babylon.

Nebuchadnezzar made an image of gold, whose height was threescore cubits, and he set it up in the plain of Dura. Then the king sent to gather the deputies, the judges, the counsellors, and all the rulers of the provinces to the dedication of the image. They stood before the image, and the herald cried: "To you it is commanded, O people, that at what time ye hear the sound of the cornet, flute, harp, psaltery, and all kinds of music, ye fall down and worship the golden image; and whoso falleth not down and worshippeth shall be cast into the midst of a fiery furnace."

Therefore the people fell down and worshipped the golden image. Certain Chaldeans said to Nebuchadnezzar: "O king, the Jews whom thou hast appointed over the affairs of the province of Babylon have not regarded thee. They serve not thy gods, nor worship the golden image which thou hast set up."

Nebuchadnezzar commanded to bring Shadrach, Meshach, and Abed-nego, and said unto them: "Is it true that ye serve not my gods, nor worship the golden image which I have set up? If ye worship not, ye shall be cast into the midst of a fiery furnace."

Shadrach, Meshach, and Abed-nego, answered: "O Nebuchadnezzar, our God whom we serve will deliver us out of thine hand. We will not serve thy gods, nor worship the golden image."

Then was Nebuchadnezzar full of fury, and he commanded that they should heat the furnace seven times more than it was wont to be heated; and he commanded the most mighty men that were in his army to bind

Shadrach, Meshach, and Abed-nego, and to cast them into the fiery furnace. Because the furnace was exceeding hot, the flame of the fire slew those men that took up Shadrach, Meshach, and Abed-nego, and cast them into the midst of the furnace.

Nebuchadnezzar said unto his counsellors: "Did not we cast three men bound into the fire? Lo, I see four men loose, walking in the midst of the fire, and they have no hurt; and the aspect of the fourth is like a son of the gods."

Nebuchadnezzar came near to the mouth of the fiery furnace, and said: "Shadrach, Meshach, and Abed-nego, ye servants of the Most High God, come forth."

They came forth out of the fire, and the deputies, and the governors, and the king's counsellors saw that the fire had no power on their bodies, nor was the hair of their heads singed, nor had the smell of fire passed on their garments. Nebuchadnezzar said: "Blessed be the God of Shadrach, Meshach, and Abed-nego, who hath sent His angel, and delivered His servants that trusted in Him. Therefore I make a decree, that every people which speaks anything amiss against the God of Shadrach, Meshach, and Abed-nego, shall be cut in pieces."

Nebuchadnezzar was at rest in his house, and he saw a dream which made him afraid; and he made a decree to bring in all the wise men of Babylon before him, that they might make known the interpretation of the dream. Then came in the magicians, the enchanters and the soothsayers, and he told the dream; but they did not make known the interpretation. At the last Daniel came, whose name was Belteshazzar, and the king told the dream before him, saying: "O Belteshazzar, master of the magicians, I saw a tree, and the tree grew, and was strong, and the height reached unto heaven. The leaves were fair, and the fruit much. The beasts of the field had shadow under it, and the fowls of heaven dwelt in the branches, and all flesh was fed of it; and, behold, a holy one came down from heaven. He cried aloud, and said: 'Hew down the tree, and cut off the branches, shake off the leaves, and scatter the fruit. Nevertheless leave the stump in the earth; and let it be wet with the dew, and let seven times* pass over it.' This dream I King Nebuchadnezzar have seen; and thou O Belteshazzar, declare the interpretation."

Then Daniel said: "My lord, the tree thou sawest is thou, O king; for thy greatness reacheth unto heaven, and thy dominion to the end of the earth. Whereas the king saw a holy one coming down, and saying: 'Hew down the tree, and destroy it; nevertheless leave the stump in the earth, and let it be wet with the dew till seven times pass;' it is the decree of the Most High, that thou shalt be driven from among men, and thy

---
*Years.

dwelling shall be with the beasts of the field, and thou shalt eat grass as oxen, and shalt be wet with the dew of heaven, and seven times shall pass over thee, till thou know that the Most High ruleth in the kingdom of men, and giveth it to whomsoever He will."

At the end of twelve months Nebuchadnezzar was walking in the palace. The king said: "Is not this great Babylon, which I have built for the royal dwelling place, and for the glory of my majesty?"

While the word was in the king's mouth, there fell a voice from heaven, saying: "O King Nebuchadnezzar, the kingdom is departed from thee."

The same hour was Nebuchadnezzar driven from men, and he did eat grass as oxen, and his body was wet with the dew till his hair was grown like eagles' feathers, and his nails like birds' claws. At the end of the days Nebuchadnezzar's understanding returned, and he blessed the Most High, and was established in his kingdom.

Belshazzar the king made a great feast to a thousand of his lords, and drank wine before the thousand. Belshazzar commanded to bring the golden and silver vessels which Nebuchadnezzar his father had taken out of the temple in Jerusalem; and the king and his lords and his wives drank in them, and praised the gods of gold, and of silver, of brass, of iron, of wood, and of stone. In the same hour came forth the fingers of a man's hand, and wrote on the wall of the king's palace.

Then the king's thoughts troubled him, and his knees smote one against another. The king cried aloud to bring in the enchanters and the soothsayers. The king said to the wise men of Babylon: "Whosoever shall read this writing, and show me the interpretation, shall be clothed with purple, and have a chain of gold about his neck, and shall be the third ruler in the kingdom."

But they could not read the writing, and the queen said: "O king, there is a man in thy kingdom, in whom is the spirit of the holy gods, and the king Nebuchadnezzar thy father made him master of the magicians. Now let Daniel be called, and he will show the interpretation."

Then was Daniel brought in before the king. The king said: "If thou canst read the writing, and make known to me the interpretation thereof, thou shalt be clothed with purple, and have a chain of gold about thy neck, and shalt be the third ruler in the kingdom."

Daniel answered: "Give thy rewards to another. Nevertheless I will read the writing unto the king, and make known the interpretation. O thou king, the Most High God gave Nebuchadnezzar thy father the kingdom. But when his heart was lifted up that he dealt proudly, he was deposed from his kingly throne, and his dwelling was with the wild asses. He was fed with grass like oxen, till he knew that God ruled in the kingdom of men. Thou his son, O Belshazzar, hast not humbled thine heart, though thou knewest all this; but hast lifted up thyself against the Lord of heaven; and they have brought the vessels of His house before thee, and thou and thy lords and thy wives have drunk wine in them; and thou hast praised the gods of silver, and gold, of brass, iron, wood, and stone, which see not, nor hear, nor know; and the God in whose hand thy breath is, hast thou not glorified. Then this writing was written, MENE, MENE, TEKEL, UPHARSIN. This is the interpretation: MENE; God hath numbered thy kingdom, and brought it to an end. TEKEL; thou art weighed in the balances, and found wanting. PERES;* thy kingdom is divided, and given to the Medes and Persians."

Then commanded Belshazzar, and they clothed Daniel with purple, and put a chain of gold about his neck, and made proclamation that he should be the third ruler in the kingdom. That night Belshazzar was slain, and Darius the Mede received the kingdom.

It pleased Darius to set over the kingdom a hundred and twenty satraps; and over them three presidents, of whom Daniel was one, and the king thought to set him over the whole realm. The presidents and the satraps sought to find occasion against Daniel; but they could find none. Then said these men: "We

---

*Mē'nē, Tē'kĕl, Ū phär'sĭn are literally translated: numbered, weighed, divisions. Pē'res is an abbreviation of the word Upharsin.

shall not find any occasion against Daniel, except we find it concerning the law of his God."

They assembled together to the king, and said: "The presidents and the satraps, the counsellors and the governors, have consulted together to establish a royal statute, that whosoever shall ask a petition of any god or man for thirty days, save of thee, O king, shall be cast into the den of lions. Now, O king, establish the decree, and sign the writing."

Wherefore King Darius signed the writing. When Daniel knew that the writing was signed, he went into his house; and the windows being open in his chamber toward Jerusalem, he kneeled three times a day, and prayed, and gave thanks before his God, as he did aforetime. These men found Daniel making supplication before his God, and they spake before the king: "Hast thou not signed a decree, that every man that shall make a petition unto any god or man, save unto thee, shall be cast into the den of lions?"

The king answered: "The thing is true, according to the law of the Medes and Persians, which altereth not."

Then they said: "Daniel regardeth thee not, O king."

The king, when he heard these words, was sore displeased, and set his heart on Daniel to deliver him; and he labored till the going down of the sun to rescue him. Then these men assembled unto the king, and said: "Know, O king, that no statute which the king establisheth may be changed."

Then the king commanded, and they brought Daniel, and cast him into the den of lions. The king went to his palace, and passed the night fasting; neither were instruments of music brought before him, and his sleep fled from him. The king arose very early in the morning, and went in haste unto the den of lions; and when he came near he cried with a lamentable voice: "Daniel, O Daniel, is thy God able to deliver thee from the lions?"

Then said Daniel: "O king, my God hath sent His angel, and hath shut the lions' mouths, and they have not hurt me."

Then was the king exceeding glad, and Daniel was taken out of the den, and no manner of hurt was found on him. The king commanded, and they brought those men that had accused Daniel, and cast them into the den of lions, them, their children, and their wives; and the lions brake all their bones in pieces, or ever they came at the bottom of the den.

Then King Darius wrote unto all peoples that dwell on the earth: "Peace be multiplied unto you. I make a decree, that in all the dominion of my kingdom men tremble and fear before the God of Daniel; for He is the living God, and steadfast for ever, and His dominion shall be even unto the end."

XVIII

QUEEN ESTHER

IT came to pass in the days of Ahasuerus, who reigned from India even unto Ethiopia, that the king made a feast unto all his princes and his servants, and he showed the riches of his glorious kingdom a hundred and fourscore days. When these days were expired, the king made a feast unto all the people that were present in Shushan the palace seven days, in the court of the garden of the king's palace. On the seventh day, when the heart of the king was merry with wine, he commanded to bring Vashti the queen before the king with the crown royal, to show the people and the princes her beauty; for she was fair to look on. But the queen Vashti refused to come at the king's commandment. Therefore was the king very wroth. Then the king said: "What shall we do unto the queen Vashti, because she hath not done the bidding of the king?"

Memucan, one of the chamberlains, answered: "Vashti the queen hath not done wrong to the king only; for this deed shall come abroad unto all women, to make their husbands contemptible in their eyes. If it please the king, let there go forth a royal commandment that Vashti come no more before King Ahasueras;

and let the king give her royal estate unto another that is better than she. When the king's decree shall be published, all the wives shall give to their husbands honor."

The saying pleased the king and the princes; and the king sent letters into all the provinces, that every man should bear rule in his own house.

Then said the king's servants that ministered unto him: "Let the king appoint officers in all the provinces of his kingdom, that they may gather together all the fair young virgins unto Shushan the palace, to the house of the women, unto Hegai the king's chamberlain, and let the maiden which pleaseth the king be queen instead of Vashti."

The king did so.

There was a certain Jew in Shushan the palace, whose name was Mordecai, who had been carried away from Jerusalem with the captives whom Nebuchadnezzar the king of Babylon had carried away. He brought up Esther, his uncle's daughter; for she had neither father nor mother, and the maid was beautiful. So when the king's commandment was heard, and many maidens were gathered unto the palace, Esther was brought unto the king's house, to the custody of Hegai, keeper of the women. The maiden pleased him, and she obtained kindness of him; and he removed her and her maidens to the best place of the house of the women; and Mordecai walked every day before the court of the women's house to know how Esther did, and what should become of her.

When the turn of Esther was come to go in unto the king, she obtained favor in the sight of all them that looked on her; and the king loved Esther above all the women, so that he set the royal crown on her head, and made her queen instead of Vashti. Esther had not yet shown her kindred nor her people; for Mordecai had charged her that she should not.

In those days, while Mordecai sat in the king's gate, two of the king's chamberlains sought to lay hands on King Ahasuerus. The thing was known to Mordecai, who told it unto Esther the queen, and Esther told the king thereof in Mordecai's name. When inquisition was made, the chamberlains were both hanged.

After these things did King Ahasuerus promote Haman the Agagite, and set his seat above all the princes that were with him. All the king's servants bowed down, and did reverence to Haman; for the king had so commanded concerning him. But Mordecai bowed not down, nor did him reverence. Then the king's servants said unto Mordecai: "Why transgressest thou the king's commandment?"

When they spake daily unto him, and he hearkened not, they told Haman. Then was Haman full of wrath. But he thought scorn to lay hands on Mordecai alone, and sought to destroy all the Jews throughout the whole kingdom. Haman said unto King Ahasuerus: "There is a certain people dispersed among the provinces of thy kingdom; and their laws are diverse from those of every people. Neither keep they the king's laws. Therefore, if it please the king, let it be written that they be destroyed; and I will pay ten thousand talents of silver into the king's treasuries."

The king took his ring from his hand, and gave it unto Haman, and said: "Do with the people as it seemeth good to thee."

Then were the king's scribes called in, and there was written according to all that Haman commanded unto the governors that were over every province, and to every people after their language. In the name of King Ahasuerus was it written, and it was sealed with the king's ring. Letters were sent into all the king's provinces to slay all Jews, both young and old, little children and women, in one day, even on the thirteenth day of the twelfth month, and to take the spoil of them for a prey. The posts went forth in haste, and the decree was given out in Shushan the palace; and the king and Haman sat down to drink.

When Mordecai knew all that was done, he rent his clothes, and put on sackcloth with ashes, and went out into the midst of the city, and cried with a loud and a bitter cry; and in every province there was great mourning among the Jews, and fasting, and weeping, and wailing. Esther's maids and her chamberlains told her; and the queen was exceedingly grieved. Then called Esther for Hatach, one of the king's chamberlains, whom he had appointed to attend on her, and charged him to go to Mordecai, to know what this was, and why it was.

So Hatach went forth to Mordecai, and Mordecai told him of all that had happened, and the exact sum of money that Haman had promised to pay to the king's treasuries for the Jews, to destroy them. Also he gave him the copy of the decree that was given out, to show unto Esther, and to charge her that she should go in unto the king, to make supplication for her people.

Hatach came and told Esther the words of Mordecai. Then Esther gave him a message unto Mordecai, saying: "Whosoever shall come unto the king into the inner court, who is not called, is put to death, except such to whom the king shall hold out the golden sceptre. I have not been called to come in unto the king these thirty days."

They told to Mordecai Esther's words. Then Mordecai commanded them to answer Esther: "Who knoweth whether thou art not come to the kingdom for such a time as this?"

Esther bade them return Mordecai this answer: "Go, gather together all the Jews that are present in Shushan, and fast ye for me, and neither eat nor drink three days, night or day. I also and my maidens will fast likewise; and I will go in unto the king, and if I perish, I perish."

So Mordecai went his way, and did according to all that Esther had commanded him.

On the third day Esther put on her royal apparel, and stood in the inner court of the king's house, and the king sat on his royal throne. When the king saw Esther the queen, she obtained favor in his sight, and the king held out the golden sceptre that was in his hand. So Esther drew near, and touched the top of the sceptre. Then said the king unto her: "What wilt thou, Queen Esther? and what is thy request? It shall be given thee even to the half of the kingdom."

Esther answered: "If it seem good unto the king, let the king and Haman come this day unto the banquet that I have prepared."

The king said: "Cause Haman to make haste, that it may be done as Esther hath said."

So the king and Haman came to the banquet, and the king said unto Esther: "What is thy petition?"

Then answered Esther: "If it please the king, let the king and Haman come to the banquet that I shall prepare for them tomorrow."

Then went Haman forth that day joyful and glad of heart; but when Haman saw Mordecai in the king's gate, that he stood not up nor moved for him, he was filled with wrath. Haman went home, and he fetched his friends and Zeresh his wife, and told them of the glory of his riches, and all the things wherein the king had promoted him. Haman said moreover: "Esther the queen did let no man come in with the king unto the banquet that she had prepared but myself. Tomorrow also am I invited by her together with the king. Yet all this availeth me nothing, so long as I see Mordecai the Jew sitting at the king's gate."

Then said Zeresh and all his friends: "Let a gallows be made fifty cubits high, and in the morning speak thou unto the king that Mordecai may be hanged thereon. Then go thou merrily with the king unto the banquet."

The thing pleased Haman, and he caused the gallows to be made.

On that night the king could not sleep, and he commanded to bring the records. They were read before the king, and it was found written that Mordecai had told of two of the chamberlains who had sought to lay hands on the king Ahasuerus. The king said: "What honor and dignity hath been done to Mordecai for this?"

Then said the king's servants: "There is nothing done for him."

The king said: "Who is in the court?"

Now Haman was come into the outward court of the king's house, to speak unto the king to hang Mordecai on the gallows that he had prepared. The king's servants said: "Behold, Haman standeth in the court."

The king said: "Let him come in."

So Haman came in, and the king said: "What shall be done unto the man whom the king delighteth to honor?"

Haman said in his heart: "To whom would the king delight to do honor more than to myself?" and Haman answered the king: "For the man whom the king delighteth to honor, let royal apparel be brought which the king useth to wear, and the horse that the king rideth on, and the crown royal; and let the apparel and the horse be delivered to the hand of one of the king's most noble princes, that they may array the man withal and cause him to ride through the city, and proclaim before him: 'Thus shall it be done to the man whom the king delighteth to honor.'"

The king said to Haman: "Make haste, and take the apparel and the horse, as thou hast said, and do even so to Mordecai the Jew, that sittest at the king's gate. Let nothing fail of all that thou hast spoken."

Then took Haman the apparel and the horse, and arrayed Mordecai, and caused him to ride through the city, and proclaimed before him: "Thus shall it be done unto the man whom the king delighteth to honor."

Mordecai came again to the king's gate; but Haman hasted to his house, mourning and having his head covered. Haman told his wife and his friends everything that had befallen him. While they were talking, came the king's chamberlains to bring Haman unto the banquet that Esther had prepared.

So the king and Haman came to banquet with Esther the queen, and the king said again: "What is thy petition, Queen Esther? Even to the half of the kingdom it shall be granted thee."

Then Esther answered: "If I have found favor in thy sight, O king, let my life be given me at my petition, and my people at my request; for we are sold, I and my people, to be destroyed."

Then spake the King Ahasuerus and said: "Who is he that durst presume to do so?"

Esther said: "An enemy, even this wicked Haman."

The king arose in his wrath and went into the palace garden, and Haman stood up to make request for his life to Esther the queen; for he saw that there was evil determined against him by the king. Then the king returned out of the garden into the place of the banquet. One of the chamberlains said: "Behold, the gallows fifty cubits high, which Haman hath made for Mordecai, standeth in the house of Haman."

The king said: "Hang him thereon."

So they hanged Haman on the gallows that he had prepared for Mordecai. Then was the king's wrath pacified; and Mordecai came before the king; for Esther had told what he was unto her. The king took off his ring, which he had taken from Haman, and gave it unto Mordecai; and Esther spake again before the king, and fell at his feet, and besought him with tears to put away the mischief Haman had devised against the Jews.

The king held out toward Esther the golden sceptre. So Esther arose, and stood before the king, and she said: "How can I endure to see the destruction of my kindred?"

The king said unto Esther the queen, and to Mordecai: "Write ye to the Jews, as it liketh you, in the king's name, and seal it with the king's ring."

Then were the king's scribes called, and it was written according to all that Mordecai commanded unto the Jews, and the governors and princes of the provinces, and unto every people after their language. He wrote in the name of King Ahasuerus, and sealed it with the king's ring, and sent letters by posts riding on swift steeds that were used in the king's service. The king granted the Jews that were in every city to gather together, and to stand for their life to cause to perish all that would assault them, and to take the spoil of them for a prey, one day, namely, on the thirteenth day of the twelfth month.

Mordecai went forth from the presence of the king in royal apparel of blue and white, and with a great crown of gold, and the city of Shushan shouted and was glad.

In the twelfth month, on the thirteenth day, the Jews gathered together to lay hands on such as sought their hurt; and all the princes of the provinces, and they that did the king's business, helped the Jews; because the fear of Mordecai was fallen on them; for Mordecai was great in the king's house, and his fame went forth throughout all the provinces. The Jews smote their enemies, and in Shushan the palace slew five hundred men. Then said Esther: "If it please the king, let it be granted to the Jews which are in Shushan to do tomorrow according unto this day's decree."

The king commanded it so to be done; and the Jews that were in Shushan gathered on the fourteenth day, and slew three hundred men.

The Jews in the provinces slew of their foes seventy and five thousand. This was done on the thirteenth day of the month; and on the fourteenth day they rested, and made it a day of feasting and gladness. But the Jews that were in Shushan made the fifteenth day a day of feasting and gladness.

XIX

THE RETURN FROM THE CAPTIVITY

THE Lord stirred up the spirit of Cyrus king of Persia, that he made a proclamation, saying: "Thus saith Cyrus king of Persia: 'All the kingdoms of the earth hath the Lord given me, and He hath charged me to build Him a house in Jerusalem. Whosoever there is among you of His people, let him go to Jerusalem, and build the house of the Lord.'"

Then rose up the leaders of Judah and Benjamin, and the priests, and the Levites; and all they that were round about them strengthened their hands with vessels of silver, with gold, with goods, and with beasts. Also Cyrus the king brought forth the vessels of the house of the Lord, which Nebuchadnezzar had brought out of Jerusalem; and the children of Israel gathered themselves together as one man to Jerusalem. They gave money unto the masons, and to the carpenters; and meat, and drink, unto them of Sidon, and to them of Tyre, to bring cedar trees from Lebanon to the sea, unto Joppa; and appointed the Levites, from twenty years old and upward, to have the oversight of the work of the house of the Lord. When the builders laid the foundation of the temple, the priests stood in their apparel with trumpets, and the Levites with cymbals, to praise the Lord; and they sang one to another giving thanks unto the Lord, saying: "For he is good, for his mercy endureth forever toward Israel."

But many of the old men that had seen the first house wept, and many shouted for joy.

When the adversaries of Judah and Benjamin heard that the children of the captivity builded a temple unto the Lord, they troubled them in building, and hired counsellors against them, to frustrate their purpose; and in the days of Artaxerxes king of Persia, wrote a letter against Jerusalem. This is the letter: "Be it known unto the king, that the Jews are building the rebellious and bad city. If this city be builded, and the walls finished, they will not pay tribute. Now because it is not meet for us to see the king's dishonor, therefore have we certified the king, that search may be made in the records of thy fathers. So shalt thou find that this is a rebellious city, for which cause was this city destroyed."

Then sent the king an answer: "The letter which ye sent hath been read before me, and search hath been made, and it is found that this city of old time hath made insurrection, and that rebellion and sedition have been made therein. There have been mighty kings also over Jerusalem. Make ye now a decree to cause these men to cease, and that this city be not builded."

Then ceased the work on the house of God unto the second year of the reign of Darius king of Persia, when Darius made a decree: "Let the governor of the Jews and the elders of the Jews build the house of God at Jerusalem. Moreover I make a decree that of the king's goods expenses be given unto these men, that they be not hindered. That which they have need of, both young bullocks, and rams, and lambs, for burnt offerings, wheat, salt, wine, and oil, according to the word of the priests, let it be given them day by day without fail, that they may offer sacrifices of sweet savor unto the God of heaven."

Then the elders of the Jews builded and prospered, and this house was finished, and the children of Israel kept the dedication with joy.

XX

THE LIFE OF JESUS

THERE was in the days of Herod king of Judæa a certain priest named Zacharias; and he had a wife named Elisabeth. They were both righteous, walking in all the commandments of the Lord blameless; but they had no child, and they were now well advanced in years.

It came to pass, while Zacharias executed the priest's office, his lot was to enter into the temple of the Lord and burn incense, and the whole multitude of the people were praying without; and there appeared unto him an angel of the Lord. Zacharias was troubled, and fear fell on him. But the angel said: "Fear not Zacharias. Thy wife shall bear a son, and thou shalt call his name John; and thou shalt have joy and gladness, for he shall be great in the sight of the Lord, and shall be filled with the Holy Spirit, and many of the children of Israel shall he turn unto the Lord their God."

Zacharias said unto the angel: "Whereby shall I know this?"

The angel said: "I am Gabriel, and am sent to bring thee these glad tidings. Behold, thou shalt be dumb and not able to speak, until the day that these things come to pass, because thou believest not my words."

The people were waiting for Zacharias, and they marvelled that he tarried so long in the temple. When he came out, he could not speak unto them, and they perceived that he had seen a vision, and he beckoned unto them, and remained speechless.

The angel Gabriel was also sent from God unto a city of Galilee, named Nazareth, to a virgin betrothed to a man whose name was Joseph, and her name was Mary. Gabriel came unto her, and said: "Hail, thou that art highly favored. The Lord is with thee."

She was greatly troubled at his saying, and cast in her mind what manner of salutation this might be. The angel said unto her: "Fear not, Mary. Behold, thou shalt have a son, and shalt call his name Jesus, and the Lord God shall give unto him the throne of David; and of his kingdom there shall be no end."

Elisabeth had a son; and her neighbors and her kinsfolk would have called him Zacharias, after the name of his father. His mother said: "Not so; but he shall be called John."

They said unto her: "There is none of thy kindred that is called by this name;" and they made signs to his father, what he would have him called.

He asked for a writing tablet, and wrote: "His name is John;" and his mouth was opened immediately, and his tongue loosed, and he spake, and praised God; and the child grew, and waxed strong in spirit.

In those days, there went out a decree from Cæsar Augustus, that all the world should be enrolled; and all went to enroll themselves, everyone to his own city. Joseph went from Galilee to the city of David, which is called Bethlehem, because he was of the family of David, to enroll himself with Mary. While they were there her son was born, and she wrapped him in swaddling clothes, and laid him in a manger, because there was no room for them in the inn.

There were shepherds in the same country abiding in the field, and keeping watch by night over their flock; and an angel of the Lord stood by them, and the glory of the Lord shone round about them, and they were sore afraid. The angel said unto them: "Fear not; for, behold, I bring you tidings of great joy which shall be to all people. There is born to you this day in the city of David a Saviour, who is Christ the Lord; and this is a sign unto you: Ye shall find the babe wrapped in swaddling clothes, lying in a manger."

Suddenly there was with the angel a multitude of the heavenly host praising God, and saying:

"Glory to God in the highest,
And on earth peace among men."

When the angels went away into heaven, the shepherds said one to another: "Let us now go unto Bethlehem, and see this thing that is come to pass, which the Lord hath made known unto us."

The star in the east

They came with haste, and found Mary and Joseph, and the babe lying in a manger; and they made known abroad the saying which was spoken to them concerning this child. All that heard wondered; but Mary kept these things, and pondered them in her heart; and the shepherds returned, glorifying and praising God.

Now, behold, wise men from the east came to Jerusalem, saying: "Where is he that is born King of the Jews? for we have seen his star, and are come to worship him."

When Herod the king heard it, he was troubled, and all Jerusalem with him; and he gathered together the chief priests and scribes, and inquired of them where the Christ should be born. They said: "In Bethlehem of Judæa."

Then Herod called the wise men, and learned of them what time the star appeared; and he said: "Go and search diligently for the young child; and when ye have found him, bring me word, that I also may come and worship him."

When they had heard the king, they departed; and lo, the star, which they saw, went before them, till it stood over where the young child was. They rejoiced with exceeding great joy, and came into the house and saw the young child with Mary, his mother; and they fell down and worshipped him. Then they opened their treasures and presented unto him gifts, gold and frankincense and myrrh. Being warned of God in a dream that they should not return to Herod, they departed into their own country another way.

When they were departed, an angel of the Lord appeareth to Joseph in a dream, saying: "Arise and take the young child and his mother, and flee into Egypt, and be thou there until I bring thee word; for Herod will seek the young child to destroy him."

Joseph arose and took the young child and his mother by night, and departed into Egypt, and was there until the death of Herod.

Herod, when he saw that he was mocked of the wise men, was exceeding wroth, and sent forth, and slew all the male children that were in Bethlehem, and in all the borders thereof, from two years old and under. Then was fulfilled that which was spoken by Jeremiah the prophet, saying:

"A voice was heard in Ramah,
Weeping and great mourning,
Rachel weeping for her children;
And she would not be comforted, because they
  were not."

When Herod was dead, an angel of the Lord appeareth in a dream to Joseph in Egypt, saying: "Arise, and take the young child and his mother, and go into the land of Israel; for they are dead that sought the young child's life." He arose, and took the child and his mother, and came into the land of Israel to Galilee, and dwelt in Nazareth.

The child grew, and was filled with wisdom; and the grace of God was on him. His parents went every year to Jerusalem at the feast of the passover. When he was twelve years old, they went after the custom of the feast; and as they were returning, the boy Jesus tarried behind in Jerusalem. His parents knew it not; but supposing him to be in the company, went a day's journey, and they sought for him among their kinsfolk and acquaintance. When they found him not, they returned to Jerusalem, seeking for him. After three days they found him in the temple, sitting in the midst of the teachers, hearing them, and asking them questions; and all that heard him were astonished at his understanding and his answers.

His mother said unto him: "Son, why hast thou thus dealt with us? Behold, thy father and I sought thee sorrowing."

He said unto them: "How is it that ye sought me? Wist ye not that I must be about my Father's business?"

They understood not the saying which he spake. He went with them to Nazareth, and was subject unto them.

In the fifteenth year of the reign of Tiberius Cæsar, Pontius Pilate being governor of Judæa, and Herod being tetrarch* of Galilee, the word of God came unto John the son of Zacharias in the wilderness; and he

---

*Herod the tetrarch or king was a subordinate ruler in the Roman Empire. He was a Jew in faith, while Pontius Pilate was an alien.

came into the country about Jordan, preaching the baptism of repentance for the remission of sins; as it is written in the book of Isaiah the prophet:

"The voice of one crying in the wilderness:
'Make ye ready the way of the Lord,
Make his paths straight,
And all flesh shall see the salvation of God.'"

John was clothed with camel's hair, and had a leathern girdle about his loins; and his food was locusts and wild honey. Multitudes went out unto him, and were baptized of him in the river Jordan, confessing their sins. But when he saw many of the Pharisees and Sadducees coming to his baptism, he said unto them: "Ye offspring of vipers, who hath warned you of the wrath to come? Bring forth fruit worthy of repentance; and think not to say within yourselves: 'We have Abraham to our father;' for I say unto you, that God is able of these stones to raise up children unto Abraham. Even now is the ax laid unto the root of the trees. Every tree that bringeth not forth good fruit is hewn down, and cast into the fire."

The people asked him, saying: "What then must we do?"

He answered and said: "He that hath two coats, let him impart to him that hath none; and he that hath food let him do likewise."

All men reasoned in their hearts concerning John, whether he were the Christ. John answered: "I indeed baptize you with water; but one mightier than I cometh, the latchet of whose shoes I am not worthy to unloose. He shall baptize you with the Holy Spirit, whose fan is in his hand, to cleanse his threshing-floor, and he will gather the wheat into his garner, but the chaff he will burn with fire unquenchable."

Then cometh Jesus from Galilee to the Jordan unto John, to be baptized; and Jesus, when he was baptized, went up straightway out of the water, and the heavens were opened, and the spirit of God descended as a dove, and lighted on him; and lo, a voice from heaven, saying: "This is my beloved Son, in whom I am well pleased."

Then was Jesus led of the Spirit into the wilderness to be tempted of the devil; and when he had fasted forty days and forty nights, he hungered. The tempter came and said: "If thou art the Son of God, command that these stones become bread."

But he answered: "It is written: 'Man shall not live by bread alone, but by every word that proceedeth out of the mouth of God.'"

Then the devil taketh him into the holy city, and set him on a pinnacle of the temple, and saith unto him: "If thou art the Son of God, cast thyself down; for it is written:

'He shall give his angels charge concerning thee;
And on their hands they shall bear thee up,
Lest haply thou dash thy foot against a stone.'"

Jesus said unto him: "It is written: 'Thou shalt not tempt the Lord thy God.'"

Again the devil taketh him unto an exceeding high mountain, and showeth him all the kingdoms of the world, and the glory of them, and saith: "All these will I give thee, if thou wilt fall down and worship me."

Then saith Jesus: "Get thee hence, Satan; for it is written: 'Thou shalt worship the Lord thy God, and Him only shalt thou serve.'"

Then the devil leaveth him, and, behold, angels came and ministered unto him.

From that time began Jesus to preach and to say: "Repent; for the kingdom of heaven is at hand;" and Jesus was about thirty years of age.

Two of John's disciples followed Jesus. One of the two was Andrew, Simon Peter's brother. He findeth his brother Simon, and saith unto him: "We have found the Messiah;" and brought him to Jesus.

On the morrow Jesus was minded to go forth into Galilee, and he findeth Philip. Jesus saith unto him: "Follow me."

Philip findeth Nathanael, and saith: "We have found him of whom Moses and the prophets did write, Jesus of Nazareth."

Nathanael saith: "Can any good thing come out of Nazareth?"

Philip saith: "Come and see."

Jesus saw Nathanael coming and saith of him: "Behold, an Israelite in whom is no guile."

The third day there was a marriage in Cana of Galilee; and the mother of Jesus was there. Jesus also was bidden, and his disciples, to the marriage. When the wine failed, the mother of Jesus saith unto him: "They have no wine."

Jesus saith: "Woman, what have I to do with thee?"

His mother saith unto the servants: "Whatsoever he saith unto you, do it."

There were six waterpots of stone set there. Jesus saith: "Fill the pots with water."

They filled them up to the brim; and he saith unto them: "Draw out now, and bear unto the steward of the feast."

They bare it, and when the steward tasted the water now become wine, and knew not whence it was, he called the bridegroom, and saith: "Every man at the beginning doth set forth good wine; and when men have drunk freely, then that which is worse. Thou hast kept the good wine until now."

The passover was at hand, and Jesus went to Jerusalem. He found in the temple those that sold oxen and sheep and doves, and the changers of money sitting; and he made a scourge of cords, and cast out all them that sold and bought in the temple, and overthrew the tables of the money-changers; and he said:

"It is written: 'My house shall be called a house of prayer;' but ye make it a den of thieves."

He taught daily in the temple, and the blind and the lame came to him, and he healed them. When the chief priests and scribes saw the wonderful things that he did, and the children that were crying in the temple: "Hosanna to the son of David;" they were moved with indignation, and sought to destroy him, and they could not find out what they might do; for the people were very attentive to hear him.

There was a man named Nicodemus, a ruler of the Jews; the same came to Jesus by night, and said: "Rabbi, we know that thou art a teacher come from God; for no man can do these miracles that thou doest, except God be with him."

Jesus answered: "Verily, verily, I say unto thee: 'Except a man be born of water and the Spirit, he cannot see the kingdom of God. The wind bloweth where it listeth, and thou hearest the sound thereof, but canst not tell whence it cometh, and whither it goeth. So is everyone that is born of the Spirit. God so loved the world, that he gave his only Son, that whosoever believeth on him should not perish, but have eternal life.'"

He cometh to a city of Samaria, called Sychar, and Jacob's well was there. Jesus, being wearied with his journey, sat by the well. There cometh a woman of Samaria to draw water. Jesus saith unto her: "Give me to drink;" for his disciples were gone into the city to buy food.

The Samaritan woman saith: "How is it that thou, being a Jew, askest drink of me?" (For Jews have no dealings with Samaritans.)

Jesus answered: "If thou knewest who it is that saith to thee: 'Give me to drink,' thou wouldest have asked of him, and he would have given thee living water."

The woman saith: "Sir, thou hast nothing to draw with, and the well is deep. Whence then hast thou that water? Art thou greater than our father Jacob, who gave us the well, and drank thereof himself, and his children, and his cattle?"

Jesus answered: "Everyone that drinketh of this water shall thirst again; but whosoever drinketh of the water that I give shall never thirst. The water that I give shall be in him a well springing up unto eternal life."

The woman saith: "Sir, give me this water, that I thirst not, neither come all the way hither to draw."

Jesus saith: "Go, call thy husband, and come hither."

The woman answered: "I have no husband."

Jesus saith unto her: "Thou hast well said; for thou hast had five husbands, and he whom thou now hast is not thy husband."

The woman saith: "Sir, I perceive that thou art a prophet."

Jesus saith: "The hour cometh, and now is, when the true worshipers shall worship the Father in spirit and truth."

The woman saith: "I know that Messiah cometh. When he is come, he will tell us all things."

Jesus saith unto her: "I that speak unto thee am he."

His disciples came. So the woman left her waterpot, and went into the city, and saith to the people: "Come, see a man who told me all things that ever I did. Is not this the Christ?"

In the meanwhile his disciples prayed him, saying: "Master, eat."

But he said unto them: "I have meat to eat that ye know not."

The disciples therefore said one to another: "Hath any man brought him aught to eat?"

Jesus saith: "My meat is to do the will of Him that sent me, and to accomplish His work."

When the Samaritans came unto him, they besought him to tarry with them; and he abode there two days, and many believed because of his word.

Jesus returned to Galilee; and a fame went out concerning him through all the region.

He came to Nazareth, where he had been brought up; and he entered, as his custom was, into the synagogue on the Sabbath Day, and stood up to read. There was delivered unto him the book of the prophet Isaiah;

and he opened the book, and found the place where it was written:

"The Spirit of the Lord is on me,
 Because He anointed me to preach the gospel to the poor;
 He hath sent me to proclaim release to the captives,
 And recovering of sight to the blind,
 To proclaim the acceptable year of the Lord."

The eyes of all in the synagogue were fastened on him, and he began to say unto them: "Today is this scripture fulfilled."

All wondered at the gracious words which proceeded out of his mouth, and they said: "Is not this the carpenter's son? Is not his mother called Mary? and his brethren and his sisters, are they not all with us? Whence then hath this man all these things?" and they were offended.

Jesus said unto them: "A prophet is not without honor, save in his own country, and among his own kin, and in his own house."

They were all filled with wrath in the synagogue, and they rose up, and thrust him out of the city, and led him unto the brow of the hill whereon their city was built, that they might throw him down headlong; but he passing through the midst of them went his way; and he could there do no mighty work, save that he laid his hands on a few sick folk, and healed them.

He came and dwelt in Capernaum, and walking by the sea of Galilee, he saw two boats by the shore. The fishermen had gone out of them, and were washing their nets, and he entered into one of the boats, which was Simon's; and he said unto Simon: "Put out into the deep, and let down your nets."

Simon answered: "Master, we have toiled all night, and taken nothing; but at thy word I will let down the nets."

When they had done this, they inclosed a great multitude of fishes; and their nets were breaking. They beckoned unto their partners in the other boat, that they should come and help; and they came, and filled both the boats, so that they began to sink. Simon Peter, when he saw it, fell down at Jesus' knees, saying: "Depart from me; for I am a sinful man."

He was astonished at the draught of the fishes which they had taken; and so were James and John, sons of Zebedee, who were partners with Simon. Jesus said unto Simon: "Fear not. Henceforth thou shalt catch men."

When they had brought their boats to land, they left all, and followed him. They went into Capernaum, and on the Sabbath Day he entered into the synagogue and taught; and in the synagogue there was a man with an unclean spirit, and he cried out, saying: "What have we to do with thee, thou Jesus of Nazareth? Art thou come to destroy us? I know thee who thou art, the Holy One of God."

Jesus rebuked the unclean spirit, saying: "Hold thy peace, and come out of him."

The unclean spirit convulsed him, and crying with a loud voice, came out of him; and they were all amazed, insomuch that they questioned among themselves, saying: "What is this? With authority he commandeth even the unclean spirits, and they obey him."

When Jesus was come into Peter's house, he saw his wife's mother lying sick of a fever; and he touched her hand, and the fever left her, and she arose, and ministered unto them.

Jesus went about in all Galilee, teaching in their synagogues, and preaching the gospel, and healing all manner of sickness among the people. While he was in one of the cities there came to him a leper, beseeching him, and kneeling down to him, and saying: "If thou wilt, thou canst make me clean."

Being moved with compassion, Jesus stretched forth his hand, and touched him, and saith: "I will. Be thou made clean;" and as soon as he had spoken, the leprosy departed from him.

When Jesus entered again into Capernaum, it was noised that he was at home; and many gathered together, so that there was no longer room for them, no, not even about the door; and he preached the word unto them. They bring unto him a man sick of the palsy, borne of four; and when they could not come nigh unto him for the crowd, they uncovered the roof where he was; and when they had broken it up, they let down the bed whereon the sick of the palsy lay. Jesus seeing their faith said unto the sick of the palsy: "Son, thy sins are forgiven. Arise, and go unto thy house."

The sick of the palsy arose, and went forth before them all, insomuch that they were all amazed, and glorified God, saying: "We have seen strange things today."

Jesus went forth, and saw a man, named Matthew, sitting at the place of toll, and saith unto him: "Follow me;" and he arose and followed him.

It came to pass, that he was sitting at meat in his house, and many publicans and sinners sat down with Jesus and his disciples. When the Pharisees saw it, they said unto his disciples: "Why eateth your Master with the publicans and sinners?"

Jesus saith unto them: "They that are whole have no need of a physician, but they that are sick. I am not come to call the righteous, but sinners to repentance."

He spake also a parable unto them: "No man putteth a piece of new cloth on an old garment; for that which should fill it up taketh from the garment, and a worse rent is made. Neither do men put new wine into old wine-skins, else the skins burst, and the wine runneth out, and the skins perish; but they put new wine into new wine-skins, and both are preserved."

After these things there was a feast of the Jews, and Jesus went up to Jerusalem. Now there is in Jerusalem by the sheep gate a pool, which is called Bethesda, having five porches. In these lay a multitude of them that were sick, blind, halt, withered, waiting for the moving of the water; for an angel of the Lord went down at certain seasons into the pool, and troubled the water. Whosoever then first stepped in was made whole, with whatsoever disease he was holden. A certain man was there who had an infirmity thirty and eight years. When Jesus saw him lying, and knew that he had been a long time in that case, he saith unto him: "Wilt thou be made whole?"

The sick man answered: "Sir, I have no man, when the water is troubled, to put me into the pool. While I am coming, another steppeth down before me."

Jesus saith unto him: "Rise, take up thy bed and walk."

Immediately the man was made whole, and took up his bed and walked.

Jesus was going on the Sabbath Day through the grainfields, and his disciples were hungry, and began to pluck ears and to eat. The Pharisees said unto him: "Behold, thy disciples do that which is not lawful to do on the Sabbath."

He said unto them: "Have ye not read what David did, when he was hungry, how he entered into the house of God and did eat the showbread, which it was not lawful for him to eat, but only for the priests. The Sabbath was made for man and not man for the Sabbath."

On another Sabbath he entered into the synagogue and taught; and a man was there whose right hand was withered. The scribes and Pharisees watched Jesus, whether he would heal on the Sabbath, that they might accuse him. But he knew their thoughts; and he said to the man that had his hand withered: "Stand forth."

He arose and stood forth; and Jesus said unto them: "Is it lawful on the Sabbath to do good, or to do evil? to save a life, or to destroy it?"

He looked round about on them all, and said unto the man: "Stretch forth thy hand."

He stretched it forth, and it was restored whole, as the other. But the Pharisees went out, and took counsel how they might destroy Jesus.

It came to pass, that he went to a mountain to pray, and he continued all night in prayer to God; and when it was day, he called his disciples, and he chose from them twelve, whom also he named apostles: Simon who is called Peter, and Andrew his brother; James the son of Zebedee, and John his brother; Philip, and Bartholomew; Thomas, and Matthew the publican; James the son of Alphæas, and Thaddæus; Simon the Canaanite, and Judas Iscariot. He came down with them and stood on a level place, and a multitude of people from all Judæa and Jerusalem, and the sea coast of Tyre and Sidon, came to hear him, and to be healed of their diseases. Seeing the multitude, he went up into the mountain, and when he had sat down, his disciples came unto him, and he taught them saying:

"Blessed are the poor in spirit; for theirs is the kingdom of heaven.

"Blessed are they that mourn; for they shall be comforted.

"Blessed are the meek; for they shall inherit the earth.

"Blessed are they that hunger and thirst after righteousness; for they shall be filled.

"Blessed are the merciful; for they shall obtain mercy.

"Blessed are the pure in heart; for they shall see God.

"Blessed are the peace-makers; for they shall be called the children of God.

"Blessed are they that have been persecuted for righteousness' sake; for theirs is the kingdom of heaven.

"Blessed are ye when men shall revile you and say all manner of evil against you falsely, for my sake. Rejoice, and be exceeding glad; for great is your reward in heaven. So persecuted they the prophets that were before you.

"Ye are the salt of the earth; but if the salt have lost its savor, it is thenceforth good for nothing, but to be cast out and trodden under foot. Ye are the light of the world. A city set on a hill cannot be hid. Neither do men light a lamp, and put it under a bushel, but on a stand; and it shineth unto all that are in the house. Even so let your light shine before men, that they may see your good works, and glorify your Father who is in heaven.

"Ye have heard that it was said: 'An eye for an eye, and a tooth for a tooth;' but I say unto you: 'Resist not him that is evil; but whosoever smiteth thee on thy right cheek, turn to him the other also. If any man would go to law with thee, and take away thy coat, let him have thy cloak also; and whosoever shall compel thee to go one mile, go with him twain. Give to him that asketh, and from him that would borrow turn not thou away.'

"Ye have heard that it was said: 'Thou shalt love thy neighbor, and hate thine enemy;' but I say unto you: 'Love your enemies, and pray for them that persecute you, that ye may be children of your Father who is in heaven;' for He maketh His sun to rise on the evil and the good, and sendeth rain on the just and the unjust. As ye would that men should do to you, do ye also to them. If ye love them that love you, what thank have ye? Even sinners love those that love them. If ye do good to them that do good to you, what thank have ye? Even sinners do the same. If ye lend to them of whom ye hope to receive, what thank have ye? Even sinners lend to sinners, to receive again as much;

and if ye salute your brethren only, what do ye more than others? Do not even the Gentiles the same?

"Take heed that ye do not your righteousness before men, to be seen of them; else ye have no reward with your Father who is in heaven. When thou doest alms, sound not a trumpet before thee, as the hypocrites do in the synagogues and in the streets, that they may have glory of men. Verily I say unto you: 'They have received their reward.' But when thou doest alms, let not thy left hand know what thy right hand doeth, that thine alms may be in secret; and thy Father who seeth in secret shall reward thee.

"When ye pray, ye shall not be as the hypocrites, for they love to stand and pray in the synagogues and on the corners of the streets, that they may be seen of men. But thou, when thou prayest, enter into thine inner chamber, and shut thy door; and in praying use not vain repetitions, as the Gentiles do; for they think that they shall be heard for their much speaking. Your Father knoweth what things ye have need of before ye ask him. After this manner therefore pray ye:

"Our Father who art in heaven, Hallowed be thy name. Thy kingdom come. Thy will be done on earth, as it is in heaven. Give us this day our daily bread; and forgive us our debts, as we forgive our debtors; and lead us not into temptation, but deliver us from evil. For Thine is the kingdom, and the power, and the glory, for ever. Amen.

"Lay not up for yourselves treasures on the earth, where moth and rust consume, and where thieves break through and steal; but lay up for yourselves treasures in heaven; for where your treasure is, there will your heart be also. No man can serve two masters; for either he will hate the one, and love the other; or else he will hold to the one and despise the other. Ye cannot serve God and mammon. Be not anxious what ye shall eat, or what ye shall drink; nor yet for your body, what ye shall put on. Behold the birds of the air; they sow not neither do they reap, nor gather into barns; and your heavenly Father feedeth them. Are not ye of more value than they? Consider the lilies of the field, how they grow. They toil not neither do they spin; yet I say unto you, that even Solomon in all his glory was not arrayed like one of these. Wherefore, if God doth so clothe the grass of the field, shall he not much more clothe you, O ye of little faith? Be not therefore anxious for the morrow. Sufficient unto the day is the evil thereof.

"Judge not that ye be not judged; for with what judgment ye judge, ye shall be judged. Give, and it shall be given unto you, good measure, pressed down, shaken together, running over.

"Can the blind guide the blind? Shall they not both fall into a ditch? and why beholdest thou the mote that is in thy brother's eye, but considerest not the beam that is in thine own eye?

"Give not that which is holy unto the dogs, neither cast your pearls before the swine, lest they trample them under their feet, and turn and rend you.

"Ask, and it shall be given you; seek, and ye shall find; knock, and it shall be opened unto you.

"What man is there of you, who, if his son shall ask him for a loaf, will give him a stone; or if he ask a fish, will give him a serpent? If ye then, being evil, know how to give good gifts unto your children, how much more shall your Father who is in heaven give good things to them that ask Him?

"Enter ye in at the narrow gate; for wide is the gate, and broad is the way, that leadeth to destruction, and many be they that enter in thereat. Narrow is the gate, and narrow is the way, that leadeth unto life, and few be they that find it.

"Beware of false prophets, who come to you in sheep's clothing, but inwardly are ravening wolves. By their fruits ye shall know them. Do men gather grapes of thorns, or figs of thistles? A good tree cannot bring forth evil fruit, neither can a corrupt tree bring forth good fruit. The good man out of the good treasure of his heart bringeth forth that which is good; and the evil man out of the evil treasure of his heart bringeth forth that which is evil. Not everyone that saith unto me: 'Lord, Lord,' shall enter into the kingdom of heaven, but he that doeth the will of my Father.

"Everyone who heareth these words of mine, and doeth them, shall be likened unto a wise man, who built his house on a rock; and the rain descended, and the floods came, and the winds blew, and beat on that house; and it fell not; for it was founded on a rock. Everyone that heareth these words of mine, and doeth them not, shall be likened unto a foolish man, who built his house on the sand; and the rain descended, and the floods came, and the winds blew, and beat on that house; and it fell, and great was the fall of it."

After he had ended all these sayings, he entered into Capernaum; and a certain centurion's servant was sick and at the point of death. When the centurion heard concerning Jesus, he came beseeching him, and saying: "Lord, my servant lieth in the house, grievously tormented."

Jesus saith: "I will come and heal him."

The centurion answered: "Lord, I am not worthy that thou shouldest come under my roof; but only speak the word, and my servant shall be healed."

Jesus said to them that followed: "Verily I say unto you, I have not found so great faith, no, not in Israel;" and Jesus said unto the centurion: "Go thy way. As thou hast believed, so be it done unto thee;" and the servant was healed in the selfsame hour.

Soon afterward, he went to a city called Nain; and his disciples went with him, and a great multitude.

When he came nigh to the gate of the city, behold, there was carried out one that was dead, the only son of his mother, and she was a widow, and much people of the city was with her. When the Lord saw her, he had compassion on her, and said unto her: "Weep not."

He came and touched the bier, and the bearers stood still; and he said: "Young man, I say unto thee: 'Arise.'"

He that was dead sat up, and began to speak, and Jesus delivered him to his mother. Fear took hold on all, and they glorified God, saying: "A great prophet is arisen among us."

The disciples of John told him of all these things; and John calling unto him two of his disciples sent them to Jesus saying: "Art thou he that cometh, or look we for another?"

Jesus said unto them: "Go and tell John the things which ye hear and see. The blind receive their sight, and the lame walk, the lepers are cleansed, and the deaf hear, and the dead are raised, and the poor have good tidings preached to them."

When the messengers were departed, he began to say unto the multitude concerning John: "What went ye out into the wilderness to behold? a reed shaken with the wind? What went ye out to see? a man clothed in soft raiment? They that are gorgeously apparelled, and live delicately, are in kings' courts. What went ye out to see? a prophet? Yea, and much more than a prophet. Verily I say unto you: 'There hath not arisen a greater than John the Baptist;' yet he that is little in the kingdom of heaven is greater than he.

"Whereunto shall I liken this generation? It is like unto children sitting in the marketplaces, that call unto their fellows, and say: 'We piped unto you, and ye did not dance; we wailed, and ye did not mourn.' For John came eating no bread nor drinking wine; and ye say: 'He hath a devil.' The Son of Man is come eating and drinking; and ye say: "Behold, a gluttonous man, and a wine-bibber.'"

Then began he to upbraid the cities wherein most of his mighty works were done, because they repented not. "Woe unto thee, Chorazin! Woe unto thee, Bethsaida! For if the mighty works had been done in Tyre and Sidon which were done in you, they would have repented long ago in sackcloth and ashes. I say unto you, it shall be more tolerable for Tyre and Sidon in the day of judgment, than for you; and thou, Capernaum, shalt go down unto hell. For if the mighty works had been done in Sodom which were done in thee, it would have remained until this day."

In that same hour he rejoiced, and said: "I thank Thee, O Father, Lord of heaven and earth, that Thou hast hid these things from the wise, and hast revealed them unto babes.

"Come unto me, all ye that labor and are heavy laden, and I will give you rest. Take my yoke on you, and learn of me; for I am meek and lowly in heart, and ye shall find rest unto your souls. For my yoke is easy, and my burden is light."

One of the Pharisees desired that he would eat with him. He entered into the Pharisee's house; and behold, a woman who was in the city, a sinner, when she knew that he was sitting at meat in the Pharisee's house, brought an alabaster cruse of ointment, and weeping, she began to wet his feet with her tears, and wiped them with the hair of her head, and anointed them with the ointment. The Pharisee spake within himself, saying: "This man, if he were a prophet, would have perceived what manner of woman this is that toucheth him."

Jesus said unto him: "Simon, I have somewhat to say unto thee. A certain lender had two debtors. The one owed him five hundred pence, and the other fifty. When they had not wherewith to pay, he forgave them both. Which of them therefore will love him most?"

Simon answered: "He, I suppose, to whom he forgave the most."

Jesus said: "Thou hast rightly judged. Seest thou this woman? I entered into thine house, thou gavest me no water for my feet; but she hath wetted my feet with her tears, and wiped them with her hair. Thou gavest me no kiss; but she, since the time I came in, hath not ceased to kiss my feet. My head with oil thou didst not anoint; but she hath anointed my feet with ointment. Wherefore I say unto thee: 'Her sins, which are many, are forgiven; for she loved much; but to whom little is forgiven, the same loveth little.'"

He said unto the woman: "Thy faith hath saved thee. Go in peace."

Soon afterward, he went about through cities and villages, preaching, and with him the twelve, and certain women who had been healed of evil spirits and infirmities, Mary that was called Magdalene, and many others, that ministered unto him of their substance.

He went into a house, and the multitude cometh together. Then was brought unto him one possessed with a devil, and he healed him. Some said: "He hath Beelzebub, and by the prince of the devils casteth he out devils."

He said unto them: "Every kingdom divided against itself is brought to desolation; and if Satan casteth out Satan, he is divided against himself. How then shall his kingdom stand? But if I by the Spirit of God cast out devils, then is the kingdom of God come unto you. He that is not with me is against me, and he that gathereth not with me scattereth. I say unto you, that every idle word that men shall speak, they shall give account thereof in the day of judgment. For by thy words thou shalt be justified, and by thy words thou shalt be condemned. This generation is an evil generation. The men of Nineveh shall stand up in the judgment, and condemn it; for they repented at the preaching of Jonah; and behold, a greater than Jonah is here. The queen of the south shall rise up in the judgment with this generation, and shall condemn it; for she came from the ends of the earth to hear the wisdom of Solomon; and behold, a greater than Solomon is here."

While he yet talked one said unto him: "Thy mother and thy brethren stand without, seeking to speak with thee."

But he said: "Who is my mother, and who are my brethren?"

He stretched forth his hand toward his disciples, and said: "Behold, my mother and my brethren! For whosoever shall do the will of my Father who is in heaven, the same is my brother, and sister, and mother."

Jesus went out of the house to the seaside, and there gathered unto him a great multitude. He went into a boat, and all the multitude stood on the shore; and he spake to them many things in parables, saying: "Behold, a sower went forth to sow; and as he sowed, some seeds fell by the wayside, and the birds came and devoured them. Some fell on rocky places, where they had not much earth; and straightway they sprang up, because they had no deepness of earth, and when the sun was risen, they were scorched; and because they had no root, they withered away. Others fell among thorns; and the thorns grew, and choked them. Others fell on the good ground, and yielded fruit, some a hundredfold, some sixty, some thirty."

As he said these things, he cried: "He that hath ears to hear, let him hear."

When he was alone, his disciples asked him what this parable might be. He answered: "Unto you it is given to know the mysteries of the kingdom of heaven. Blessed are your eyes, for they see; and your ears, for they hear. Verily I say unto you, that many prophets and righteous men desired to see the things which ye see, and saw them not, and to hear the things which ye hear, and heard them not.

"Hear then the parable of the sower. When anyone heareth the word of the kingdom, and understandeth it not, then cometh the evil one, and snatcheth away that which was sown in his heart. This is he that was sown by the wayside. He that was sown on the rocky places is he that heareth the word, and straightway with joy receiveth it; yet hath he not root in himself, but endureth for a while; and when tribulation or persecution ariseth, he stumbleth. He that was sown among the thorns is he that heareth the word; and the care of the world, and the deceitfulness of riches, choke the word, and he becometh unfruitful. He that was sown on the good ground is he that heareth the word, and understandeth it; who beareth fruit, and bringeth forth, some a hundredfold, some sixty, some thirty."

Another parable put he forth unto them, saying: "The kingdom of heaven is likened unto a man that sowed good seed in his field; but while men slept, his enemy came and sowed tares among the wheat, and went away. When the blade sprang up, and brought forth fruit, then appeared the tares also. So the servants of the householder came and said: "Sir, didst thou not sow good seed in thy field? Whence then hath it tares?"

He said: "An enemy hath done this."

The servants say unto him: "Wilt thou then that we go and gather them up?"

He said: "Nay, lest while ye gather up the tares, ye root up the wheat with them. Let both grow together until the harvest, and in the time of the harvest I will say to the reapers: 'Gather up first the tares, and bind them in bundles to burn them; but gather the wheat into my barn.'"

Another parable set he before them, saying: "The kingdom of heaven is like unto a grain of mustard seed, which a man took, and sowed in his field; which indeed is the least of all seeds; but when it is grown, it is the greatest among herbs, so that the birds of the air come and lodge in the branches thereof."

His disciples said: "Explain unto us the parable of the tares of the field."

He answered: "He that soweth the good seed is the Son of Man. The field is the world. The good seed are the children of the kingdom, and the tares are the children of the evil one. The enemy that sowed them is the devil. The harvest is the end of the world, and the reapers are the angels. As therefore the tares are gathered up and burned with fire, so shall it be in the end of the world. The Son of Man shall send forth his angels, and they shall gather out of his kingdom all things that cause stumbling, and them that do iniquity, and shall cast them into a furnace of fire. There shall be weeping and gnashing of teeth. Then shall the righteous shine forth as the sun in the kingdom of their Father.

"Again, the kingdom of heaven is like unto a merchant seeking goodly pearls, who found one pearl of great price, and went and sold all that he had, and bought it."

When even was come, he went into a boat with his disciples; and he said: "Let us go over unto the other side of the lake;" and they launched forth.

But as they sailed he fell asleep; and there came a storm of wind on the lake, and the waves beat into the boat, insomuch that it was now filling. He himself was in the stern, asleep. They came to him, and awoke him, saying: "Lord, save us. We perish."

He saith unto them: "Why are ye fearful, O ye of little faith?"

Then he arose, and rebuked the winds and the sea; and there was a calm; and the men marvelled, saying:

"What manner of man is this, that even the winds and the sea obey him?"

They came to the other side of the sea, and there met him a man with an unclean spirit, who had his dwelling in the tombs. He had been often bound with fetters and chains, and the chains had been rent asunder by him, and the fetters broken in pieces; and no man had strength to tame him. Always, night and day, in the tombs and in the mountains, he was crying out, and cutting himself with stones. When he saw Jesus, he ran and worshipped him; and cried with a loud voice, and said: "What have I to do with thee, Jesus, thou Son of the Most High God? I adjure thee, torment me not."

Jesus asked him: "What is thy name?"

He said: "My name is Legion;" for many devils were entered into him.

Now there was afar off a herd of many swine feeding; and the devils besought Jesus, saying: "If thou cast us out, send us into the herd of swine."

He said unto them: "Go;" and they came out, and went into the swine; and behold, the whole herd rushed down the steep into the sea, and perished in the waters.

When they that fed them saw what had come to pass, they fled, and went away into the city, and told everything. The whole city came to Jesus, and found the man, from whom the devils were gone out, sitting, clothed and in his right mind, at the feet of Jesus; and they besought Jesus that he would depart from their borders.

Jesus had crossed over again in the boat, and there cometh one of the rulers of the synagogue, Jairus by name, and fell at his feet, and besought him greatly, saying: "My little daughter is at the point of death. I pray thee, that thou come and lay thy hands on her, that she may live."

Jesus went, and a great multitude followed, and they thronged him. A woman having an issue of blood twelve years, who had spent all her living on physicians, and could not be healed of any, but rather grew worse, having heard concerning Jesus, came behind him, and touched the border of his garment; for she said within herself: "If I do but touch his garment I shall be made whole."

Immediately the issue of her blood stanched. Jesus said: "Who touched me?"

His disciples said unto him: "Thou seest the multitude thronging thee, and sayest thou: 'Who touched me?'"

He looked round about to see who had done this thing. The woman fearing and trembling, came and fell down before him, and told him all. He said unto her: "Daughter, thy faith hath made thee whole."

While he yet spake, there cometh one from the ruler of the synagogue's house, saying: "Thy daughter is dead. Trouble not the Master."

But Jesus hearing it, answered: "Fear not. Only believe."

When he came to the house, he suffered not any man to go in with him, save Peter, and John, and James, and the father of the maiden and her mother; and all were weeping, and bewailing her. He said: "Weep not, for she is not dead, but sleepeth."

They laughed him to scorn, knowing that she was dead; but he took her by the hand, and called, saying: "Maiden, arise;" and her spirit returned, and she rose up immediately; and he commanded that something be given her to eat.

When Jesus saw the multitudes, he was moved with compassion for them, because they were distressed and scattered, as sheep not having a shepherd. Then saith he unto his disciples: "The harvest truly is plenteous, but the laborers few;" and he began to send forth his twelve disciples by two and two, and he gave them authority over unclean spirits, and to heal all manner of sickness.

He charged them that they should take nothing for their journey, save a staff, and to go shod with sandals, and said: "Whosoever shall not receive you, nor hear your words, as ye go forth out of that house or that city, shake off the dust of your feet for a testimony against them. Behold, I send you forth as sheep in the midst of wolves. Be ye therefore wise as serpents, and harmless as doves. They will deliver you up to councils, and in their synagogues they will scourge you; yea and before governors and kings shall ye be brought for my sake.

But when they deliver you up, be not anxious how or what ye shall speak. It shall be given you in that hour what ye shall speak; for it is not ye that speak, but the Spirit of your Father that speaketh in you. Ye shall be hated of all men for my sake; but he that endureth to the end, shall be saved. Be not afraid of them that kill the body, but are not able to kill the soul. Rather fear Him who is able to destroy both soul and body in hell. Are not two sparrows sold for a farthing? and not one of them shall fall on the ground without your Father. The very hairs of your head are numbered. Fear not therefore. Ye are of more value than many sparrows. Everyone who shall confess me before men, him will I also confess before my Father who is in heaven. But whosoever shall deny me before men, him will I also deny before my Father who is in heaven.

"He that receiveth you receiveth me, and he that receiveth me receiveth Him that sent me; and whosoever shall give to drink unto one of these little ones a cup of cold water, in the name of a disciple, verily I say unto you, he shall in no wise lose his reward."

When Jesus had made an end of commanding his twelve disciples, they departed, and went through the villages preaching the gospel and healing everywhere.

Herod the tetrarch heard of all that was done, and he was much perplexed, because it was said by some, that John was risen from the dead; and by some, that

Elijah had appeared. Herod said: "John I beheaded. Who is this?"

For Herod had laid hold on John, and bound him, and put him in prison for the sake of Herodias, his brother Philip's wife. He had married her, and John had said unto him: "It is not lawful for thee to have her."

When Herod would have put John to death, he feared the multitude, because they counted him as a prophet. Herod on his birthday made a supper to his lords, and the high captains, and the chief men of Galilee; and when the daughter of Herodias came in and danced, she pleased Herod and them that sat at meat with him. The king said unto the damsel: "Ask of me whatsoever thou wilt, and I will give it thee, unto the half of the kingdom."

She went out, and said to her mother: "What shall I ask?"

Her mother said: "The head of John the Baptist."

She came in straightway unto the king, saying: "I will that thou give me on a platter the head of John the Baptist."

The king was exceeding sorry; but for the sake of his oath, and of them that sat at meat, he would not reject her; and the king sent forth a soldier of his guard; and he went and beheaded John in the prison, and brought his head on a platter, and gave it to the damsel, and the damsel gave it to her mother. John's disciples came and took up his corpse, and laid it in a tomb, and they went and told Jesus.

The apostles, when they returned, declared unto Jesus what things they had done, and he said unto them: "Come ye apart into a desert place and rest a while;" for there were many coming and going, and they had no leisure so much as to eat.

They went away in a boat, and the people saw them going, and they followed on foot from all the cities. He came forth, and he began to teach them many things. When the day was far spent, his disciples came unto him, and said: "Send them away, that they may go into the villages round about, and buy themselves somewhat to eat."

He answered: "Give ye them to eat."

They say unto him: "Shall we go and buy two hundred pennyworth of bread, and give them to eat?"

Andrew saith: "There is a lad here who hath five barley loaves, and two fishes; but what are these among so many?"

Jesus commanded that all should sit down by companies on the green grass; and they sat down in ranks, by hundreds, and by fifties, and he took the five loaves and the two fishes, and looking up to heaven, blessed them, and brake, and gave to his disciples to set before the multitude. They did eat, and were all filled, and he saith unto his disciples: "Gather up the fragments which remain over, that nothing be lost."

So they gathered them up, and filled twelve baskets; and they that did eat were about five thousand men, besides women and children.

When the people saw the miracle that Jesus did, they said: "This is of a truth the prophet that cometh into the world."

Jesus perceived that they were about to take him by force, to make him king, and he withdrew into a mountain alone. His disciples entered into a boat, and were going over to Capernaum. It was now dark, and the sea arose by reason of a great wind that blew. The boat was in the midst of the sea, tossed by the waves, and in the fourth watch of the night Jesus came, walking on the sea. When the disciples saw him, they were troubled, saying: "It is an apparition;" and they cried out for fear.

But Jesus spake unto them, saying: "Be of good cheer. It is I."

Peter said: "Lord, if it be thou, bid me come unto thee on the water."

Jesus said: "Come."

Peter went from the boat, and walked on the water; but when he saw that the wind was boisterous, he was afraid. He began to sink, and he cried out: "Lord, save me."

Immediately Jesus stretched forth his hand, and caught him, and said: "O thou of little faith, wherefore didst thou doubt?"

When they were come into the boat, the wind ceased, and straightway the boat was at the land whither they were going. When they were come out of the boat, the people knew him, and ran about that whole region, and began to carry on their beds those that were sick, where they heard he was. Wheresoever he entered, into villages, or into cities, or into the country, they laid the sick in the market places, and besought him that they might touch if it were but the border of his garment; and as many as touched it were made whole.

Jesus withdrew into the borders of Tyre and Sidon, and behold, a Canaanitish woman came, and cried, saying: "O Lord, my daughter is grievously vexed with a devil."

But he answered not a word. His disciples besought him, saying: "Send her away; for she crieth after us."

She came and worshipped him, saying: "Lord, help me."

He answered: "It is not meet to take the children's bread, and cast it to the dogs."

She said: "Yea, Lord; yet the dogs eat of the crumbs which fall from their masters' table.

Then Jesus said: "O woman, great is thy faith. Be it done unto thee even as thou wilt;" and her daughter was healed from that hour.

Jesus came nigh unto the sea of Galilee; and he went up into a mountain. They bring unto him one that was deaf, and had an impediment in his speech; and they beseech him to lay his hand on him. He took him aside from the multitude, and put his fingers into his ears, and he spat, and touched his tongue, and looking up to heaven, he sighed, and saith: "Be opened;" and his ears were opened, and the bond of his tongue was loosed, and he spake plain.

Jesus called unto him his disciples, and said: "I have compassion on the multitude, because they continue with me now three days and have nothing to eat, and I would not send them away fasting, lest they faint on the way."

The disciples say unto him: "Whence should we have so much bread in a desert place, as to fill so great a multitude?"

Jesus saith: "How many loaves have ye?"

They said: "Seven, and a few little fishes."

He commanded the multitude to sit down, and he took the seven loaves and the fishes, and gave thanks and brake, and gave to the disciples, and the disciples to the multitude. They did all eat, and were filled; and they took up that which remained over of the broken pieces, seven baskets full; and they that did eat were about four thousand.

Jesus came to Bethsaida, and they bring to him a blind man, and beseech him to touch him. He took the blind man by the hand, and led him out of the village; and when he had spit on his eyes, and put his hands on him, he asked: "Seest thou aught?"

He looked up, and said: "I see men as trees, walking."

Then again Jesus laid his hands on his eyes; and he looked steadfastly, and was restored, and saw all things clearly.

Jesus asked his disciples: "Who do men say that I am?"

They answered: "John the Baptist; and others, that one of the old prophets is risen."

He saith unto them: "But who say ye that I am?"

Simon Peter answered: "Thou art the Christ, the Son of the living God."

Jesus said unto him: "Blessed art thou, Simon. Thou art Peter, and on this rock I will build my church. I will give unto thee the keys of the kingdom of heaven."

From that time began Jesus to show his disciples that he must go unto Jerusalem, and suffer many things of the elders and chief priests and scribes, and be killed, and the third day be raised up. Peter began to rebuke him, saying: "Be it far from thee, Lord. This shall never be unto thee."

But he turned, and said unto Peter: "Get thee behind me, Satan. Thou art an offence unto me; for thou mindest not the things of God, but those that be of men."

Then said Jesus unto his disciples: "If any man would come after me, let him deny himself, and take up his cross, and follow me. For whosoever would save his life shall lose it; and whosoever shall lose his life for my sake shall find it. What is a man profited if he gain the whole world, and forfeit his life? For the Son of Man shall come in the glory of his Father with his angels, and then shall he render unto every man according to his deeds. Verily I say unto you: 'There be some standing here, who shall not taste of death, till they see the Son of Man coming in his kingdom.'"

Jesus taketh Peter, and James, and John his brother, and bringeth them up into a high mountain apart; and he was transfigured before them. His face did shine as the sun, and his garments became white as the light, and there appeared Moses and Elijah talking with him. Peter said unto Jesus: "Lord, it is good for us to be here. If thou wilt, I will make three tabernacles, one for thee, and one for Moses, and one for Elijah."

While he was yet speaking, a bright cloud overshadowed them; and behold, a voice out of the cloud, which said: "This is my beloved Son, in whom I am well pleased. Hear ye him."

The disciples fell on their faces, and were sore afraid, and Jesus came and touched them, and said: "Arise, and be not afraid;" and lifting up their eyes, they saw no one, save Jesus only.

When they were come down from the mountain, a great multitude met them, and a man from the multitude cried, saying: "Master, I beseech thee to look on my son; for he is mine only child, and he is epileptic and suffereth grievously. Oft-times he falleth into the fire, and oft-times into the water; and I brought him to thy disciples, and they could not cure him."

Jesus said: "Bring him to me."

They brought him, and straightway the spirit tare him, and he fell on the ground, and wallowed foaming. Jesus asked his father: "How long time is it since this hath come unto him?"

He said: "From a child. If thou canst do anything, have compassion on us, and help us."

Jesus saith: "All things are possible to him that believeth."

The father of the child cried out, and said: "I believe. Help thou mine unbelief."

Jesus rebuked the unclean spirit, saying: "I command thee, come out of him."

Having convulsed him much, it came out; and the child became as one dead; insomuch that many said: "He is dead."

But Jesus took him by the hand, and the boy arose, and was cured from that hour. Then came the disciples to Jesus apart, and said: "Why could not we cast it out?"

He said unto them: "Because of your little faith."

There arose a reasoning among the disciples, which of them should be greatest in the kingdom of heaven.

Jesus took a little child, and set him in the midst of them, and said: "Verily I say unto you: 'Except ye become as little children, ye shall in no wise enter into the kingdom of heaven. Whosoever therefore shall humble himself as this little child, the same is the greatest in the kingdom of heaven; and whoso shall receive one such little child in my name receiveth me. But whoso shall cause one of these little ones that believe on me to stumble, it is better for him that a millstone should be hanged about his neck, and that he should be sunk in the depth of the sea.'"

Peter said to him: "Lord, how oft shall my brother sin against me, and I forgive him?—until seven times?"

Jesus saith: "I say not unto thee: 'Until seven times;' but: 'Until seventy times seven.' Therefore is the kingdom of heaven likened unto a certain king, who would make a reckoning with his servants. One was brought unto him, that owed him ten thousand talents. But forasmuch as he had not wherewith to pay, his lord commanded him to be sold, and his wife, and children, and all that he had, and payment to be made. The servant fell down and worshipped him, saying: 'Lord, have patience with me, and I will pay thee all.'

"Then the lord of that servant was moved with compassion, and forgave him the debt. But that servant went out, and found one of his fellow-servants, who owed him a hundred pence, and he laid hold on him, and took him by the throat, saying: 'Pay that thou owest.'

"His fellow-servant fell down and besought him, saying: 'Have patience with me, and I will pay thee.'

"He would not; but cast him into prison, till he should pay that which was due. When his fellow-servants saw what was done, they were very sorry, and came and told their lord all that was done. Then his lord called him, and said: 'Thou wicked servant, I forgave thee all that debt, because thou besoughtest me. Shouldest not thou also have had mercy?' and his lord was wroth, and delivered him to the tormentors, till he should pay all that was due.

"So shall my heavenly Father do unto you, if ye forgive not every one his brother."

It came to pass that Jesus steadfastly set his face to go to Jerusalem; and on the way, a certain man said unto him: "I will follow thee whithersoever thou goest."

Jesus said: "The foxes have holes, and the birds have nests; but the Son of Man hath not where to lay his head."

He said unto another: "Follow me."

But he said: "Lord, suffer me first to go and bury my father."

Jesus said unto him: "Leave the dead to bury their own dead; but go thou and preach the kingdom of God."

Another said: "I will follow thee, Lord; but first suffer me to bid farewell to them that are at my house."

Jesus said unto him: "No man having put his hand to the plough, and looking back, is fit for the kingdom of God."

After these things the Lord appointed seventy others, and sent them two and two into every city and place, whither he himself was about to come; and he said: "Carry no purse, no wallet, no shoes; and into whatsoever house ye enter, in that house remain, eating and drinking such things as they give; for the laborer is worthy of his hire."

A certain lawyer tempted Jesus, saying: "Master, what shall I do to inherit eternal life?"

Jesus said unto him: "What is written in the law?"

He answering said: "Thou shalt love the Lord thy God with all thy heart, and thy neighbor as thyself."

Jesus said: "Thou hast answered right. This do and thou shalt live."

He said: "And who is my neighbor?"

Jesus made answer: "A certain man was going from Jerusalem to Jericho; and he fell among thieves, who stripped him and beat him, and departed, leaving him half dead. By chance a priest was going that way; and when he saw him, he passed by on the other side. In like manner a Levite, when he came to the place and saw him, passed by on the other side. But a Samaritan, as he journeyed, came where he was; and was moved with compassion, and bound up his wounds, pouring on them oil and wine; and he set him on his own beast, and brought him to an inn, and took care of him. On the morrow he took out two shillings, and gave them to the host, and said: 'Take care of him, and whatsoever thou spendest more, I will repay thee, when I come again.'

"Which of these three, thinkest thou, proved neighbor unto him that fell among the thieves?"

The lawyer said: "He that showed mercy on him."

Jesus said: "Go, and do thou likewise."

Jesus entered into a village, and a woman named Martha received him into her house. She had a sister Mary, who sat at the Lord's feet, and heard his words. But Martha was cumbered with much serving; and she came, and said: "Lord, dost thou not care that my sister did leave me to serve alone? Bid her therefore that she help me."

Jesus answered: "Martha, Martha, thou art anxious and troubled about many things; but Mary hath chosen the good part, which shall not be taken away from her."

As Jesus passed by, he saw a man blind from his birth; and he spat on the ground, and made clay of the spittle, and anointed the eyes of the blind man with the clay, and said: "Go, wash in the pool of Siloam."

The man went away therefore, and washed, and came seeing. The neighbors said: "Is not this he that sat and begged?"

Some said: "This is he."

Others said: "No, but he is like him."

He said: "I am he."

They said unto him: "How then were thine eyes opened?"

He answered: "The man that is called Jesus made clay, and anointed mine eyes, and said: 'Go to Siloam and wash.' So I went and washed, and I received sight."

They brought to the Pharisees him that aforetime was blind. Now it was the Sabbath when Jesus opened his eyes. The Pharisees also asked him how he received his sight. He said unto them: "He put clay on mine eyes, and I washed, and do see."

Some of the Pharisees said: "This man is not from God, because he keepeth not the Sabbath."

Others said: "How can a man that is a sinner do such miracles?" and there was a division among them.

They say unto the man again: "What sayest thou of him, in that he opened thine eyes?"

He said: "He is a prophet."

The Jews did not believe that the man had been blind, and had received his sight, until they called his parents, and asked them: "Is this your son, who ye say was born blind? How then doth he now see?"

His parents answered: "We know that this is our son, and that he was born blind; but by what means he now seeth, we know not. Ask him. He shall speak for himself."

The Jews called a second time the man that was blind, and said unto him: "We know that this man is a sinner."

He answered: "Whether he be a sinner, I know not. One thing I know, that, whereas I was blind, now I see."

They said unto him: "What did he to thee? How opened he thine eyes?"

He answered: "I have told you already. Wherefore would ye hear it again? Would ye also become his disciples?"

They reviled him, and said: "Thou art his disciple, but we are disciples of Moses. We know that God spake unto Moses; but as for this fellow, we know not whence he is."

The man answered: "Why, herein is the marvel, that ye know not whence he is, and yet he opened mine eyes. Since the world began it was never heard that anyone opened the eyes of a man born blind. If this man were not of God, he could do nothing."

They said unto him: "Thou wast altogether born in sins, and dost thou teach us?" and they cast him out.

Jesus heard that they had cast him out; and finding him, said: "Dost thou believe on the Son of God?"

He said: "Lord, I believe;" and he worshipped him.

Jesus said: "For judgment came I into this world, that they who see not may see; and that they who see may become blind."

Some of the Pharisees who were with him said: "Are we also blind?"

Jesus said: "Verily, verily, I say unto you: 'He that entereth not by the door into the sheepfold, but climbeth up some other way, the same is a thief and a robber. But he that entereth in by the door is the shepherd of the sheep. To him the porter openeth, and he calleth his own sheep by name, and leadeth them out. When he hath put forth all his own, he goeth before them, and the sheep follow him; for they know his voice. A stranger will they not follow, but will flee from him. I am the good shepherd. The good shepherd layeth down his life for the sheep. He that is a hireling seeth the wolf coming, and leaveth the sheep, and fleeth, and the wolf catcheth them, and scattereth them. I am the good shepherd; and other sheep I have, which are not of this fold. Them also I must bring, and they shall hear my voice.'"

There arose a division among the Jews because of these words; and many of them said: "He hath a devil, and is mad. Why hear ye him?"

Others said: "These are not the words of one that hath a devil. Can a devil open the eyes of the blind?"

It was the feast of the dedication at Jerusalem; and Jesus walked in the temple in Solomon's porch. The Jews came round about him, and said: "If thou art the Christ, tell us plainly."

Jesus answered: "I told you, and ye believe not. The works that I do in my Father's name—these bear witness of me. I and my Father are one."

The Jews took up stones to stone him. Jesus said: "Many good works have I showed you. For which of those works do ye stone me?"

The Jews answered: "For a good work we stone thee not, but for blasphemy, and because thou, being a man, makest thyself God."

Jesus answered: "If I do not the works of my Father, believe me not. But if I do them, though ye believe not me, believe the works, that ye may know that the Father is in me, and I in the Father."

They sought to take him; but he escaped out of their hand.

At another time, when many thousands were gathered together, one said unto him: "Master, bid my brother divide the inheritance with me."

But he said: "Man, who made me a judge or a divider over you?" and he said unto the multitude: "Take heed, and keep yourselves from covetousness; for a man's life consisteth not in the abundance of the things which he possesseth."

He spake a parable saying: "The ground of a certain rich man brought forth plentifully; and he reasoned with himself: 'What shall I do, because I have not where to bestow my fruits?' He said: 'This will I do: I will pull down my barns, and build greater, and there will I bestow all my goods; and I will say to my soul: "Soul, thou hast much goods laid up for many years. Take thine ease, eat, drink, and be merry."

"But God said unto him: 'Thou fool, this night is thy soul required of thee, and the things which thou hast provided, whose shall they be?'

"So is he that layeth up treasure for himself, and is not rich toward God."

Jesus was teaching in one of the synagogues on the Sabbath Day; and behold, a woman that had a spirit of infirmity eighteen years, and she was bowed together, and could in no wise lift herself up. Jesus called her, and said: "Woman, thou art loosed from thine infirmity."

He laid his hands on her, and immediately she was made straight, and glorified God.

The ruler of the synagogue, being moved with indignation because Jesus had healed on the Sabbath, said to the people: "There are six days in which men ought to work. In them therefore come and be healed, and not on the Sabbath."

But the Lord said: "Doth not each one of you on the Sabbath loose his ox or his ass from the stall, and lead him away to watering? and ought not this woman, whom Satan had bound, lo, these eighteen years, to have been loosed from this bond on the Sabbath?"

As he said these things, his adversaries were put to shame, and the people rejoiced for all the glorious things that were done by him.

He went on his way through cities and villages, and one said unto him: "Lord, are they few that be saved?"

He said: "Strive to enter in by the narrow door; for many shall seek to enter in, and shall not be able. When once the master of the house is risen up, and hath shut the door, and ye stand without, and knock, saying: 'Lord, open to us;' he shall answer: 'I know not whence ye are.' Then shall ye say: 'We did eat and drink in thy presence, and thou didst teach in our streets.' He shall say: 'I know not whence ye are. Depart from me, all ye workers of iniquity.'"

Jesus went into the house of one of the rulers of the Pharisees to eat; and he spake a parable unto those that were bidden, when he marked how they chose out the chief seats, saying: "When thou art bidden to a marriage feast, sit not down in the chief seat; lest a more honorable man than thou be bidden, and he that bade thee shall come and say: 'Give this man place.' But sit in the lowest place, that when he that hath bidden thee cometh, he may say: 'Friend, go up higher.' Then shalt thou have glory in the presence of all that sit at meat with thee. For whosoever exalteth himself shall be humbled, and he that humbleth himself shall be exalted."

One of them that sat at meat said: "Blessed is he that shall eat bread in the kingdom of God."

Jesus said: "A certain man made a great supper, and bade many; and he sent forth his servant at supper time to say to them that were bidden: 'Come; for all things are now ready.' They all began to make excuse. The first said: 'I have bought a field, and I must needs go and see it. I pray thee have me excused.' Another said: 'I have bought five yoke of oxen, and I go to prove them. I pray thee have me excused.' Another said: 'I have married a wife, and therefore I cannot come.' The servant came and told his lord these things. Then the master of the house being angry said to his servant: 'Go out quickly into the streets and lanes of the city, and bring in hither the poor and maimed and blind and lame; for none of those men that were bidden shall taste of my supper.'"

There went with Jesus great multitudes; and the Pharisees and scribes murmured, saying: "This man receiveth sinners, and eateth with them."

He spake unto them, saying: "What man of you, having a hundred sheep, if he lose one of them, doth not leave the ninety and nine in the wilderness, and go after that which is lost, until he find it? When he hath found it, he layeth it on his shoulders, rejoicing; and when he cometh home, he calleth together his friends and his neighbors, saying unto them: 'Rejoice with me, for I have found my sheep which was lost.' I say unto you, that even so there shall be joy in heaven over one sinner that repenteth, more than over ninety and nine righteous persons, who need no repentance.

"Or what woman having ten pieces of silver, if she lose one piece, doth not light a lamp, and sweep the house, and seek diligently until she find it; and when she hath found it, she calleth together her friends and neighbors, saying: 'Rejoice with me; for I have found the piece which I had lost.' Even so, I say unto you, there is joy in the presence of the angels of God over one sinner that repenteth.

"A certain man had two sons; and the younger said to his father: 'Give me the portion of thy substance that falleth to me.' The father divided unto them his living, and the younger son gathered all together, and took his journey into a far country; and there he wasted his substance with riotous living. When he had spent all, there arose a mighty famine in that country; and he began to be in want, and he went and joined himself to a citizen of that country, who sent him into his fields to feed swine. He would fain have been filled with the husks that the swine did eat, and no man gave unto him. He said: 'How many servants of my father's have bread enough and to spare, and I perish here with hunger! I will arise and go to my father, and will say unto him: "Father, I have sinned against heaven, and in thy sight, and am no more worthy to be called thy son. Make me as one of thy hired servants."

"He arose, and came to his father. While he was yet afar off, his father saw him, and was moved with compassion, and ran, and fell on his neck, and kissed him. The son said: 'Father, I have sinned against heaven, and in thy sight, and am no more worthy to be called thy son.'

The prodigal son

"But the father said to his servants: 'Bring forth the best robe, and put it on him; and put a ring on his hand, and shoes on his feet; and bring the fatted calf, and kill it, and let us eat and make merry; for this my son was dead, and is alive; he was lost, and is found;' and they began to be merry.

"Now his elder son was in the field, and as he came and drew nigh to the house, he heard music and dancing. He called one of the servants and asked what these things meant. The servant said: 'Thy brother is come, and thy father hath killed the fatted calf, because he hath received him safe and sound.' The elder son was angry, and would not go in; and his father came out and entreated him. He said to his father: 'Lo, these many years do I serve thee, and I never transgressed a commandment of thine; and yet thou never gavest me a kid, that I might make merry with my friends. But as soon as this thy son came who hath devoured thy living with sinners, thou killed for him the fatted calf.' His father said: 'Son, thou art ever with me, and all that I have is thine. But it was meet to make merry and be glad; for this thy brother was dead, and is alive; and was lost, and is found.'"

The Pharisees heard all these things, and they derided. Jesus said unto them: "Ye are they that justify yourselves in the sight of men; but God knoweth your hearts. There was a certain rich man, and he was clothed in purple and fine linen, and fared sumptuously every day; and a beggar named Lazarus was laid at his gate, full of sores, and desiring to be fed with the crumbs that fell from the rich man's table. It came to pass, that the beggar died, and he was carried away by the angels into Abraham's bosom. The rich man also died, and in hell he lifted up 'his eyes, being in torments, and seeth Abraham afar off, and Lazarus in his bosom. He cried and said: 'Father Abraham, have mercy on me, and send Lazarus, that he may dip the tip of his finger in water, and cool my tongue; for I am in anguish in this flame.' But Abraham said: 'Son, remember that thou in thy lifetime receivedst thy good things, and Lazarus evil things; but now he is comforted, and thou art in anguish. Besides all this, between us and you there is a great gulf fixed, so that they who would pass hence to you cannot.' The rich man said: 'I pray thee, that thou wouldest send him to my father's house; for I have five brethren, that he may testify unto them, lest they also come unto this place of torment.' Abraham saith: 'They have Moses and the prophets. Let them hear them.' He said: 'Nay, father Abraham; but if one go to them from the dead, they will repent.' Abraham said unto him: 'If they hear not Moses and the prophets, neither will they be persuaded, if one rise from the dead.'"

Lazarus, the brother of Mary and Martha, was sick. His sisters therefore sent, saying: "Lord, behold, he whom thou lovest is sick."

When Jesus heard it, he abode two days in the place where he was. Then he saith to the disciples: "Let us go into Judæa again."

The disciples say unto him: "Rabbi, the Jews of late sought to stone thee; and goest thou thither again?"

Jesus saith: "Our friend Lazarus is fallen asleep. I go, that I may awake him."

The disciples said: "Lord, if he is fallen asleep, he will recover."

Howbeit Jesus had spoken of his death; but they thought he spake of taking rest in sleep. Then Jesus said unto them plainly: "Lazarus is dead. Let us go unto him."

When Jesus came, he found that he had been in the tomb four days. Many of the Jews had come to Martha and Mary, to comfort them concerning their brother. Martha, as soon as she heard that Jesus was coming, went and met him; but Mary still sat in the house. Martha said unto Jesus: "Lord, if thou hadst been here, my brother had not died."

Jesus saith unto her: "Thy brother shall rise."

Martha saith: "I know that he shall rise in the resurrection at the last day."

Jesus said: "I am the resurrection, and the life. He that believeth on me, though he die, yet shall he live."

Martha went and called Mary her sister secretly, saying: "The Master is here, and calleth thee."

Mary arose quickly, and went unto him. (Jesus was not yet come into the village, but was where Martha met him.) The Jews who were with Mary in the house, when they saw that she rose and went out, followed her, supposing that she was going unto the tomb to weep there. Mary, when she came where Jesus was, and saw him, fell down at his feet, saying unto him: "Lord, if thou hadst been here, my brother had not died."

When Jesus saw her weeping, and the Jews also weeping who came with her, he said: "Where have ye laid him?"

They say: "Lord, come and see."

Jesus wept. The Jews said: "Behold how he loved him!"

Jesus cometh to the tomb. It was a cave, and a stone lay against it. Jesus saith: "Take ye away the stone."

So they took away the stone; and Jesus lifted up his eyes, and said: "Father, I thank thee that thou hast heard me;" and he cried with a loud voice: "Lazarus, come forth."

He that was dead came forth, bound hand and foot with grave-clothes. Jesus saith unto them: "Loose him, and let him go."

Many of the Jews, who beheld that which he did believed on him. But some of them went away to the Pharisees, and told them what things Jesus had done. The chief priests therefore and the Pharisees gathered a council, and said: "This man doeth many miracles. If we let him alone, all men will believe on him; and the Romans will come and take away our nation. Caiaphas, being high priest that year, said: "It is expedient that one man should die for the people, and that the whole nation perish not."

So from that day they took counsel that they might put Jesus to death. Jesus therefore walked no more openly among the Jews; but departed into the country near to the wilderness, into a city called Ephraim; and there he tarried with his disciples.

As he entered a certain village, there met him ten men that were lepers, who stood afar off, and lifted up their voices, saying: "Jesus, Master, have mercy on us."

He said unto them: "Go and show yourselves unto the priests."

As they went, they were cleansed; and one of them, when he saw that he was healed, turned back, glorifying God, and giving Jesus thanks; and he was a Samaritan.

Jesus said: "Were not ten cleansed? But where are the nine? Were there none that returned to give glory to God, save this stranger?" and he said unto him: "Arise, and go thy way. Thy faith hath made thee whole."

Being asked by the Pharisees, when the kingdom of God should come, he answered: "The kingdom of God cometh not with observation. Neither shall they say: 'Lo, here!' or, 'Lo, there!' For the kingdom of God is within you."

He spake a parable unto his disciples to the end that men ought always to pray, and not to faint, saying: "There was in a city a judge, who feared not God, and regarded not man; and there was a widow in that city; and she came oft unto him, saying: 'Avenge me of mine adversary.' He would not for a while; but afterward he said within himself: 'Though I fear not God, nor regard man; yet because this widow troubleth me, I will avenge her, lest she wear me out by her continual coming.' The Lord said: 'Hear what the unrighteous judge saith; and shall not God avenge his elect, that cry to him day and night?' I say unto you, that he will avenge them speedily."

He spake also this parable unto certain who trusted in themselves that they were righteous, and set all others at naught. "Two men went up into the temple to pray, the one a Pharisee, and the other a publican. The Pharisee stood and prayed thus with himself: 'God, I thank thee, that I am not as the rest of men, extortioners, unjust, or even as this publican. I fast twice in the week. I give tithes of all that I get.' But the publican, standing afar off, would not lift up so much as his eyes unto heaven, but smote his breast, saying: 'God, be merciful to me a sinner.' I tell you: 'This man went to his house justified rather than the other.'"

They brought unto him little children, that he should touch them; and the disciples rebuked them. But Jesus was moved with indignation, and said: "Suffer the little children to come unto me, and forbid them not; for of such is the kingdom of God;" and he took them in his arms, and blessed them.

As he was going forth on his way, there ran one to him, and kneeled, and asked: "Good master, what shall I do that I may inherit eternal life?"

Jesus said unto him: "Thou knowest the commandments."

He said: "Master, all these have I observed from my youth."

Jesus looking on him loved him, and said: "One thing thou lackest. Go, sell whatsoever thou hast, and give to the poor, and thou shalt have treasure in heaven; and come, follow me."

But his countenance fell at the saying; and he went away sorrowful; for he had great possessions. Jesus saith unto his disciples: "It is easier for a camel to go through the eye of a needle than for a rich man to enter into the kingdom of God."

They were astonished exceedingly, saying unto him: "Who then can be saved?"

Jesus said: "With men this is impossible; but with God all things are possible."

Peter said: "Lo, we have left all, and followed thee What then shall we have?"

Jesus said: "Verily I say unto you that every one that hath left houses, or brethren, or sisters, or father, or mother, or children, or lands, for my name's sake, shall receive a hundredfold, and shall inherit eternal life. But many shall be last that are first. For the kingdom of heaven is like unto a man that is a householder, who went out early in the morning to hire laborers into his vineyard; and when he had agreed with them for a shilling a day, he sent them into his vineyard. He went out about the third hour, and saw others standing idle in the marketplace; and to them he said: 'Go ye also into the vineyard, and whatsoever is right I will give you;' and they went. Again he went out about the sixth and the ninth hour, and did likewise. About the eleventh hour he went out, and found others standing; and he saith unto them: 'Why stand ye here all the day idle?' They say: 'Because no man hath hired us.' He saith: 'Go ye also into the vineyard.'

"When even was come, the lord of the vineyard saith unto his steward: 'Call the laborers, and pay them their hire, beginning from the last unto the first.' They that were hired about the eleventh hour received every man a shilling. The first likewise received every man a shilling; and they murmured against the householder, saying: 'These last have spent but one hour, and thou hast made them equal unto us, who have borne the burden of the day and the scorching heat.' He said to one of them: 'Friend, I do thee no wrong. Didst not thou agree with me for a shilling? Take that which is thine, and go thy way. It is my will to give unto this last, even as unto thee. Is it not lawful for me to do what I will with mine own?' So the last shall be first, and the first last."

Jesus took unto him the twelve, and said: "Behold, we go to Jerusalem, and the Son of Man shall be delivered up unto the Gentiles, and shall be shamefully treated; and they shall scourge and kill him, and the third day he shall rise."

There came near unto him James and John, the sons of Zebedee, saying: "Master, we would that thou shouldest do for us whatsoever we shall ask of thee."

He said: "What would ye that I should do for you?"

They said: "Grant unto us that we may sit, one on thy right hand, and one on thy left hand, in thy glory."

Jesus said: "Ye know not what ye ask. Are ye able to drink the cup that I drink? and be baptized with the baptism that I am baptized with?"

They said: "We are able."

Jesus said: "The cup that I drink ye shall drink; and with the baptism that I am baptized withal shall ye be baptized; but to sit on my right hand and on my left hand is not mine to give; but it is for them for whom it hath been prepared of my Father."

The ten were moved with indignation concerning the two brethren; but Jesus said: "Ye know that the rulers of the Gentiles lord it over them, and their great ones exercise authority over them. Not so shall it be among you. Whoever would be first among you shall be your servant; even as the Son of Man came not to be ministered unto, but to minister, and to give his life a ransom for many."

Jesus was passing through Jericho; and behold, a man named Zacchæus, who was a chief publican, and rich, sought to see Jesus, and could not for the crowd, because he was little of stature; and he ran on before, and climbed up into a sycamore tree to see him. When Jesus came to the place, he looked up, and said: "Zacchæus, make haste, and come down; for today I must abide at thy house."

He made haste, and came down, and received Jesus joyfully. They all murmured, saying: "He is gone in to lodge with a man that is a sinner."

Zacchæus said unto the Lord: "The half of my goods I give to the poor; and if I have wrongfully exacted aught of any man, I restore fourfold."

Jesus said unto him: "Today is salvation come to this house."

Jesus came to Bethany, and they made him a supper there, and Martha served. Mary took a pound of ointment, very costly, and anointed the feet of Jesus; and the house was filled with the odor of the ointment. Judas Iscariot saith: "Why was not this ointment sold for three hundred pence, and given to the poor?"

This he said, not because he cared for the poor, but because he was a thief, and having the bag took away what was put therein. But Jesus said: "Let her alone. She hath wrought a good work on me. Ye have the poor always with you, and whensoever ye will ye can do them good; but me ye have not always. Verily I say unto you: 'Wherever the gospel shall be preached throughout the whole world, that which this woman hath done shall be spoken of for a memorial of her.'"

When they drew nigh unto Jerusalem, and came to the mount of Olives, Jesus sent two disciples, saying: "Go into the village that is over against you, and ye shall find a colt tied, whereon no man ever yet sat. Loose him, and bring him; and if anyone say unto you: 'Why do ye this?' say: 'The Lord hath need of him.'"

They went, and found a colt tied in the street; and they loose him. Certain of them that stood there said: "What do ye, loosing the colt?"

They said unto them even as Jesus had said; and they brought the colt to Jesus, and he sat on him. A great multitude that had come to the feast, when they heard that Jesus was coming to Jerusalem, took branches of palm trees, and went forth to meet him; and many spread their garments in the way, and others branches, which they had cut from the trees; and they that went before, and they that followed, cried: "Hosanna to the son of David: Blessed is he that cometh in the name of the Lord; Hosanna in the highest."

When Jesus drew nigh, he beheld the city and wept over it, saying: "The days shall come, when thine enemies shall dash thee to the ground, and they shall not leave in thee one stone on another."

He entered into Jerusalem, into the temple; and when he had looked round about on all things, it being now eventide, he went out unto Bethany with the twelve. In the morning as he returned to the city, he hungered; and seeing a fig tree by the wayside, he came to it, and found nothing thereon, but leaves only; and he said unto it: "Let no fruit grow on thee henceforward forever."

Immediately the fig tree withered away. The disciples marvelled, and Jesus said unto them: "Verily I say unto you: 'If ye have faith and doubt not, ye shall not only do what is done to the fig tree, but even if ye shall say unto this mountain: "Be thou taken up and cast into the sea," it shall be done. All things whatsoever ye shall ask in prayer, believing, ye shall receive.'"

When he was come into the temple, the chief priests and elders came unto him as he was teaching, and said: "By what authority doest thou these things?"

Jesus answered: "I also will ask you one question, which if ye tell me, I likewise will tell you by what authority I do these things. The baptism of John, whence was it? from heaven or from men?"

They reasoned with themselves, saying: "If we shall say: 'From heaven;' he will say: 'Why then did ye not believe him?' But if we shall say: 'From men;'

we fear the people; for all hold John as a prophet;" and they answered: "We cannot tell."

He said unto them: "Neither tell I you by what authority I do these things. But what think ye? A man had two sons; and he came to the first, and said: 'Son, go work today in the vineyard;' and the son said: 'I will not;' but afterward he repented, and went. He came to the second, and said likewise; and the son said: 'I go, sir;' and went not. Which of the twain did the will of his father?"

They say: "The first."

Jesus saith unto them: "Verily I say unto you, that the publicans and sinners go into the kingdom of God before you. For John came unto you in the way of righteousness, and ye believed him not; but the publicans and sinners believed him; and ye did not even repent afterward.

"Hear another parable. A man planted a vineyard, and let it out to husbandmen, and went into another country for a long time. At the season he sent unto the husbandmen a servant, that they should give him of the fruit of the vineyard; but the husbandmen beat him, and sent him away empty. He sent another servant; and him also they beat, and handled shamefully, and sent him away empty. He sent yet a third, and him they wounded, and cast forth. The lord of the vineyard said: 'What shall I do? I will send my beloved son. It may be they will reverence him.'

But when the husbandmen saw him, they reasoned among themselves, saying: 'This is the heir. Let us kill him, that the inheritance may be ours;' and they killed him. What therefore will the lord of the vineyard do unto them?"

They say unto him: "He will destroy those miserable men, and will let out the vineyard unto other husbandmen, who shall render him the fruits in their seasons."

Jesus saith: "Did ye never read in the scriptures:
'The stone which the builders rejected,
The same was made the head of the corner?'
I say unto you: 'The kingdom of God shall be taken away from you, and shall be given to a nation bringing forth the fruits thereof.' "

The scribes and the chief priests watched him, and sent forth spies, who feigned themselves to be righteous, that they might take hold of his words, so as to deliver him up to the authority of the governor; and they say unto him: "Master, we know that thou art true, and teachest the way of God, and carest not for anyone; for thou regardest not the person of men. Tell us therefore: Is it lawful to give tribute unto Cæsar, or not?"

Jesus perceived their wickedness, and said: "Why tempt ye me, ye hypocrites? Show me the tribute money."

They brought him a penny; and he saith: "Whose is this image and superscription?"

They say unto him: "Cæsar's."

Then saith he unto them: "Render unto Cæsar the things that are Cæsar's, and unto God the things that are God's."

When they heard these words, they marvelled, and went their way.

The Jews said unto him: "What sign showest thou unto us?"

Jesus answered: "Destroy this temple, and in three days I will raise it up."

The Jews said: "Forty and six years was this temple in building, and wilt thou raise it up in three days?"

But he spake of the temple of his body. Then spake Jesus to the multitude, saying: "The scribes and the Pharisees bind heavy burdens and grievous to be borne, and lay them on men's shoulders; but they themselves will not move them with their finger. All their works they do to be seen of men; for they desire to walk in long robes, and love salutations in the marketplaces, and the chief seats in the synagogues, and the chief places at feasts; who devour widows' houses, and for a pretence make long prayers. These shall receive greater condemnation. Woe unto you, scribes and Pharisees, hypocrites! because ye shut the kingdom of heaven against men; for ye go not in yourselves, neither suffer ye them that are entering to go in. Woe unto you, scribes and Pharisees, hypocrites! Ye blind guides, that strain at a gnat, and swallow a camel. Ye are like unto whited sepulchres, which outwardly appear beautiful, but inwardly are full of dead men's bones, and of all uncleanness. Even so ye also outwardly appear righteous unto men, but within ye are full of hypocrisy and iniquity. O Jerusalem, Jerusalem, that killeth the prophets, and stoneth them that are sent unto thee! How often would I have gathered thy children together, even as a hen gathereth her chickens under her wings, and ye would not! Behold, your house is left unto you desolate."

He sat down, and beheld how the people cast money into the treasury; and many that were rich cast in much; and there came a poor widow, and she threw in two mites, which make a farthing. He called his disciples, and said: "Verily I say unto you: 'This poor widow cast in more than all they that are casting into the treasury; for they did cast in of their abundance; but she of her want did cast in all that she had, even all her living.'"

Jesus went out from the temple, and as he sat on the mount of Olives, he began to say unto his disciples: "Ye shall hear of wars and rumors of wars, and there shall be famines and earthquakes, and many false prophets shall arise, and shall lead many astray. After the tribulation of those days, the sun shall be darkened, and the moon shall not give her light, and the stars shall fall from heaven. Then shall all the tribes of the earth see the Son of Man coming on the clouds with power and great glory; and he shall send forth his angels with a great sound of a trumpet, and they shall gather together his elect from one end of heaven to the other. But of that day knoweth no one. Therefore be ye ready; for in an hour that ye think not the Son of Man cometh.

"Then shall the kingdom of heaven be likened unto ten virgins, who took their lamps, and went forth to meet the bridegroom. Five of them were foolish, and five were wise. The foolish, when they took their lamps, took no oil with them; but the wise took oil with their lamps. While the bridegroom tarried, they all slumbered and slept. But at midnight there was a cry: 'Behold, the bridegroom! Come ye out to meet him.' Then all those virgins arose, and trimmed their lamps: and the foolish said unto the wise: 'Give us of your oil, for our lamps are going out.' But the wise answered: 'Not so; lest there be not enough for us and you. Go ye rather to them that sell, and buy for yourselves.' While they went away to buy, the bridegroom came; and they that were ready went in with him to the marriage feast; and the door was shut. Afterward come the other virgins, saying: 'Lord, Lord, open to us.' But he said: 'I know you not.'

"It is as when a man, going into a far country, called his servants, and delivered unto them his goods. Unto one he gave five talents, to another two, to another one; to each according to his ability; and he went on his journey. Then he that received the five talents went and traded with them, and made other five talents. In like manner he also that received the two gained other two. But he that received the one went and digged in the earth, and hid his lord's money. After a long time the lord of those servants cometh, and reckoneth with them. He that received the five talents came and brought other five talents, saying: 'Lord, thou deliveredst unto me five talents. Lo, I have gained other five talents.' His lord said unto him: 'Well done, good and faithful servant. Thou hast been faithful over a few things, I will set thee over many things. Enter thou into the joy of thy lord.' He also that received the two talents came and said: 'Lord, thou deliveredst unto me two talents. Lo, I have gained other two talents.' His lord said unto him: 'Well done, good and faithful servant. Thou hast been faithful over a few things, I will set thee over many things. Enter thou into the joy of thy lord.' He also that had received the one talent came and said: 'Lord, I knew thee that thou art a hard man, reaping where thou didst not sow, and gathering where thou didst not scatter; and I was afraid, and went and hid thy talent in the earth. Lo, thou hast thine own.' But his lord said: 'Thou wicked and slothful servant, thou knewest that I reap where I sowed not, and gather where I did not scatter. Thou oughtest therefore to have put my money to the bankers, and at my coming I should have received mine own with interest. Take ye therefore the talent from him, and give it unto him that hath the ten talents. For unto every one that hath shall be given, and he shall have abundance; but from him that hath not, even that which he hath shall be taken away; and cast ye out the unprofitable servant into the outer darkness.'

"When the Son of Man shall come, and all the angels with him, then shall he sit on the throne of his glory; and before him shall be gathered all nations, and he shall separate them one from another, as a shepherd separateth the sheep from the goats. He shall set the sheep on his right hand, but the goats on the left. Then shall the King say unto them on his right hand: 'Come, ye blessed of my Father, inherit the kingdom prepared for you from the foundation of the world; for I was hungry, and ye gave me meat; I was thirsty, and ye gave me drink; I was a stranger, and ye took me in; naked, and ye clothed me; I was sick, and ye visited me; I was in prison, and ye came unto me.' Then shall the righteous answer, saying: 'Lord, when saw we thee hungry, and fed thee? or thirsty, and gave thee drink? When saw we thee a stranger, and took thee in? or naked, and clothed thee? and when saw we thee sick, or in prison, and came unto thee?' The King shall answer: 'Inasmuch as ye did it unto one of these my brethren, ye did it unto me.' Then shall he say unto them on the left hand: 'Depart from me, ye cursed, into the everlasting fire prepared for the devil and his angels; for I was hungry, and ye gave me no meat; I was thirsty, and ye gave me no drink; I was a stranger, and ye took me not in; naked, and ye clothed me not; sick, and in prison, and ye visited me not.' Then shall they say: 'Lord, when saw we thee hungry, or athirst, or a stranger, or naked, or sick, or in prison, and did not minister unto thee?' Then shall he answer: 'Verily I say unto you, inasmuch as ye did it not to one of the least of these, ye did it not to me;' and these shall go away into eternal punishment, but the righteous into eternal life."

Every day Jesus was teaching in the temple; and every night he went out, and lodged in the mount of Olives; and all the people came early in the morning to him in the temple, to hear him. The chief priests and the scribes sought how they might put him to death. Then Judas Iscariot, one of the twelve, went unto the chief priests, and said: "What are ye willing to give me, and I will deliver him unto you?"

They weighed unto him thirty pieces of silver; and from that time he sought opportunity to deliver Jesus unto them.

The day of unleavened bread came, and Jesus sent Peter and John, saying: "Go and make ready for us the passover, that we may eat."

They said unto him: "Where wilt thou that we make ready?"

He said: "Behold, when ye are entered into the city,

there shall meet you a man bearing a pitcher of water. Follow him, and wheresoever he shall enter in, say to the goodman of the house: 'The Master saith unto thee: "Where is the guest-chamber, where I shall eat the passover with my disciples?" He will show you a large upper room furnished. There make ready."

They went, and found as he had said unto them; and they made ready the passover. When it was evening he cometh, and he sat down, and the apostles with him. During supper, Jesus riseth, and he took a towel, and girded himself. Then he poureth water into the basin, and began to wash the disciples' feet, and to wipe them with the towel. When he had washed their feet and sat down again, he said unto them: "Ye call me, 'Master,' and, 'Lord;' and ye say well; for so I am. If I then, the Lord and the Master, have washed your feet, ye also ought to wash one another's feet."

When Jesus had thus said, he was troubled in spirit, and said: "Verily, verily, I say unto you, that one of you shall betray me."

The disciples looked one on another, doubting of whom he spake. There was at the table reclining on Jesus' bosom one of his disciples, whom Jesus loved. Simon Peter therefore beckoneth to him, that he should ask who it should be.

He, leaning back on Jesus' breast, saith: "Lord who is it?"

Jesus answered: "He it is, for whom I shall dip the sop,* and give it to him."

So when he had dipped the sop, he gave it to Judas, and Satan entered into him. Jesus said unto him: "That thou doest, do quickly."

No man at the table knew for what intent he spake this. Some thought, because Judas had the bag, that Jesus said unto him: "Buy what things we have need of for the feast;" or that he should give something to the poor. He then having received the sop went out straightway; and it was night.

As they were eating, Jesus took bread, and blessed and brake it; and he gave it to the disciples, and said: "Take, eat; this is my body;" and he took a cup, and gave thanks, and gave it to them saying: "Drink ye all of it; for this is my blood, which is shed for many;" and when they had sung a hymn, they went out unto the mount of Olives.

Then saith Jesus unto them: "All ye shall be offended in me this night."

Peter said: "I will never be offended."

Jesus said: "This night, before the cock crow, thou shalt deny me thrice."

Peter saith: "Even if I must die with thee, yet will I not deny thee."

Likewise said all the disciples.

Jesus said unto them: "Let not your heart be

---

*A morsel of bread, or the like, dipped in a liquid, before eating.

troubled. In my Father's house are many mansions. I go to prepare a place for you; and I will come again, and receive you unto myself, that where I am, there ye may be also."

Then cometh Jesus with them unto a place called Gethsemane, and saith unto the disciples: "Sit ye here, while I go yonder and pray."

He took with him Peter and the two sons of Zebedee. Then saith he unto them: "My soul is exceeding sorrowful. Abide ye here, and watch with me."

He went forward a little and fell on his face, and prayed, saying: "My Father, if it be possible, let this cup pass from me. Nevertheless, not as I will, but as Thou wilt."

He cometh unto the disciples, and findeth them sleeping, and saith unto Peter: "What, could ye not watch with me one hour? Watch and pray, that ye enter not into temptation. The spirit indeed is willing, but the flesh is weak."

A second time he went away, and prayed, saying: "My Father, if this cannot pass away, Thy will be done."

He came again and found them sleeping, for their eyes were heavy; and they wist not what to answer him. He left them, and went away, and prayed a third time, saying again the same words. Then cometh he to the disciples, and saith: "Sleep on now. Behold, the hour is at hand, and the Son of Man is betrayed into the hands of sinners."

Judas knew the place; for Jesus ofttimes resorted thither, and while Jesus yet spake, lo, Judas came, and with him a great multitude with lanterns and torches and weapons. Judas had given them a token, saying: "Whomsoever I kiss, that is he."

Straightway he came to Jesus, and said: "Hail, Master;" and kissed him.

Jesus said unto him: "Friend, do that for which thou art come."

Then they laid hands on Jesus, and took him. Simon Peter having a sword drew it, and struck the high priest's servant, and cut off his right ear. Jesus touched the ear, and healed it, and said unto Peter: "Put up thy sword into the sheath. The cup which the Father hath given me, shall I not drink it? Thinkest thou that I cannot pray to my Father, and he shall send me more than twelve legions of angels?"

In that hour said Jesus to the multitude: "Are ye come out as against a thief with swords and staves to seize me? I sat daily in the temple teaching, and ye took me not."

Then all the disciples forsook him and fled. So the officers of the Jews bound Jesus, and led him to Annas, father-in-law to Caiaphas, the high priest.

Simon Peter followed Jesus, and so did another disciple. That disciple entered with Jesus into the court of the high priest; but Peter stood at the door without. The damsel that kept the door saith unto Peter: "Art thou also one of this man's disciples?"

He saith: "I am not."

The servants and officers were standing there, having made a fire of coals; and they were warming themselves; and Peter was with them warming himself.

The high priest asked Jesus of his disciples, and of his teaching. Jesus answered him: "I have spoken openly to the world. I ever taught in synagogues, and in the temple, where all the Jews come together; and in secret spake I nothing. Why askest thou me? Ask them that have heard me, what I spake unto them."

One of the officers standing by struck Jesus with his hand, saying: "Answerest thou the high priest so?"

Jesus answered him: "If I have spoken evil, bear witness of the evil; but if well, why smitest thou me?"

Annas sent him away to the house of Caiaphas, where the scribes and the elders were assembled. Peter followed afar off, unto the court of the high priest, and went in, and sat with the officers, to see the end. The whole council sought false witness against Jesus, that they might put him to death, and found it not. For many bare false witness against him, yet their witness agreed not together. Afterward came two, and said: "This fellow said: 'I am able to destroy the temple of God, and to build it in three days.'"

The high priest arose and said: "Answerest thou nothing?"

But Jesus held his peace; and the high priest said: "I adjure thee by the living God, that thou tell us whether thou be the Christ, the Son of God."

Jesus said: "I am."

Then the high priest rent his garments, saying: "He hath spoken blasphemy. What further need have we of witnesses. Ye have heard the blasphemy. What think ye?"

They answered: "He is worthy of death."

Then did they spit in his face and buffet him; and some smote him with the palms of their hands; and they blindfolded him, and asked him, saying: "Prophesy unto us, thou Christ: who is he that struck thee?"

Peter was sitting without in the court; and a maid came unto him, saying: "Thou also wast with the Nazarene."

But he denied before them all, saying: "Woman, I know him not."

After a little while they that stood by said to Peter: "Surely thou also art one of them; for thy speech bewrayeth thee."

Then began he to curse and to swear, saying: "I know not the man."

Straightway the cock crew, and Peter remembered the words which Jesus had said: "Before the cock crow, thou shalt deny me thrice;" and he went out, and wept bitterly.

Judas, when he saw that Jesus was condemned,

repented, and brought back the thirty pieces of silver to the chief priests and elders, saying: "I have sinned in that I betrayed innocent blood."

But they said: "What is that to us?"

He cast down the pieces of silver in the temple, and he went away and hanged himself. The chief priests took the pieces of silver, and said: "It is not lawful to put them into the treasury, because they are the price of blood;" and they took counsel, and bought with them the potter's field, to bury strangers in.

They led Jesus away to Pilate the governor into the hall of judgment, and they themselves entered not. Pilate went out unto them, and saith: "What accusation bring ye against this man?"

They said: "We found him perverting our nation, and forbidding to give tribute to Cæsar, and saying that he is Christ a king."

Pilate said: "Take him yourselves, and judge him according to your law."

The Jews said: "It is not lawful for us to put any man to death."

Pilate entered into the judgment hall, and called Jesus, and said unto him: "Art thou the king of the Jews?"

Jesus answered: "My kingdom is not of this world. If my kingdom were of this world, then would my servants fight, that I should not be delivered to the Jews. I came into the world, that I should bear witness unto the truth. Everyone that is of the truth heareth my voice."

Pilate went out again unto the Jews, and saith: "I find no crime in him."

But they were the more urgent, saying: "He stirreth up the people."

Pilate asked whether the man were a Galilæan; and and when he knew that he was of Herod's jurisdiction, he sent him to Herod, who was at Jerusalem in those days. When Herod saw Jesus, he was exceeding glad; for he was a long time desirous to see him, because he had heard concerning him, and hoped to see some miracle done by him. He questioned him in many words, but Jesus answered nothing; and the chief priests and scribes stood vehemently accusing him. Herod with his soldiers set him at naught, and mocked him, and arraying him in gorgeous apparel sent him back to Pilate.

Pilate called together the chief priests and the rulers and the people, and said: "Ye brought unto me this man, as one that perverteth the people, and behold, I, having examined him, found no fault in this man touching those things whereof ye accuse him. No, nor yet Herod; for he sent him back. Nothing worthy of death hath been done by him. I will therefore chastise him, and release him."

At the feast the governor was wont to release unto the people a prisoner, whom they asked of him; and there was one named Barabbas, who for a certain insurrection made in the city, and for murder, was cast into prison. Pilate said: "Whom will ye that I release unto you? Barabbas, or Jesus who is called Christ?"

While he was sitting on the judgment-seat, his wife sent unto him, saying: "Have thou nothing to do with that righteous man; for I have suffered many things this day in a dream because of him."

But the chief priests and the elders persuaded the multitude that they should ask for Barabbas, and destroy Jesus. The governor said: "Which of the twain shall I release unto you?"

They said: "Barabbas."

Pilate saith unto them: "What then shall I do with Jesus who is called Christ?"

They all say: "Let him be crucified."

Pilate said: "Why, what evil hath he done?"

But they cried out exceedingly, saying: "Crucify him."

When Pilate saw that he prevailed nothing, but rather that a tumult was arising, he took water, and washed his hands before the multitude, saying: "I am innocent of the blood of this just person. See ye to it."

All the people answered: "His blood be on us, and on our children."

Then released he unto them Barabbas; but Jesus he scourged and delivered to be crucified.

The soldiers of the governor took Jesus into the palace, and put on him a scarlet robe, and they platted a crown of thorns and put it on his head, and a reed in his right hand; and they kneeled before him, and mocked him, saying: "Hail, King of the Jews!" and they spat on him, and took the reed and smote him on the head. After they had mocked him, they took off the robe, and led him away to crucify him; and they compel one passing by, coming from the country, to go with them, and laid on him the cross, to bear it after Jesus. There followed a great multitude of the people, and of women who bewailed and lamented him.

They bring him unto a place called Golgotha, which is, being interpreted, the place of a skull. Jesus said: "Father, forgive them; for they know not what they do."

They crucified him, and with him two robbers; one on his right hand, and one on his left. The soldiers took his garments, and made four parts, to every soldier a part. Now the coat was without seam, woven from the top throughout. They said therefore one to another: "Let us not rend it, but cast lots for it, whose it shall be."

These things the soldiers did, and they sat and watched him there.

Pilate wrote a title, and put it on the cross; and there was written: "JESUS OF NAZARETH, THE KING OF THE JEWS." This title read many of the Jews; for the place where Jesus was crucified was nigh to the city;

and it was written in Hebrew, and in Latin, and in Greek. The chief priests said to Pilate: "Write not: 'The King of the Jews;' but, that he said: 'I am King of the Jews.'"

Pilate answered: "What I have written I have written."

They that passed by reviled Jesus, wagging their heads, and saying: "Ha! thou that destroyest the temple, and buildest it in three days, save thyself. If thou art the Son of God, come down from the cross."

In like manner also the chief priests mocking him, with the scribes and elders, said: "He saved others; himself he cannot save. Let him come down from the cross, and we will believe on him."

One of the malefactors that were crucified with him railed on him, saying: "If thou be Christ save thyself and us."

But the other rebuking him said: "Dost thou not fear God, seeing thou art in the same condemnation? and we indeed justly; for we receive the due reward of our deeds; but this man hath done nothing amiss;" and he said: "Lord, remember me when thou comest into thy kingdom."

Jesus said unto him: "Today shalt thou be with me in Paradise."

There were standing by the cross of Jesus his mother, and his mother's sister, and Mary Magdalene. When Jesus saw his mother, and the disciple standing by, whom he loved, he saith unto his mother: "Woman, behold, thy son!"

Then saith he to the disciple: "Behold, thy mother!" and the disciple took her unto his own home.

From the sixth hour there was darkness over all the land until the ninth hour; and about the ninth hour Jesus cried with a loud voice, saying: "My God, my God, why hast thou forsaken me?"

Some of them that stood there said: "This man calleth Elijah."

One of them ran, and took a sponge, and filled it with vinegar, and put it on a reed, and gave him to drink. The rest said: "Let be; let us see whether Elijah will come to save him."

Jesus cried again with a loud voice, and yielded up his spirit; and behold, the veil of the temple was rent in twain from the top to the bottom; and the earth did quake; and the rocks were rent; and the tombs were opened; and many bodies of the saints were raised, and coming forth out of the tombs after his resurrection they entered into the holy city and appeared unto many. The centurion, and they that were with him watching Jesus, when they saw the earthquake, and the things that were done, feared exceedingly, saying: "Truly this was the Son of God."

All the multitudes that came together, when they beheld the things that were done, returned smiting their breasts. The soldiers saw that Jesus was dead, and one of them with a spear pierced his side, and straightway there came out blood and water.

When even was come, there came a rich man from Arimathæa, named Joseph, a good man and righteous. This man went to Pilate, and asked for the body of Jesus. Then Pilate commanded it to be delivered; and Joseph took the body, and wrapped it in a clean linen cloth. In the place where Jesus was crucified there was a garden; and in the garden a new tomb which had been hewn out of a rock, wherein was never man yet laid. Joseph laid the body in this tomb, and he rolled a great stone to the door of the tomb, and departed.

The women who had come with Jesus out of Galilee beheld the tomb, and they returned, and prepared spices and ointments.

On the morrow, the chief priests and the Pharisees were gathered together unto Pilate, saying: "Sir, we remember that deceiver said: 'After three days I rise.' Command therefore that the sepulchre be made sure until the third day, lest his disciples come and steal him away, and say unto the people: 'He is risen from the dead;' and the last error will be worse than the first."

Pilate said unto them: "Ye have a guard. Go your way. Make it as sure as ye can."

So they went, and made the sepulchre sure, sealing the stone, and setting a guard.

On the first day of the week, at early dawn, Mary Magdalene, and Mary the mother of James, came unto the tomb, bringing the spices which they had prepared; and behold, an angel of the Lord descended from heaven, and rolled away the stone, and sat on it. His appearance was like lightning, and his raiment white as snow; and for fear of him the watchers became as dead men. The angel said unto the women: "Fear not ye; for I know that ye seek Jesus who was crucified. He is not here; for he is risen, even as he said. Go quickly and tell his disciples."

They departed from the tomb with fear and great joy, and ran, and told the eleven and all the rest. These words appeared as idle talk to the apostles and they believed them not; but Peter arose, and ran to the tomb; and stooping and looking in, he seeth the linen cloths, and he departed wondering at that which was come to pass.

Mary was standing at the tomb weeping. She stooped and looked in; and she beholdeth two angels in white sitting, one at the head, and one at the feet, where the body of Jesus had lain. They say unto her: "Woman, why weepest thou?"

She saith: "Because they have taken away my Lord, and I know not where they have laid him."

When she had thus said, she turned herself, and saw Jesus standing, and knew not that it was Jesus. Jesus saith unto her: "Woman, whom seekest thou?"

She, supposing him to be the gardener, saith: "Sir,

if thou hast borne him hence, tell me where thou hast laid him, and I will take him away."

Jesus saith: "Mary."

She saith unto him: "Master."

Jesus saith: "Go to my brethren, and say, I ascend unto my Father."

Mary Magdalene came and told the disciples that she had seen the Lord, and that he had said these things unto her.

Some of the guard came into the city, and told unto the chief priests all the things that were come to pass; and the chief priests gave large money unto the soldiers, saying: "Say ye: 'His disciples came by night, and stole him away while we slept;' and if this come to the governor's ears, we will persuade him, and rid you of care."

So they took the money, and did as they were taught; and this saying spread abroad among the Jews.

Two of Jesus' followers were going to a village named Emmaus; and while they communed and questioned together, Jesus himself drew near, and went with them. But their eyes were holden that they should not know him. He said unto them: "What communications are these that ye have one with another, as ye walk?"

One of them answering said: "Dost thou sojourn in Jerusalem and not know the things which are come to pass there in these days?"

He said: "What things?"

They said: "The things concerning Jesus of Nazareth, who was a prophet mighty in deed and word; and how the chief priests and our rulers delivered him up to be condemned to death, and crucified him. We hoped that it was he who should redeem Israel. It is now the third day since these things were done. Moreover certain women of our company amazed us, having been early at the tomb, when they found not his body, they came, saying that they had seen a vision of angels, who said that he was alive. Certain of them that were with us went to the tomb, and found it even so as the women had said; but him they saw not."

He said unto them: "O foolish men, and slow of heart to believe all that the prophets have spoken. Ought not Christ to have suffered these things, and to enter into his glory?"

They drew nigh unto the village, whither they were going, and he made as if he would go further. They constrained him, saying: "Abide with us; for it is toward evening, and the day is far spent."

He went in with them, and when he had sat down with them to meat, he took the bread, and blessed it, and brake, and gave to them; and their eyes were opened, and they knew him; and he vanished out of their sight. They said one to another: "Did not our heart burn within us, while he spake to us in the way?"

They rose up that very hour, and returned to Jerusalem, and found the eleven, and them that were with them, and they told the things that happened. As they spake, Jesus himself stood in the midst of them, and saith: "Peace be unto you."

But they were terrified and affrighted, and supposed that they beheld a spirit. He said unto them: "Why are ye troubled? and wherefore do reasonings arise in your hearts? Behold my hands and my feet; handle me; for a spirit hath not flesh and bones, as ye behold me having."

While they still disbelieved for joy, and wondered, he said: "Have ye here anything to eat?"

They gave him a piece of broiled fish; and he took it, and did eat before them.

But Thomas, one of the twelve, called Didymus, was not with them when Jesus came. The other disciples therefore said unto him: "We have seen the Lord."

He said: "Except I shall see in his hands the print of the nails, and put my finger into the print of the nails, and thrust my hand into his side, I will not believe."

After eight days again his disciples were within, and Thomas with them. Jesus cometh, the doors being shut, and stood in their midst, and said: "Peace be unto you." Then saith he to Thomas: "Reach hither thy finger, and see my hands; and reach hither thy hand, and put it into my side; and be not faithless, but believing."

Thomas said unto him: "My Lord and my God."

Jesus saith: "Because thou hast seen me, thou hast believed. Blessed are they that have not seen, and yet have believed."

Jesus showed himself again to the disciples at the sea of Tiberias. There were together Simon Peter, and Thomas, and Nathanael, and the sons of Zebedee, and two others of his disciples. Simon Peter saith: "I go a-fishing."

They say: "We also go with thee."

They entered into the boat; and that night they took nothing; but when day was breaking, Jesus stood on the shore. Howbeit the disciples knew not that it was Jesus. He saith unto them: "Children, have ye aught to eat?"

They answered: "No."

He said unto them: "Cast the net on the right side of the boat, and ye shall find."

They cast therefore, and now they were not able to draw it for the multitude of fishes. That disciple whom Jesus loved saith unto Peter: "It is the Lord."

When Simon Peter heard that it was the Lord, he girt his coat about him, and cast himself into the sea; but the other disciples came in the little boat dragging the net full of fishes. As soon as they got out on the land, they saw a fire of coals, and fish laid thereon, and bread. Simon Peter drew the net to land, full of great fishes, a hundred and fifty and three; and for all there were so many, the net was not broken. Jesus saith unto them: "Come and break your fast."

None of the disciples durst ask him: "Who art thou?" knowing that it was the Lord.

Jesus taketh the bread, and giveth them, and the fish likewise. When they had broken their fast, Jesus saith to Simon Peter: "Simon, lovest thou me more than these?"

Peter saith: "Yea, Lord; thou knowest that I love thee."

Jesus saith: "Feed my lambs."

He saith to him a second time: "Simon, lovest thou me?"

Peter saith: "Yea, Lord; thou knowest that I love thee."

Jesus saith: "Feed my sheep."

He saith the third time: "Simon, lovest thou me?"

Peter was grieved, and he said: "Lord, thou knowest all things. Thou knowest that I love thee."

Jesus saith unto him: "Feed my sheep. Verily, verily, I say unto thee: 'When thou wast young, thou girdest thyself, and walkedst whither thou wouldest; but when thou shalt be old, thou shalt stretch forth thy hands, and another shall gird thee, and carry thee whither thou wouldest not.' "

This he spake, signifying by what manner of death Peter should glorify God.

The eleven disciples went into Galilee, unto the mountain where Jesus had appointed them; and Jesus came to them and spake, saying: "All authority hath been given unto me in heaven and on earth. Go ye therefore, and make disciples of all the nations, baptizing them to the name of the Father and of the Son and of the Holy Spirit: teaching them to observe all things I commanded you; and lo, I am with you always, even unto the end of the world."

He lifted up his hands, and blessed them; and it came to pass while he blessed them, he was carried up into heaven; and they returned to Jerusalem with great joy.

XXI

THE ACTS OF THE APOSTLES

JESUS showed himself alive after his passion by many proofs, appearing unto the apostles whom he had chosen by the space of forty days, and he charged them not to depart from Jerusalem, but to wait for the promise of the Father. When they were come together, he said: "Ye shall be my witnesses in all Judæa and Samaria, and unto the uttermost part of the earth."

As they were looking, he was taken up, and a cloud received him out of their sight. While they were looking steadfastly toward heaven, behold, two men stood by them in white apparel, who said: "Ye men of Galilee, why stand ye gazing up into heaven? This Jesus shall come in like manner as ye beheld him going."

Then returned they unto Jerusalem from the mount called Olivet; and they went into the upper chamber where they were abiding. In these days Peter stood up, and said: "Brethren, it was needful that the scripture should be fulfilled concerning Judas, who was guide to them that took Jesus. It is written in the book of Psalms:

> 'Let his habitation be made desolate,
> And let no man dwell therein.
> His office let another take.'

Of the men therefore who have companied with us must one become a witness with us of the resurrection."

They gave lots, and the lot fell on Matthias; and he was numbered with the eleven apostles.

When the day of Pentecost was come, they were all gathered together; and suddenly there came from heaven a sound as of the rushing of a mighty wind, and it filled all the house where they were sitting; and there appeared tongues like as of fire, and sat on each one of them; and they were filled with the Holy Spirit, and began to speak with other tongues. There were dwelling at Jerusalem Jews, devout men, from every nation under heaven; and when this sound was heard, the multitude came together, and were confounded, because every man heard them speaking in his own language. They were all amazed and marvelled, saying: "Are not all these that speak Galilæans? and how hear we, every man in our own language?"

Others mocking said: "They are filled with new wine."

Peter, standing up, spake forth, saying: "Ye men of Judæa, and all ye that dwell at Jerusalem, hearken to my words. This is that which hath been spoken by the prophet Joel:

'And it shall come to pass in the last days,' saith God,
'I will pour forth of my Spirit on all flesh;
And your sons and your daughters shall prophesy,
And I will show wonders in the heaven above,
And signs on the earth beneath.'

"Ye men of Israel; Jesus of Nazareth, ye did crucify by the hand of lawless men. This Jesus hath God raised up, whereof we are all witnesses. Let all the house of Israel know assuredly, that God hath made him both Lord and Christ."

When they heard this, they were pricked in their heart, and said unto Peter and the rest of the apostles: "Brethren, what shall we do?"

Peter said: "Repent ye, and be baptized every one of you in the name of Jesus Christ;" and with many other words he testified and exhorted, and there were added unto them in that day about three thousand souls.

Peter and John were going into the temple at the hour of prayer; and a certain man that was lame from his birth, and who was laid daily at the door of the temple which is called "Beautiful," to ask alms, seeing Peter and John, asked to receive an alms.

Peter said: "Silver and gold have I none; but what I have that I give thee. In the name of Jesus Christ of Nazareth, rise up and walk."

He took him by the right hand, and lifted him up. Immediately his feet and his ankle-bones received strength. He stood, and began to walk; and he entered with them into the temple, walking, and leaping, and praising God. As he held Peter and John, all the people ran together unto them greatly wondering; and Peter said: "Why marvel ye at this man? or why look ye so earnestly on us, as though by our own power we had made him to walk? The God of Abraham, and of Isaac, and of Jacob, hath glorified his Son Jesus; whom ye killed. Faith in his name hath made this man strong; and now, brethren, I wot that in ignorance ye did it. Repent ye therefore, that your sins may be blotted out."

The priests and the captain of the temple and the Sadducees, being sore troubled because they proclaimed in Jesus the resurrection from the dead, laid hands on them and put them in ward. On the morrow, the rulers and elders and scribes gathered together, and when they had set Peter and John in the midst, they asked: "By what power, or in what name, did ye do this?"

Peter said: "In the name of Jesus Christ of Nazareth, whom ye crucified. In none other is there salvation."

They conferred among themselves, saying: "What shall we do to these men? for that a notable miracle hath been done by them, is manifest to all that dwell in Jerusalem; and we cannot deny it. But that it spread no further among the people, let us threaten them, that they speak henceforth to no man in this name."

So they commanded them not to speak at all in the name of Jesus; but Peter and John answered: "Whether it be right to hearken unto you rather than unto God, judge ye; for we cannot but speak the things which we saw and heard."

The rulers and the elders, when they had further

threatened them, let them go, finding nothing how they might punish them, because of the people; for all men glorified God for that which was done.

The multitude of them that believed were of one heart and soul; and they had all things common. As many as were possessors of lands or houses sold them, and brought the money, and laid it at the apostles' feet; and distribution was made unto each, according as anyone had need. But a man named Ananias, with Sapphira his wife, sold a possession, and kept back part of the price, and brought a certain part, and laid it at the apostles' feet. Peter said: "Ananias, why hath Satan filled thy heart to keep back part of the price? Thou hast not lied unto men, but unto God."

Ananias hearing these words fell down and gave up the ghost; and the young men arose and wrapped him up, and they carried him out and buried him.

About the space of three hours after, his wife, not knowing what was done, came in. Peter said: "Tell me whether ye sold the land for so much."

She said: "Yea, for so much."

Peter said unto her: "How is it that ye have agreed together to tempt the Spirit of the Lord? Behold, the feet of them who have buried thy husband are at the door, and they shall carry thee out."

She fell down, and the young men came in and found her dead, and they carried her out and buried her by her husband; and great fear came on as many as heard these things.

By the hands of the apostles were many signs and wonders wrought among the people; and believers were added to the Lord, multitudes both of men and women; insomuch that they brought out the sick into the streets, and laid them on beds and couches, that, as Peter came by, at the least his shadow might overshadow them. There also came together a multitude from the cities round about Jerusalem, bringing sick folk, and they were healed every one.

The high priest and all they that were with him were filled with jealousy, and laid hands on the apostles, and put them in prison. But an angel of the Lord by night opened the prison doors, and brought them forth, and said: "Go ye, and speak in the temple to the people."

They entered into the temple about daybreak, and taught. The high priest called the council together, and sent to the prison to have them brought; but the officers found them not in the prison, and returned saying: "The prison we found shut, and the keepers standing at the doors; but when we had opened, we found no man within."

When the captain of the temple and the chief priests heard these words, they were much perplexed; and there came one and told them: "Behold, the men whom ye put in prison are in the temple teaching the people."

Then went the captain with the officers, and brought

them. The high priest said: "We straitly charged you not to teach in this name; and ye have filled Jerusalem with your teaching, and intend to bring this man's blood on us."

Peter and the apostles answered: "We must obey God rather than men. The God of our fathers raised up Jesus, whom ye slew, to be a Prince and a Savior."

When they heard this, they were minded to slay them; but there stood up one of the council, named Gamaliel, and commanded to put the apostles forth a little while; and he said: "Ye men of Israel, take heed to yourselves what ye are about to do. Before these days rose up Theudas, boasting himself to be somebody; to whom a number of men, about four hundred, joined themselves. He was slain, and all who obeyed him were scattered, and came to nought. Now I say unto you: 'Refrain from these men, and let them alone; for if this work be of men, it will be overthrown; but if it is of God, ye will not be able to overthrow them.'"

To him they agreed, and when they had called the apostles, they beat them and charged them not to speak in the name of Jesus, and let them go. They therefore departed from the presence of the council, rejoicing that they were counted worthy to suffer dishonor for his name; and every day, in the temple and at home, they ceased not to preach Jesus as the Christ.

There arose a murmuring of the Grecian Jews against the Hebrews, because their widows were neglected in the daily ministration. The twelve called the multitude of the disciples unto them, and said: "It is not fit that we should forsake the word of God, and serve tables. Look ye out from among you seven men of good report, whom we may appoint over this business."

The saying pleased the multitude; and they chose Stephen, a man full of faith and of the Holy Spirit, and Philip, and five others. Stephen, full of grace and power, wrought great wonders and miracles among the people; but there arose certain disputing with Stephen, and they were not able to withstand the wisdom and the Spirit by which he spake. Then they stirred up the people, and the elders, and the scribes, and seized him, and brought him to the council, and set up false witnesses, who said: "This man ceaseth not to speak against this holy place, and the law; for we have heard him say, that Jesus of Nazareth shall destroy this place, and shall change the customs which Moses delivered unto us."

All that sat in the council saw his face as it had been the face of an angel; and the high priest said: "Are these things so?"

He said: "As your fathers did, so do ye. Which of the prophets did not your fathers persecute? and they killed them that showed the coming of the Righteous One; of whom ye have become betrayers and murderers."

When they heard these things, they were cut to the

heart, and they gnashed on him with their teeth. But he, being full of the Holy Spirit, looked up steadfastly into heaven, and said: "Behold, I see the heavens opened, and the Son of Man standing on the right hand of God."

They cried out with a loud voice, and stopped their ears, and rushed on him with one accord; and they cast him out of the city, and stoned him; and the witnesses laid their garments at the feet of a young man named Saul. Stephen kneeled down, and cried with a loud voice: "Lord, lay not this sin to their charge."

When he had said this, he fell asleep; and Saul was consenting unto his death.

There arose a great persecution against the church which was in Jerusalem; and they were all scattered abroad throughout the regions of Judæa and Samaria, except the apostles. Saul laid waste the church, entering into every house, and dragging away men and women committed them to prison. They that were scattered abroad went about preaching the word; and Philip went to the city of Samaria, and proclaimed unto them the Christ.

An angel of the Lord spake unto Philip, saying: "Arise, and go toward the south unto the way that goeth from Jerusalem to Gaza."

He arose and went; and behold, a man of Ethiopia, an officer of great authority, who had come to Jerusalem to worship, and was returning sitting in his chariot, and reading the prophet Isaiah. Philip ran to him, and said: "Understandest thou what thou readest?"

He said: "How can I, except someone shall guide me?" and he besought Philip to come up and sit with him.

The place of the scriptures which he read was this:

"He was led as a sheep to the slaughter;
And as a lamb before his shearer is dumb,
So he opened not his mouth."

The officer said: "I pray thee, of whom speaketh the prophet this?"

Philip, beginning from this scripture, preached unto him Jesus. As they went on their way, they came unto a certain water; and the officer said: "What doth hinder me to be baptized?"

He commanded the chariot to stand still; and they both went down into the water, and Philip baptized him. When they came up out of the water, the Spirit of the Lord caught away Philip, and the officer saw him no more. But Philip was found at Azotus; and he preached the gospel to all the cities, till he came to Cæsarea.

Saul, breathing threatening and slaughter against the disciples of the Lord, went unto the high priest, and asked of him letters to Damascus unto the synagogues, that if he found any that were of the Way, he might bring them bound to Jerusalem. As he drew nigh unto Damascus, suddenly there shone round about him a light out of heaven; and he fell to the earth, and heard a voice saying unto him: "Saul, Saul, why persecutest thou me?"

He said: "Who art thou, Lord?"

The voice said: "I am Jesus whom thou persecutest. Arise and go into the city, and it shall be told thee what thou must do."

The men that journeyed with him stood speechless, hearing the voice, but beholding no man. Saul arose from the earth; and he saw nothing; and they led him by the hand and brought him into Damascus. He was three days without sight, and did neither eat nor drink.

There was a certain disciple at Damascus, named Ananias, and the Lord said unto him in a vision: "Arise, and go to the street which is called Straight, and inquire in the house of Judas for one named Saul; for behold, he prayeth; and he hath seen in a vision a man named Ananias coming in, and laying his hands on him, that he might receive his sight."

Ananias answered: "Lord, I have heard from many of this man, how much evil he hath done to Thy saints at Jerusalem; and here he hath authority from the chief priests to bind all that call on Thy name."

But the Lord said unto him: "Go thy way; for he is a chosen vessel unto me, to bear my name before the Gentiles and kings, and the children of Israel."

Ananias departed, and entered into the house; and

laying his hands on him said: "Brother Saul, the Lord, who appeared unto thee in the way which thou camest, hath sent me, that thou mayest receive thy sight, and be filled with the Holy Spirit."

Straightway there fell from his eyes as it were scales, and he received his sight; and he arose and was baptized; and he took food and was strengthened. He was certain days with the disciples who were at Damascus; and in the synagogues he proclaimed Jesus. All that heard him were amazed, and said: "Is not this he that in Jerusalem made havoc of them that called on this name?"

The Jews took counsel together to kill him; but their plot became known to Saul. They watched the gates day and night; but his disciples took him by night, and let him down through the wall in a basket.

When he was come to Jerusalem, he assayed to join himself to the disciples; and they were all afraid of him. But Barnabas brought him to the apostles; and declared unto them how Saul had seen the Lord in the way, and how at Damascus he had preached boldly in the name of Jesus; and Saul was with them going in and going out, preaching in the name of the Lord.

Peter came to the saints that dwelt at Lydda. Now there was at Joppa a certain disciple named Tabitha, which by interpretation is called Dorcas. This woman was full of good works, and she fell sick, and died, and they laid her in an upper chamber. As Lydda was nigh to Joppa, the disciples, hearing that Peter was there, sent two men entreating him that he would not delay to come to them.

Peter went with them; and when he was come, they brought him into the upper chamber. All the widows stood by him weeping, and showing the coats and garments which Dorcas made. But Peter put them all forth, and kneeled down, and prayed; and turning to the body, he said: "Tabitha, arise."

She opened her eyes; and he gave her his hand, and raised her up; and calling the saints and widows, he presented her alive. It became known throughout all Joppa, and many believed on the Lord; and Peter tarried many days in Joppa with one Simon a tanner.

There was a man in Cæsarea, Cornelius by name, a centurion, a devout man that feared God with all his house, who gave much alms to the people. He saw in a vision an angel of God coming in unto him, and saying: "Cornelius, thy prayers and thine alms are gone up for a memorial before God. Now send men to Joppa, and fetch one Peter. He lodgeth with Simon a tanner, whose house is by the seaside."

When the angel was departed, Cornelius called two of his household-servants, and a devout soldier of them that waited on him continually; and having rehearsed all things unto them, he sent them to Joppa.

On the morrow, as they were on their journey, and drew nigh unto the city, Peter went up on the housetop to pray, about the sixth hour; and he became hungry and desired to eat: but while they made ready, he fell into a trance; and he saw the heaven opened, and a vessel descending, as it were a great sheet, let down by four corners on the earth; wherein were all manner of fourfooted beasts and creeping things of the earth and fowls of the air. There came a voice to him: "Rise, Peter; kill and eat."

But Peter said: "Not so, Lord; for I have never eaten anything that is common and unclean."

The voice spake unto him the second time: "What God hath cleansed, call not thou common."

This was done thrice, and the vessel was received up into heaven. While Peter was much perplexed what the vision might mean, behold, the men that were sent by Cornelius stood before the gate, and asked whether Peter were lodging there. While Peter thought on the vision, the Spirit said unto him: "Behold, three men seek thee. Go with them, nothing doubting; for I have sent them."

Peter went down to the men, and said: "I am he whom ye seek. What is the cause wherefore ye are come?"

They said: "Cornelius a centurion was warned of God to send for thee into his house, and to hear words from thee."

So Peter called them in and lodged them, and on the morrow he went forth with them. They entered into

Cæsarea, and Cornelius was waiting for them, and had called together his kinsmen and near friends. When Peter entered, Cornelius fell down at his feet, and worshipped him. But Peter raised him up, saying: "Stand up. I myself also am a man."

He found many come together; and he said unto them: "Ye know that it is unlawful for a Jew to come unto one of another nation; and yet unto me hath God showed that I should not call any man common or unclean. Therefore I came, when I was sent for. Of a truth I perceive that God is no respecter of persons; but in every nation he that feareth Him, and worketh righteousness, is acceptable to Him."

While Peter yet spake, the Holy Spirit fell on all them that heard the word.

The apostles and the brethren that were in Judæa heard that the Gentiles also had received the word of God; and when Peter was come to Jerusalem, they contended with him; but Peter expounded the matter unto them; and they glorified God, saying: "Then to the Gentiles also hath God granted repentance unto life."

Herod the king killed James the brother of John; and when he saw that it pleased the Jews, he proceeded to seize Peter. He put him in prison, and delivered him to four quaternions of soldiers to guard him; intending after the passover to bring him forth to the people. Peter therefore was kept in the prison; but prayer was made earnestly of the church unto God for him. When Herod was about to bring him forth, the same night Peter was sleeping between two soldiers, bound with chains; and guards before the door kept the prison; and behold, an angel stood by him, and a light shined in the cell. The angel smote Peter on the side, and awoke him, saying: "Rise up quickly."

His chains fell off, and the angel said: "Gird thyself, and bind on thy sandals."

He did so, and the angel saith: "Follow me."

Peter followed; and he wist not that it was true which was done by the angel, but thought he saw a vision. When they were past the first and the second ward, they came unto the iron gate that leadeth into the city; which opened to them of its own accord. They went out, and passed through one street, and the angel departed. When Peter was come to himself, he said: "Now I know of a truth, that the Lord hath sent his angel and delivered me out of the hand of Herod."

He came to the house of Mary the mother of Mark; where many were together praying. When he knocked at the gate, a damsel came to answer; and when she knew Peter's voice, she opened not the gate for gladness, but ran in, and told that Peter stood before the gate. They said unto her: "Thou art mad."

But she confidently affirmed that it was even so; and they said: "It is his angel."

Peter continued knocking; and when they had

opened, they saw him, and were astonished. But he, beckoning unto them to hold their peace, declared how the Lord had brought him forth out of the prison; and he departed to another place.

As soon as it was day, there was no small stir among the soldiers, what was become of Peter; and when Herod sought for him, and found him not, he examined the guards, and commanded that they should be put to death.

Herod was highly displeased with them of Tyre and Sidon; and they came to him, and asked for peace. Herod arrayed himself in royal apparel, and sat on the throne, and made an oration unto them; and the people shouted, saying: "It is the voice of a god, and not of a man."

Immediately an angel of the Lord smote him, because he gave not God the glory; and he was eaten of worms, and gave up the ghost.

There were at Antioch in the church that was there, Barnabas and Saul, and they, being sent forth by the Holy Spirit, sailed to Cyprus, and proclaimed the word of God. When they had gone through the whole island, Saul, who is also called Paul, and his company, set sail, and came to Perga, and they went thence to Iconium. Long time they tarried there speaking boldly in the Lord. But the multitude of the city was divided, and part held with the Jews, and part with the apostles; and when there was made an onset both of the Gentiles and of the Jews to stone them, they fled unto Lystra. At Lystra there sat a man impotent in his feet, who had never walked. The same heard Paul speaking; and Paul seeing that he had faith said: "Stand upright on thy feet."

He leaped up and walked, and the multitude lifted up their voices, saying: "The gods are come down to us in the likeness of men."

They called Barnabas, "Jupiter;" and Paul, "Mercury," because he was the chief speaker; and the priest of Jupiter whose temple was before the city, brought oxen and garlands and would have done sacrifice with the multitude. When Barnabas and Paul heard of it, they rent their garments, and ran in among the people, crying out and saying: "Sirs, why do ye these things? We are men of like passions with you, and bring you good tidings, that ye should turn from these vanities unto the living God, who made the heaven and the earth and the sea, and all that in them is."

With these sayings scarce restrained they the people from doing sacrifice unto them. There came Jews thither from Iconium, and having persuaded the multitude, they stoned Paul, and dragged him out of the city, supposing that he was dead. But as the disciples stood round about him, he rose up, and the next day he went with Barnabas to Derbe. They preached the gospel to that city, and after visiting various other cities, they returned to Antioch, and rehearsed all things that God had done with them, and how he had opened a door of faith unto the Gentiles.

After some time Paul chose Silas, and went through Syria and Cilicia, confirming the churches. He came also to Lystra, and a certain disciple was there, named Timothy. Him would Paul have to go with him; and they went to Philippi, which is a city of Macedonia. On the Sabbath Day they went forth by a river side, and they sat down, and spake unto the women who were come together. A woman named Lydia heard them, whose heart the Lord opened, to give heed unto the things which were spoken by Paul. When she was baptized, she besought them, saying: "Come into my house, and abide there;" and she constrained them.

As they were going to the place of prayer, a certain maid having a spirit of divination met them, who brought her masters much gain by soothsaying. The same followed after them, and cried out: "These men are servants of the Most High God, who proclaim unto us the way of salvation."

This she did for many days. Paul, being sore troubled, turned and said to the spirit: "I charge thee in the name of Jesus Christ to come out of her."

It came out that very hour; but when her masters saw that the hope of their gain was gone, they laid hold on Paul and Silas, and dragged them into the marketplace before the rulers, and said: "These men do exceedingly trouble our city, and teach customs which it is not lawful for us to observe."

The magistrates commanded to beat them with rods; and when they had laid many stripes on them, they cast them into prison, and the jailor made their feet fast in the stocks. About midnight Paul and Silas were praying and singing hymns unto God, and the prisoners were listening to them. Suddenly there was a great earthquake, so that the foundations of the prison were shaken; and immediately all the doors were opened, and everyone's bands were loosed. The jailor being roused out of sleep, and seeing the prison doors open, drew his sword, and was about to kill himself, supposing that the prisoners had escaped. But Paul cried with a loud voice, saying: "Do thyself no harm; for we are all here."

The jailor called for lights, and fell down before Paul and Silas, and brought them out, and said: "Sirs, what must I do to be saved?"

They said: "Believe on the Lord Jesus."

They spake the word of the Lord unto him, and to all that were in his house; and he took them the same hour of the night, and washed their stripes, and was baptized, he and all his; and he brought them into his house, and set meat before them, and rejoiced greatly.

When it was day, the magistrates sent, saying: "Let those men go."

The jailor reported the words to Paul; but Paul said:

"They have beaten us publicly, uncondemned, men that are Romans, and have cast us into prison. Let them come themselves and fetch us out."

The magistrates feared, when they heard that they were Romans; and they came and besought them; and when they had brought them out, they asked them to depart out of the city.

They departed, and Paul journeyed until he came to Athens. His spirit was provoked within him, as he beheld the city full of idols. So he reasoned in the synagogue with the Jews and the devout persons, and in the marketplace every day with them that met with him. Certain also of the Epicurean and Stoic philosophers encountered him; and some said: "What would this babbler say?" Others: "He seemeth to be a setter forth of strange gods."

They took hold of him and brought him unto the Areopagus,* saying: "May we know what this new teaching is, whereof thou speakest?"

Now all the Athenians and the strangers sojourning there spent their time in nothing else, but either to tell or to hear some new thing. Paul stood, and said: "Ye men of Athens, I perceive that ye are somewhat superstitious. For as I passed along, and observed the objects of your worship, I found an altar with this inscription: 'TO AN UNKNOWN GOD.' Whom therefore

---

*A hill where the Athenians held an open-air political and religious court.

ye worship in ignorance, him declare I unto you. The God that made the world dwelleth not in temples made with hands, though He is not far from each one of us; for in Him we live, and move, and have our being. We ought not to think that the Godhead is like unto gold, or silver, or stone, graven by art and device of man. The times of ignorance God overlooked; but now He commandeth men that they should all repent, inasmuch as He hath appointed a day, in the which He will judge the world by the man whom He hath ordained; whereof He hath given assurance, in that He hath raised him from the dead."

When they heard of the resurrection of the dead, some mocked, but others said: "We will hear thee concerning this again."

So Paul went out from among them, but certain men clave unto him, and believed. After these things he departed to Corinth, where he found a certain Jew named Aquila, with his wife Priscilla. Because he was of the same trade, he abode with them, and they wrought; for by their occupation they were tentmakers; and he reasoned in the synagogue every Sabbath. When he departed thence, he continued from city to city until he came to Ephesus; and God wrought special miracles by the hands of Paul, insomuch that unto the sick were carried away from his body handkerchiefs or aprons, and the diseases departed from them. Not a few that practiced magical arts brought their books, and burned them. So mightily grew the word of the Lord and prevailed.

A man named Demetrius, who made silver shrines of Diana, brought no small gain unto the craftsmen; whom he gathered together, and said: "Sirs, ye know that by this business we have our wealth; and ye see and hear, that not alone at Ephesus, but almost throughout all Asia, this Paul hath persuaded and turned away much people, saying that they be no gods, which are made with hands. Not only is there danger that our trade come into disrepute; but also that the temple of the great goddess Diana should be despised and her magnificence destroyed."

When they heard this, they were filled with wrath, and cried out, saying: "Great is Diana of the Ephesians."

The city was filled with the confusion; and they rushed with one accord into the theatre. Some cried one thing, and some another; and the more part knew not wherefore they were come together. They brought Alexander out of the multitude, and he saith: "Ye men of Ephesus, ye ought to do nothing rash. If Demetrius, and the craftsmen that are with him, have a matter against any man, the courts are open. We are in danger to be accused concerning this day's riot, there being no cause for it."

When he had thus spoken, he dismissed the assembly. After the uproar was ceased, Paul departed, and came into Greece. He spent three months there, and travelled through Macedonia, and he and his company sailed away from Philippi, and came unto Troas, where they abode seven days. On the first day of the week, when they were gathered together to break bread, Paul discoursed with them of Troas, intending to depart on the morrow; and prolonged his speech until midnight. There were many lights in the upper chamber, where they were, and there sat in a window a certain young man. Being sunk down with sleep he fell from the third story; and was taken up dead. Paul went down, and embracing him said: "Trouble not yourselves; for his life is in him."

When he was come up again, and had broken the bread, and eaten, and had talked a long while, even till break of day, he departed; and they brought the young man alive, and were not a little comforted.

Paul came to Jerusalem, and the brethren received him gladly; but the Jews from Asia saw him in the temple, and stirred up the multitude, and laid hands on him, crying out: "Men of Israel, help. This is the man that teacheth all men everywhere against the people, and the law, and this place. Moreover he brought Greeks also into the temple, and hath polluted this holy place." For they had seen with him in the city Trophimus an Ephesian, whom they supposed that Paul had brought into the temple.

The people ran together, and they laid hold on Paul, and dragged him out of the temple. As they were seeking to kill him, tidings came to the chief captain of the band, that all Jerusalem was in an uproar Forthwith he took soldiers, and ran down on them. They, when they saw the chief captain and the soldiers, left off beating Paul. Then the chief captain came near, and commanded him to be bound with two chains, and demanded who he was, and what he had done. Some shouted one thing, some another; and when he could not know the certainty for the tumult, he commanded him to be carried into the castle. The multitude followed after, crying out: "Away with him. Away with such a fellow from the earth."

As they cried out, and threw off their garments, and cast dust into the air, the chief captain brought him into the castle, and bade that he should be examined by scourging, that he might know for what cause they so shouted against him. When they had tied him with the thongs, Paul said unto the centurion that stood by: "Is it lawful for you to scourge a Roman, and uncondemned?"

The centurion went to the chief captain, saying: "Take heed what thou doest; for this man is a Roman."

The chief captain came, and said: "Tell me, art thou a Roman?"

He said: "Yea."

The chief captain said: "With a great sum obtained I this citizenship."

Paul said: "But I am a Roman born."

They then who were about to examine him departed; and the chief captain also was afraid, when he knew that Paul was a Roman, and because he had bound him. On the morrow he commanded the chief priests and the council to come together, and brought Paul, and set him before them. When Paul perceived that the one part were Sadducees, and the other Pharisees, he cried out: "Brethren, I am a Pharisee, the son of Pharisees. Touching the resurrection of the dead I am called in question."

When he had so said, there arose a dissension between the Pharisees and Sadducees; and the assembly was divided. For the Sadducees say that there is no resurrection, neither angel, nor spirit; but the Pharisees confess both. There arose a great clamor; and some of the Pharisees stood up, saying: "We find no evil in this man."

The chief captain, fearing lest Paul should be torn in pieces by them, commanded the soldiers to bring him into the castle. The night following the Lord stood by him, and said: "Be of good cheer. As thou hast testified concerning me at Jerusalem, so must thou bear witness also at Rome."

When it was day, the Jews banded together, and bound themselves under a curse, saying that they would neither eat nor drink till they had killed Paul. They were more than forty who made this conspiracy; and they came to the chief priests and elders, and said:

"Signify to the chief captain that he bring Paul unto you, as though ye would judge of his case more exactly; and we are ready to kill him."

Paul's sister's son heard of their lying in wait, and he entered into the castle, and told Paul, who called one of the centurions, and said: "Bring this young man unto the chief captain; for he hath something to tell him."

So the centurion took him to the chief captain, who went aside with him privately and asked: "What is that thou hast to tell me?"

He said: "The Jews have agreed to ask thee to bring Paul unto the council. Do not thou yield unto them; for there lie in wait more than forty men, who have bound themselves with an oath, neither to eat nor to drink till they have slain him."

The chief captain let the young man go; and he called two centurions, and said: "Make ready two hundred soldiers to go to Cæsarea, and horsemen threescore and ten, and spearmen two hundred, at the third hour of the night. Provide them beasts, that they may set Paul thereon, and bring him safe unto Felix the governor."

They came to Cæsarea, and after five days the high priest came with certain elders, and with an orator, who said: "We have found this man a pestilent fellow, and a mover of insurrections, and a ringleader of the sect of the Nazarenes; who moreover assayed to profane the temple."

When the governor had beckoned unto him to speak, Paul answered: "Neither in the temple did they find me disputing with any man or stirring up a crowd, nor in the synagogues, nor in the city. But this I confess, that after the Way which they call heresy, so worship I the God of our fathers."

Felix deferred Paul's accusers, saying: "When the chief captain shall come, I will determine your matter."

After certain days Felix sent for Paul, and heard him concerning the faith in Christ. As he reasoned of righteousness, and temperance, and the judgment to come, Felix was terrified, and said: "Go thy way for this time; and when I have a more convenient season, I will call thee unto me."

He hoped that money would be given him of Paul, that he might loose him; wherefore he sent for him the oftener and communed with him. After two years were fulfilled, Felix was succeeded by Festus; and desiring to gain favor with the Jews, Felix left Paul in bonds.

Festus went to Jerusalem, and the chief priests and the principal men of the Jews informed him against Paul; and they besought him, that he would send for him to Jerusalem, laying a plot to kill him on the way. But Festus answered, that Paul was kept in charge at Cæsarea, and that he himself was about to depart thither. "Let them therefore," saith he, "who are of power among you, go with me, and if there is anything amiss in the man, let them accuse him."

He went unto Cæsarea, and sat on the judgment-seat, and commanded Paul to be brought. When Paul was come, the Jews from Jerusalem stood round about, bringing many and grievous charges; while Paul said in his defence: "Neither against the law of the Jews, nor against the temple, nor against Cæsar, have I sinned at all."

Festus said: "Wilt thou go to Jerusalem, and there be judged of these things?"

Paul said: "I stand at Cæsar's judgment-seat, where I ought to be judged. If I am a wrong-doer, and have committed anything worthy of death, I refuse not to die; but if none of those things is true, whereof these accuse me, no man can deliver me unto them. I appeal unto Cæsar."

Then Festus answered: "Thou hast appealed unto Cæsar; unto Cæsar shalt thou go."

When certain days were passed, Agrippa the king arrived at Cæsarea, and Festus laid Paul's case before the king, saying: "There is a man left a prisoner by Felix; concerning whom, his accusers, the chief priests and the elders of the Jews, brought no charge of such evil things as I supposed; but had certain questions against him of their own religion, and of one Jesus, who was dead, whom Paul affirmed to be alive."

Agrippa said: "I also could wish to hear the man."

So on the morrow, when they were entered into the place of hearing, with the chief captains, and the principal men of the city, Paul was brought in. Festus said: "Ye see this man about whom the Jews made suit to me. As he appealed to the emperor I brought him before you that, after examination, I may have somewhat to write. For it seemeth to me unreasonable, to send a prisoner, and not to signify the charges against him."

Agrippa said unto Paul: "Thou art permitted to speak for thyself."

Then Paul answered: "I think myself happy, King Agrippa, that I am to make my defence before thee, because thou art expert in all customs and questions which are among the Jews. My manner of life from my youth up know all the Jews. After the straitest sect of our religion I lived a Pharisee. Now I stand here to be judged for the hope of the promise made of God unto our fathers. I verily thought, that I ought to do many things contrary to the name of Jesus of Nazareth; and I shut up many of the saints in prisons, and I persecuted them even unto foreign cities. As I journeyed to Damascus, at midday, O king, I saw a light from heaven, above the brightness of the sun, shining round about me and them that journeyed with me. When we were all fallen to the earth, I heard a voice, saying: 'Saul, Saul, why persecutest thou me?' I said: 'Who art thou, Lord?' The voice said: 'I am

The Acts of the Apostles

Jesus whom thou persecutest. But arise; for I have appeared unto thee to appoint thee a minister and a witness both of the things wherein thou hast seen me, and of the things wherein I will appear unto thee; delivering thee from the people, and from the Gentiles, unto whom I send thee, that they may turn from darkness to light, and from the power of Satan unto God.' Wherefore, O King Agrippa, I was not disobedient unto the heavenly vision; but declared to them of Damascus first, and throughout all the country of Judæa, and also to the Gentiles, that they should repent and turn to God, and do works worthy of repentance."

As he thus spake for himself, Festus said: "Paul, much learning doth make thee mad."

Paul saith: "I am not mad, most excellent Festus; but speak words of truth and soberness. The king knoweth of these things; for this was not done in a corner."

Agrippa said unto Paul: "Almost thou persuadest me to be a Christian."

Paul said: "I would to God, that not only thou, but all that hear me this day, might become such as I am, except these bonds."

The king rose up, and the governor, and they that sat with them. When they had withdrawn, they spake one to another, saying: "This man doeth nothing worthy of death or of bonds."

Agrippa said unto Festus: "This man might have been set at liberty, if he had not appealed unto Cæsar."

When it was determined that Paul should sail for Italy, they delivered him and certain other prisoners to a centurion named Julius; who embarked in a ship, and came to Myra, a city of Lycia. There the centurion found a ship sailing for Italy, and he put the prisoners therein. They sailed under the lee of Crete, and came unto a place called Fair Havens. When the south wind blew softly, they weighed anchor and sailed along Crete, close in shore. But after no long time there arose a tempestuous wind; and the ship was caught, and could not face the wind, and they were driven. As they labored exceedingly with the storm, the next day they began to throw the freight overboard; and the third day they cast out the tackling of the ship. Neither sun nor stars shone on them for many days, and all hope that they should be saved was taken away. Then Paul stood forth in the midst of them, and said: "Sirs, I exhort you to be of good cheer. There shall be no loss of life among you, but only of the ship. For there stood by me this night an angel of the God whom I serve, saying: 'Fear not, Paul. Thou must be brought before Cæsar; and lo, God hath granted thee all them that sail with thee.' Wherefore, sirs, be of good cheer."

When the fourteenth night was come, about midnight the sailors surmised that they were drawing near to some country. They sounded, and found twenty

Paul's shipwreck

fathoms; and after a little space, they sounded again, and found fifteen fathoms. Fearing lest they should be cast ashore on rocks, they let go four anchors from the stern, and prayed for the day. As the sailors were seeking to flee out of the ship, and had lowered the boat into the sea, as though they would lay out anchors from the foreship, Paul said to the centurion and to the soldiers: "Except these abide in the ship, ye cannot be saved."

Then the soldiers cut away the ropes of the boat, and let her fall off. While the day was coming on, Paul besought them all to take some food, saying: "This day is the fourteenth day that ye continue fasting. Wherefore I beseech you to take some food."

When he had thus spoken, he took bread, and gave thanks to God in the presence of all; and he brake it, and began to eat. Then were they all of good cheer, and took food. When it was day, they knew not the land; but they perceived a bay with a beach, and they took counsel whether they could drive the ship on it. Casting off the anchors, they left them in the sea, at the same time loosing the bands of the rudders; and hoisting up the foresail to the wind, they made for the beach. But lighting on a place where two seas met, they ran the vessel aground. The forepart struck and remained immovable, but the stern began to break up by the violence of the waves. The soldiers' counsel was to kill the prisoners, lest any of them should swim, and escape. But the centurion, desiring to save Paul, kept them from their purpose, and commanded that they who could swim should cast themselves overboard, and get first to the land; and the rest, some on planks, and some on other things from the ship. So it came to pass, that they all escaped safe.

When they were escaped, they knew that the island was called Melita; and the barbarians showed them no little kindness; for they kindled a fire, and received them all, because of the rain and the cold. Paul gathered a bundle of sticks, and laid them on the fire, and a viper came out by reason of the heat; and fastened on his hand. When the barbarians saw the beast hanging from his hand, they said one to another: "No doubt this man is a murderer, whom, though he hath escaped from the sea, yet Justice hath not suffered to live."

Howbeit he shook off the beast into the fire, and felt no harm. They expected that he would have swollen, or fallen down dead suddenly; but when they had looked a great while, and beheld nothing amiss come to him, they changed their minds, and said that he was a god.

In the neighborhood of that place were lands belonging to the chief man of the island, named Publius; who received them, and lodged them three days courteously. The father of Publius lay sick of fever and dysentery; unto whom Paul entered in, and prayed, and laid his hands on him and healed him. When this was done, others also who had diseases in the island came, and were cured. These honored them with many honors; and when they sailed, put on board such things as they needed.

When they came to Rome, Paul was suffered to dwell by himself with the soldier that guarded him; and after three days he called together those that were chief of the Jews, and said unto them: "I, brethren, though I had done nothing against the people, or the customs of our fathers, yet was delivered prisoner from Jerusalem into the hands of the Romans; who, when they had examined me, desired to set me at liberty, because there was no cause of death in me. But when the Jews spake against it, I was constrained to appeal unto Cæsar. Because of the hope of Israel I am bound with this chain."

They said unto him: "We neither received letters concerning thee, nor did any of the brethren come hither and speak harm of thee. We desire to hear what thou thinkest; for concerning this sect, we know that everywhere it is spoken against."

When they had appointed a day, there came many to him into his lodging; to whom he expounded the matter, persuading them concerning Jesus from morning till evening. Some believed the things which were spoken, and some disbelieved; and when they agreed not among themselves, they departed.

Paul dwelt two whole years in his own hired house, and received all that came in unto him, preaching the kingdom of God, and teaching those things which concern the Lord Jesus Christ with all boldness.

Names of Persons and Places

The pronunciation generally adopted in the public reading of the Bible is here indicated. The following words furnish a key to the markings: tāme, arm, fâre; hăt, a͞a = a of am; a͡a = a of care; mediæval, a͡isle, ha̱il, a͞o = o of alone; ma͡ul, çell, e̱c̱ho, mēte, mĕt, he͡ed, ne͡uter, le͞wd, ġem, fīne, hĭm, peculịar, ōld, nôr, ŏn, so̱n, haṡ, adhe͞sion, t͞hyme, ac͞tion, tūne, rûde, tûrn, ŭs, lȳre, hy̆mn.

A͡a'rŏn
Ăb'dŏn
Ă bĕd'-nĕ gō
Ā'bĕl
Ă bī'ă thar
Ăb'ĭ ga̱il
Ă bī'jăh
Ă bī jăm
Ă bĭm'ĕ lĕc̱h
Ă bĭn'ă dăb
Ă bĭn'ŏ ăm
Ă bī'răm
Ăb'ĭ sha͡i
Ăb'nĕr
Ā'bră hăm
Ăb'să lo̱m
Ā'c̱hĭsh
Ăd'ăm
Ăd ō nī'jăh
Ăd'ō nī-zē'dec
Ă dŭl'lăm
Ā'găg
Ăg'ă gīte
Ă grĭp'pă
Ā'hăb
Ă hăs ū ē'rŭs
Ā'hăz
Ā hă zī'ăh
Ă hī'jăh
Ă hī mă ăz
Ă hĭm ĕ lĕc̱h
Ă hī'ō
Ă hĭth'ŏ phĕl
Ăj'ă lŏn
Ăl ĕx ăn'dĕr
Ăl phæ'ŭs
Ăm'ă lĕk
Ăm ă zī ăh
Ăm'mo̱n
Ăm'nŏn
Ā'mŏn
Ăm'ō rīte

Names of Persons and Places

Ā′năk
Ăn ă nī′ăs
Ăn′drew
Ăn′năs
Ăn′tĭ ŏch
Ă quĭl′ă
Ăr′ă răt
Är chīte
Ăr ĕ ŏp′ă gŭs
Ăr ĭ mă thæ′ă
Ăr′ĭ ŏch
Ăr tă xĕrx′ēs
Ā′să
Ăs′ĕ năth
Ăsh′dŏd
Ăsh′ĕr
Ā′sĭă
Ăsh′kĕ lon
Ăs sȳr′ĭ ă
Ăth ă lī′ăh
Ăth′ĕns
Aû gŭs′tŭs
Ăz ă rī′ăh
Ă zō′tŭs
Bā′ăl
Bā′ăl-hā′zôr
Bā ăsh′ă
Bā′bĕl
Băb′ў lon
Bă hū′rĭm
Bā′laām
Bā′lăk

Bär ăb′băs
Bâr′ăk
Bar′nă băs
Bar thŏl′ŏ mew
Bā′shăn
Băth-shĕ′bă
Bē ĕl′zĕ bŭb
Beêr-shē′bă
Bĕ nâı′ăh
Bĭn-hā′dăd
Bē′ôr
Bĕl shăz′zar
Bĕl tē shăz′zar
Bĕn′jă mĭn
Bĕth′ă nў
Bĕth′ĕl
Bĕth ĕs′dă
Bĕth′-lĕ hĕm
Bĕth sā′ĭ dă
Bĕth-shē′mĕsh
Bĕ thū′ĕl
Bĭl′dăd
Bō ăz
Cæ′sär
Cæs ă rē′ă
Câı′ă phăs
Cain
Cā′lĕb
Cā nă
Cā′naân
Că pĕr′nă ŭm

Names of Persons and Places

Car′mĕl
Chăl dē′ăns
Chē′rĭth
Chĭ′lĭ ŏn
Chō rā′zĭn
Christ
Cĭ lĭc′ĭ ă
Cŏr′ĭnth
Côr nēl′ĭŭs
Crēte
Cū′shīte
Cū′thăh
Cȳ′prŭs
Cȳ′rus
Dā′gŏn
Dă măs′cŭs
Dăn
Dăn′iĕl
Dă rī′ŭs
Dā′thăn
Dā′vĭd
Dĕb′ŏ răh
Dĕ lī′lăh
Dē mē′trĭ ŭs
Dĕr′bē
Dī ăn′ă
Dĭd′ȳ mŭs
Dôr′căs
Dō′thăn
Dū′ră
Ē dĕn

Ĕg′lŏn
Ē′gўpt
Ē′hŭd
Ĕk′rŏn
Ē′lăh
Ĕl ē ā′zàr
Ē′lī
Ē lī′ăb
Ē lī′ă kĭm
Ē lī′jăh
Ē lĭm′ĕ lĕch
Ĕ lī′phăz
Ē lĭś′ă bĕth
Ē lī′shă
Ĕl kā′năh
Ē′lŏn
Ĕm mā′ŭs
Ĕn ġē′dī
Ĕph′ĕ sŭs
Ē′phră ĭm
Ĕp ĭ cū rē′ăn
Ē′saû
Ĕsh′cŏl
Ĕs′thĕr
Ē′tăm
Ē thĭ ō′pĭ ă
Eû phrā′tēś
Ēve
Ē′zĕl
Fē′lĭx
Fĕs′tŭs
Gā′brĭ ĕl

Names of Persons and Places

Găd
Gā'dī
Găl'ĭ leê
Gā mā'lĭ ĕl
Găth
Gā'ză
Gĕ hā'zī
Gĕn'tīle
Gē'shur
Gĕth sĕm'ă nē
Gĭb'bĕ thŏn
Gĭb'ĕ ăh
Gĭb'ĕ on
Gĭd'ĕ on
Gī'hŏn
Gĭl bō'ă
Gĭl'ĕ ăd
Gĭl'găl
Gĭt'tīte
Gŏl'gō thă
Gō lī'ăth
Gō mŏr'răh
Gō'shĕn
Greêce
Hā'gär
Hăm
Hā'măn
Hā'măth
Hăn ă nī'ăh
Hăn'năh
Hâr'ăn
Hā'tăch

Hē'bĕr
Hē'brew
Hē'brŏn
Hē'gâi
Hĕr'od
Hĕ rō'dĭ ăs
Hĕsh'bŏn
Hĕz ē kī'ăh
Hī'răm
Hĭl'lĕl
Hĭt'tīte
Hī'vīte
Hôr
Hôr'ĕb
Hō shē'ă
Hur
Hū'shâi
Ĭb'zăn
Ī cō'nĭ ŭm
Ĭn'dĭ ă
Ī'saac
Ī sâi'ăh
Ĭsh-bŏsh'ĕth
Ĭsh'mā ĕl
Ĭs'rā ĕl
Ĭs'să char
Ĭt'ă lў
Ĭt'tā ī
Jăb'bok
Jā'bĕsh
Jā'bĭn

Names of Persons and Places

Jā′cǒb
Jā′ĕl
Jā′ĭr
Jā ĭ′rŭs
Jāmes
Jā′phĕth
Jā′zẽr
Jĕb′ū sīte
Jĕ hō′ă hăz
Jĕ hō′ăsh
Jĕ hôı̆′ă chı̆n
Jĕ hôı̆′ă dă
Jĕ hôı̆′ă kı̆m
Jĕ hō′răm
Jĕ hŏsh′ă phăt
Jē hŏsh′ĕ bă
Jē′hū
Jĕph′thăh
Jĕr ē mī′ăh
Jĕr′ĭ chō
Jĕr ĕ bō′ăm
Jĕ rû′să lĕm
Jĕs′sĕ
Jē′sŭs
Jĕth′rō
Jēws
Jĕz′ĕ bĕl
Jĕz′reêl
Jō′ăb
Jō′ăsh
Jōb
Jō′ĕl

Jǒhn
Jǒn′ă dăb
Jō′năh
Jǒn′ă thăn
Jǒp′pă
Jō′răm
Jôr dăn′
Jō′sĕph
Jŏsh′ū ă
Jō sī′ăh
Jō′thăm
Jû dæ′ă
Jû dăh
Jû′dăs Ĭs căr′ĭ ot
Jûl′ĭŭs
Jû′pĭ tẽr
Kā′dĕsh
Kē′dĕsh
Kē′nīte
Kı̆r′jăth-jē′ă rı̆m
Kı̆sh
Kō′răh
Lā băn
Lăz′ă rŭs
Lē ăh
Lĕb′ă nǫn
Lē′vī
Lō′dĕ bar
Lǒt
Lўç′ĭ ă
Lўd′dă
Lўd′ĭ ă

Names of Persons and Places

Lўs'tră
Măc ē dō'nĭ ă
Mā'chĭr
Măg'dă lēne
Mā hă nā'ĭm
Mah'lŏn
Măk kē'dah
Măm'rē
Mă năs'seh
Mă nō'ăh
Mär'ăh
Mark
Mär'thă
Mâr'ў
Mătth'ew
Mătth ī'ăs
Mēde
Měl'chī shû'ă
Měl'ĭ tă
Mě mū'căn
Mě phĭb'ŏ shěth
Měr'cū rў
Mē'shăck
Mě thū'sě lăh
Mī'chăl
Mĭd'ĭ ăn
Mĭg'dŏl
Mĭr'ĭ ăm
Mī'shā ĕl
Mĭz'pěh
Mō'ăb
Môr dě cā'ī
Mō rī'ăh
Mō'sěs
My'ră
Nā'ă măn
Nā'băl
Nā'bŏth
Nā'dăb
Nā hăsh
Nā'hôr
Nā'ĭn
Nā'ō mī
Năph'tă lī
Nā'thăn
Nă thăn'ă ĕl
Năz'ă rēne
Năz'ă rīte
Năz'ă rĕth
Nē'bō
Něb ū chăd ṇěz'zar
Nĭc ŏ dē'mŭs
Nīle
Nĭm'shī
Nĭn'ĕ věh
Nō'ăh
Nŏb
Nŏd
Nŭn
Ō bă dī'ăh
Ō'bed-ē'dom
Ŏg
Ŏl'ĭ vět
Ŏm'rī

Names of Persons and Places

Ŏn
Ŏph′răh
Ôr′păh
Ŏth′nĭ ĕl
Pâr′ăn
Paûl
Pē′kah
Pĕk ă hī′ăh
Pĕn′tē cŏst
Pĕr′gă
Pĕr′ĭz zīte
Pĕr′sĭă
Pē′tĕr
Phâr′aoh
Phăr′ĭ sêe
Phĭl′ĭp
Phĭ lĭp′pī
Phĭl ĭs′tĭne
Phĭn′ĕ hăs
Phū′răh
Pĭs′găh
Pŏn′tĭŭs Pī′lăte
Pŏt′ĭ phar
Pŏ tĭ′-phĕr ăh
Prĭs çĭl′lă
Pŭb′lĭ ŭs
Răb′băh
Rā′chĕl
Rā′hăb
Rā′măh
Rā′mŏth-gĭl′ĕ ăd

Rĕ bĕk′ăh
Rē hŏ bō′ăm
Rĕph′ĭ dĭm
Reû′bĕn
Rōme
Rûth
Să bē′ăns
Săd′dū cêe
Să mâr′ĭ ă
Săm′son
Săm′ū ĕl
Săpph ī′ră
Sâr′ăh
Sā′tăn
Saûl
Sē′ĭr
Sĕn năch′ĕr ĭb
Sĕth
Shā′drăch
Shăl′lŭm
Shā′phăt
Shē′bă
Shē′chĕm
Shĕm
Shī′lōh
Shī′nar
Shī′shăk
Shur
Shû′shăn
Sī′dŏn
Sī′hŏn
Sī′lăs

Names of Persons and Places

Sī lŏ'ăm
Sĭm'ĕ on
Sī'mon
Sĭn
Sī'nâi
Sĭs'ĕ ră
Sôr'ĕk
Sŏd'om
Sŏl ŏ mon
Stē'phĕn
Stō'ĭc
Sŭc'cōth
Sȳ'chàr
Sy̆r'ĭ ă
Tăb'ĭ thă
Tā'bôr
Tā'mär
Tar'shĭsh
Thăd dæ'ŭs
Theû'dăs
Thŏm'ăs
Tī bē'rĭ ŭs
Tim'năth
Tĭm'ŏ thy̆
Tĭr'zăh
Tĭsh'bīte

Trō'ăs
Trŏph'ĭ mŭs
Tȳre
Ū rī'ăh
Ŭz
Ŭz'zăh
Văsh'tī
Zăc chæ'ŭs
Zăch ă rī'ăh
Zăch ă rī'ăs
Zā'dok
Zăr'ĕ phăth
Zĕb'ĕ dêe
Zĕ bū'lŭn
Zĕd ē kī'ăh
Zē-rĕsh
Zĕr ū ī'ăh
Zī'bă
Zĭm'rī
Zĭn
Zĭp'pŏ răh
Zī'on
Zō'ar
Zō'phär
Zŭph

GOLDEN BOOKS
FOR CHILDREN

FIRST ISSUES

Robin Hood
The Arabian Nights

IF YOU READ ONE BOOK IN THIS
SERIES YOU WILL WANT OTHERS.
ASK YOUR BOOKSELLER TO SHOW
YOU ALL THE VOLUMES THAT
HAVE BEEN ISSUED IN THIS
LIBRARY OF

GOLDEN BOOKS FOR CHILDREN

Or write for descriptive circular to the publishers
THE BAKER AND TAYLOR COMPANY
33 East 17th Street New York

www.ingramcontent.com/pod-product-compliance
Lightning Source LLC
LaVergne TN
LVHW011254081225
827303LV00032B/518